ALSO BY CAROL GILLIGAN

In a Different Voice (1982)

Meeting at the Crossroads
(with Lyn Mikel Brown, 1992)

Between Voice and Silence
(with Jill McLean Taylor and Amy M. Sullivan, 1995)

EDITED BY CAROL GILLIGAN

Mapping the Moral Domain:
A Contribution of Women's Thinking to Psychological
Theory and Education
(with Janie Victoria Ward, Jill McClean Taylor,
and Betty Bardige, 1988)

Making Connections
(with Nona P. Lyons and Trudy J. Hanmer, 1990)

Women, Girls, and Psychotherapy: Reframing Resistance
(with Annie G. Rogers and Deborah L. Tolman, 1991)

THE BIRTH OF PLEASURE

THE BIRTH OF
PLEASURE

Carol Gilligan

Alfred A. Knopf
New York
2002

THIS IS A BORZOI BOOK
PUBLISHED BY ALFRED A. KNOPF

www.aaknopf.com

Knopf, Borzoi Books, and the colophon are registered trademarks
of Random House, Inc.

Owing to limitations of space, acknowledgments of permission to reprint
previously published material can be found following the index.

Library of Congress Catalogue-in-Publication Data
Gilligan, Carol, [date]
The birth of pleasure / Carol Gilligan.—1st ed.
p.   cm.
Includes bibliographical references and index.
ISBN 0-679-44037-2 (alk. paper)
1. Love.   2. Man-woman relationships.   3. Intimacy (Psychology)
I. Title.
BF575.L8   G56   2002
152.4'1—dc21   2001050329

Manufactured in the United States of America
First Edition

For Jim

The power of love upsets the order of things.

GENESIS RABBAH LV8

Contents

Acknowledgments

*T*HIS BOOK was conceived in love, and I am grateful to the many people who encouraged and inspired me. I would like to thank the couples who opened their lives to me, the girls who showed me a path, and the young boys and their parents who filled in a vital part of the map. Their voices were the grounding to which I repeatedly returned. My thanks to the students who became my colleagues in these projects; their perceptions and insights were a great gift. Thanks also to the writers whose books became so integral to my exploration.

Normi Noel was my soul's companion on this journey; hers was the ear on which I relied. At the final stages of writing, I walked with Tina Packer every morning, and her insights into the larger themes of the book opened many doors for me. She too has drawn deeply from the well of Psyche and Cupid and tracked Shakespeare's women in her play *Women of Will.* Kristin Linklater's illumination of "the natural voice" and the process of freeing it lit my way into the psyche; as co–artistic directors of the theater troupe The Company of Women, we joined our work.

Mary Hamer was a writing pal and her bold work, an inspiration. Terry Real became a best friend; his invitation to join him in doing couples therapy was an invitation into understanding how deeply truth is entwined with love. David

Acknowledgments

Richards also became a best friend, and teaching with him, a special pleasure. His work on the Abolitionist Feminists, his interpretation of the Constitution, and his analysis of the liberation movements of the twentieth century spurred me to think about the relationship between love and democracy. Jean Baker Miller opened my life to new ways of seeing and has stood as a beacon for me.

Several people encouraged this project at crucial junctures: Kate Medina above all. I am grateful to Rachel Kadish for her novelist's eye and to the other members of my writers' workshop in Cambridge—Kathleen Cleaver, Laura Harrington, and Florence Ladd. Thanks to Helaine and Yorick Blumenfeld, Peggy Davis, Tova and Moshe Halbertal, Marsha Levy-Warren, Lisby Mayer, Wendy Puriefoy, and Joel Revzen for their insights and wisdom; to Denise DeCosta for alerting me to Anne Frank's editing of her diary; to Simon Goldhill, Mary Beard, and Froma Zeitlin for discussing Apuleius with me; to Bessel van der Kolk for conversations about trauma; to Jonathan Gilligan for conversations about action at a distance; and to Ruby Blondell, Emily Hass, Wendy Kesselman, Nanci Kincaid, and Dennis Krausnick.

Elizabeth Debold, Diana de Vegh, Dana Jack, Donald Levy, Deborah Luepnitz, Cindy Ness, Christina Robb, and Daniella Varon generously read and commented on early drafts. I benefited from the opportunity to present parts of this work and from the discussions that followed at Princeton University, the University of Cambridge in England, the Cambridge Hospital/Stone Center conferences on learning from women, the Austen Riggs Center, Robert Jay Lifton's Wellfleet Seminar, the symposium commemorating the Institute of Pennsylvania Hospital, the Northwestern Family Therapy Institute, the Women's Therapy Center, Facing History and Ourselves, the Ms. Foundation board retreat, the Roger Williams Law School in Rhode Island, and the Examiners Club in Boston. I also benefited from the thoughtful responses of members of my seminar at the NYU law school.

For encouraging and supporting the research on girls' development and the women teaching girls/girls teaching women projects, I am grateful to the Boston Foundation, the Cleveland Foundation, the Geraldine Rockefeller Dodge Foundation, the Gund Foundation, the Lily Endowment, and the Spencer Foundation. Emily Fisher and Elizabeth Hobbs, together with Nancy Aronson and an anonymous donor initiated and endowed Harvard's first chair in Gender Studies at the Graduate School of Education. My thanks to Patricia Albjerg Graham, Jerry Murphy, and my colleagues at Harvard for making this happen; the research endowment given to the Chair by the Spencer Foundation supported the research with boys. An anonymous donor funded the study of marriages in crisis, and the Cambridge Family Institute and the Gender Studies program at Harvard supported the project with couples in therapy. To Jane Fonda, my thanks for her vision and generosity, for taking the map of this book and working to make its vision a reality.

A special thanks to Virgina Kahn, to the principals and teachers who welcomed and joined my research, to Jane Rabb and the late Frances West, and to Judy Chu, Miriam Raider-Roth, Ilina Singh, and Renee Spencer—graduate students at Harvard—and Carol Kaplan and Eliza Patten at New York University School of Law for work that inspired me. I am grateful to my colleagues at NYU for their friendship; special thanks to John Sexton for asking me what I needed and providing it.

In the course of writing, I relied on Nancy Costerisan, Gloria Rieger, Marion Rutledge, and Sarah Thorne to remind me of the beauty of houses and gardens and the wisdom of the body. My heartfelt thanks to Willie Mae Jackson for keeping the spirit of my parents alive along with her own, to my

Acknowledgments

cousin Bette Caminez Kroening, to Alexia Panayiotou and her parents for offering their beach house in Cyprus as a writing retreat, to David Hartman and the Shalom Hartman Institute in Jerusalem, and to my stellar research assistant, Tatiana Bertsch.

Thanks to John Brockman for his steadying presence and to Sonny Mehta for being a friend to this writer. Most of all, I have relied on the talents of Victoria Wilson, who brought her discerning eye to this work and urged me to walk into those places where I hesitated to go.

My family has inspired me to write about pleasure. I thank my sons, Jon, Tim, and Chris Gilligan, for all the pleasures they have brought me and for bringing Vicki Greene, Heather Gornik, and Golbarg Niknejad into my life. Nora Gilligan, my granddaughter, embodies joy. Jacob Gilligan's birth gives new meaning to pleasure. To Jim, my thanks for encouraging me always to realize my dreams; he is my deepest friend, my love.

THE BIRTH OF PLEASURE

I

A Radical Geography
of Love

Let it be
Like wild flowers,
Suddenly, an imperative of the field . . .

—YEHUDA AMICHAI

FOR YEARS, without knowing why, I have been drawn to maps of the desert, drawn by descriptions of the winds and the wadi—dry watercourses that suddenly fill with rain. I began following an ancient story about love told in North Africa in the second century, written in the coastal city of Carthage, carried into Europe as the winds carry the desert sand, falling like rain into a tradition whose origins lie in the birth of tragedy, coursing through the centuries like an underground stream. Set in the landscape of tragedy, this story leads to the birth of pleasure.

Maybe love is like rain. Sometimes gentle, sometimes torrential, flooding, eroding, quiet, steady, filling the earth, collecting in hidden springs. When it rains, when we love, new life grows. So that to say, as Moses coming down from Sinai said, that there are two roads, one leading to life and one to death, and therefore choose life, is to say in effect: choose love. But what is the way?

I PICKED UP the ancient road map of love at a time when relationships between women and men were changing. The waves of liberation that swept through American society in the second half of the twentieth century, freeing love from many constraints, set in motion a process of transformation. In a historic convergence, the civil rights movement, which galvanized a moral consensus against enslavement, was followed by the anti-war movement and the women's movement, initiating a conversation about freedom that included freedom from long-standing ideals of manhood and womanhood. For a man to be a man, did he have to be a soldier, or at least prepare himself for war? For a woman to be a woman, did she have to be a mother, or at least prepare herself to raise children? Soldiers and mothers were the sacrificial couple, honored by statues in the park, lauded for their willingness to give their lives to others. The gay liberation movement drew people's attention to men's love for men and women's for women and also men's love for women who were not the objects of their sexual desire and women's love for men who were not their economic protectors. In the 1990s, for the first time since suffrage, women's votes elected the president, more women were gaining an economic foothold, and wealth began shifting into the hands of young men who bypassed the usual channels of advancement. The tension between democracy and patriarchy was out in the open.

Democracy rests on an ideal of equality in which everyone has a voice. Patriarchy, although frequently misinterpreted to mean the oppression of women by men, literally means a hierarchy—a rule of priests—in which the priest, the *hieros,* is a father. It describes an order of living that elevates fathers, separating fathers from sons (the men from the boys) and placing both sons and women under a father's authority. With the renaissance of women's voices in the late twentieth century, with sons questioning the authority of fathers, especially with respect to war, with the revolution in technology reducing the need for a priesthood by providing direct access to knowledge, the foundations of patriarchy were eroding.

I was searching at the time for a washed-out road. Picking up the voice of pleasure in men's and women's stories about love and also among adolescent girls and young boys, I came to the places where this voice drops off and a tragic story takes over. The tragic story where love leads to loss and pleasure is associated with death was repeated over and over again, in operas, folk songs, the blues, and novels. We were in love with a tragic story of love. It was "our story."

If we have a map showing where pleasure is buried and where the seeds of tragedy are planted, then we can see an order of living that was presumed to be natural or inevitable as a road we have taken and trace alternative routes. Piecing together an ancient love story with the findings of contemporary research, I found myself led into the heart of a mystery and then to a new mapping of love. This book is a record of that journey.

IN THE MID-1980s, I began a study with women and men whose intimate relationships with one another had reached a point of crisis. People were asking new questions about love, finding their way alone and together across a shifting societal and psychic terrain. More women were speaking openly about their experiences of love, saying what they knew about pleasure. The double standard, or what Freud had called "a *double* morality," had led to "concealment of the truth, false optimism, self-deception and deception of others" on the part of both women and men. The poet Jorie Graham's questions became everyone's questions:

*How far is true
enough?
How far into the
earth
can vision go and
still be*

love?

A search for truth was uncovering a buried history, revealing the extent to which neither men nor women felt authentic. How had this happened? Where had they split with their souls, their desires, their connection to each other?

Led by an awareness of this disconnection, I began to explore the roots of what seemed a pervasive trauma. Trauma is the shock to the psyche that leads to dissociation: our ability to separate ourselves from parts of ourselves, to create a split within ourselves so that we can know and also not know what we know, feel and yet not feel our feelings. It is our ability, as Freud put it in *Studies on Hysteria,* to hold parts of our experience not as a secret from others but as a "foreign body" within ourselves.

The foundational stories we tell about Western civilization are stories of trauma. Oedipus is wounded and abandoned by his parents, who drive a stake through his feet (hence the name Oedipus, which means "swollen foot") and give him to a herdsman with instructions to leave the baby on a hillside to die. Saved by the herdsman, Oedipus is fated to kill his father, Laius, and marry his mother, Jocasta—a fate decreed by Apollo as retribution for Laius' having sexually violated a young boy.

The *Oresteia,* Aeschylus' trilogy about the founding of Athenian democracy, tells a story so horrible it is almost unspeakable. Atreus, the father of Agamemnon (the king who will lead the Greek army to Troy), had a brother Thyestes, who ran off with Atreus' wife. In response to this loss and the blow to male honor it carries, Atreus invites Thyestes to a banquet and serves him his children, cut up and cooked into a stew. Athenian democracy is the civic order created to contain the seemingly endless cycle of violence that follows in the wake of this trauma. The *Oresteia* links the establishment of democracy with the reinstatement of patriarchy, as Orestes, Agamemnon's son, is acquitted for the crime of killing his mother at the first recorded trial. Athena (born from the head of Zeus) casts the deciding vote in his favor, giving priority to fathers by saying: "The death of a wife who killed her husband is bad, but not so bad as the death of a father and king."

In the Book of Genesis, the trauma is the expulsion of Adam and Eve from the Garden of Eden; it too leaves a legacy of violence and betrayal. Cain, the son of Adam and Eve, murders his brother Abel. In the story of Noah, God brings a flood to wipe out this history and start over, but the residue of trauma returns in Noah's drunkenness and incestuous sexuality. Jacob, with the help of his mother, steals his brother Esau's birthright. And Jacob's son Joseph is sold into slavery by his brothers, who envy his relationship with his father.

In these foundational stories, a trauma occurs in a triangle composed of two men and a woman. When we focus more closely on what actually happens, we see that a father or a husband's authority is challenged. Oedipus is wounded by his father and mother because he is fated to kill his father; Atreus is betrayed by his wife and his brother; Adam and Eve disobey God. What follows has the cast of tragedy, as if what happens had to happen. The order of the triangle has been challenged (father over son, man over woman), and a man, wounded in his love, responds by unleashing a cycle of violence.

Perhaps patriarchy, by establishing hierarchy in the heart of intimacy, is inherently tragic, and like all trauma survivors, we keep telling the story we need to listen to and understand. At the same time, we look for ways to break what quickly becomes a vicious cycle, searching for "a new truth . . . [that would] establish the whole relation between man and woman on a surer ground of mutual happiness." The quotation is from *The Scarlet Letter,* where Nathaniel Hawthorne's narrator makes the observation that the new truth must be brought by a woman, echoing a thought that, once spoken, becomes inescapable: the presence of women in a democratic society contains the seeds of transformation—a second coming, a new beginning, a civilization that is not patriarchal. This is the radical geography of love, the wildflower seeded from generation to generation, the messiah perpetually in our midst.

In Greek, the word for "soul" is *psyche;* it also means "breath" or "life." This ancient word carries the wisdom that we are more than our genetic makeup, more than our life histories, more than our cultural lineage. Whether conceived as a divine spark or as part of the natural wonder of the human being, the soul is the wellspring of our minds and our hearts, our voice and our capacity for resistance. But Psyche is also the name of the young woman in the ancient story about love.

My research has centered on listening for the voice of the psyche as it speaks directly and indirectly, in language and in silence—a voice often hidden in the structure of a sentence. I developed a method to guide this listening, inspired by the early work of Freud and Piaget, by literature and music, and spurred by the challenge of listening to women within a cultural acoustic that distorts their experience. I was drawn by the sound of an unmediated voice, a voice that broke free, a wild voice or what Kristin Linklater, an expert on voice in the theater, has called "the natural voice": the voice that carries rather than covers a person's inner world. I found that in order to hear this voice I had to create a resonance that would encourage the impulse to speak, and also to signal in one way or another my answer to the implicit question that I was asked explicitly one day by a woman who said: "Do you want to know what I think? Or do you want to know what I really think?" I became interested precisely in this doubling of thoughts and feelings and in the conditions under which we will reveal to others and to ourselves what we know.

In the journal he kept on his voyage to the Galápagos Islands, Darwin sketched the variation he saw among finches, collecting the first of the evidence that would lead him to posit the mechanism of natural selection as a way of explaining the origin and the extinction of species. Modifications in the beaks of birds who had migrated to a particular island in the archipelago represented adaptations to the food source of the island, making it possible for them to eat and survive. Species, although considered to be God-given, could arise and disappear through a similar process of evolution.

Adolescent girls became the Galápagos on my journey. With them, I first glimpsed evidence suggesting that what psychologists had taken to be human nature was an adaptation to a particular human landscape. Talking with girls, I heard and experienced sudden shifts between not knowing and knowing, lassitude and intense feeling, a cover story and an under-reality. In girls' intricately layered stories of love and betrayal, I saw evidence pointing to the origin of dissociative processes—splits in consciousness that were familiar to me, that became surprising only when I realized that they occurred in response to a break in relationship that girls experienced with shock. It was like working on a geological fault, the ground of relationship suddenly shifting and girls marking the shifts, registering what was happening, so that in their presence I found it easy to distinguish the experience of relationship (being in sync with another person) from what are often called relationships. As I came back to a knowing I had learned to distance myself from or discredit, I saw girls beginning not to know what they knew. Dissociation was an adaptation to a shocking break in relationship; it was a way of holding a loss often said not to be a loss, a way of holding a love that quickly came to seem incredible.

"Ourself behind ourself concealed / Should startle most," Emily Dickinson wrote, conveying the startling discovery of a hidden self. "I hid myself within myself . . . and quietly wrote down all my joys, sorrows and contempt in my diary." This is Anne Frank. In *The Land of Look Behind,* in the section "Claiming an Identity They Taught Me to Despise," in a passage called "Obsolete Geography," Michelle Cliff, the Jamaican-born poet, associates her twelve-year-old discovery of pleasure (the taste of mangoes, the feel of water, the stirring of longing within her body) with watching a pig's throat being cut: "as her cries cease, mine begin."

"If I were to say what I was feeling and thinking, no one would want to be with me, my voice would be too loud," seventeen-year-old Iris says, half to me and half to herself. And then looking straight at me, she adds with an edge of defiance, "But you have to have relationships." "Yes," I agree. We had been listening to the honest, outspoken voices of younger girls. "But if you are not saying what you are feeling and thinking, then where are you in these relationships?" It is my question for girls and women; it is my question for myself. Iris sees the paradox in what she is saying: she has given up relationship in order to have relationships, muting her voice and concealing herself so that "she" could be with other people. Her pleasure in these relationships is compromised by her awareness of having sacrificed herself, or pleasure takes on a different meaning, referring to bodily sensations that have become divorced from or a stand-in for the pleasure of being a soul in a body living in connection with others.

In suggesting an analogy to Darwin's work on natural selection and positing dissociation as a psychic mechanism that serves an adaptive function on a cultural level, I also noticed a difference. The self that girls and women conceal, like the voice they mute or the identity they are taught to despise, is a vital, curious, pleasure-loving soul that also has adaptive value. Dissociation is a brilliant although costly way of ensuring this soul's survival. If dissociation is also the psychic mechanism that allows survival in patriarchy, an adaptation to the splits in relationship among and between men and women, the soul in its affinity to life and to love will resist this adaptation.

I remembered my own resistance at the age of twelve, my fights with my mother over how to act with boys who had turned from boys or friends into "boyfriends," and the suffocating experience of being corralled by a teacher named Sybil, who urged me to become a "constructive leader," to tone down my high-spirited nature. I remembered the sounds of my mother's voice and the voices of women teachers telling me what I needed to know, their voices often sounding as if they were speaking for someone other than themselves. But it was only later, when I was working with girls, that I felt again the pleasure of moving freely in a girl's body and heard again the sound of a voice that was free from second thoughts and instant revision, a voice that was at once familiar and surprising—my voice at the age of twelve.

Witnessing girls beginning a process of revision that I am coming to remember, I dream I am wearing my glasses over my contact lenses. I am literally seeing double, although it does not seem like that in the dream. A woman, my therapist, says to me, "I cannot offer you myself," and I am instantly filled with shame and remorse for wanting what seems so unreasonable, so extreme. Until, in the dream, I take off my glasses. My head spins around 180 degrees like an owl's, and I feel an overwhelming sensation of vertigo, as if I have been struck by lightning or suffered a severe shock, as I say "No." Because suddenly I know. This isn't it. This endless wanting of what is being withheld. Without the second set of corrective lenses, my desire loses its overlay of shame. I want what I had wanted with my mother and my women teachers: I want her to be herself. I do not want to enter the subtle and surreptitious competition among women that I remember from my adolescence—not the open contests that I knew as an athlete and a good student at school, but a competition that is said not to be a competition, a competition hidden in the guise of love. "I do not want you to compete with me," I say to the woman in the dream. When I wake up, I realize that I feel dizzy in the dream not when I am seeing double—when I am wearing my glasses over my contact lenses—but when I take off my glasses and am seeing clearly.

When I subsequently read W. E. B. DuBois' essay "The Souls of Black Folk," I understand what he calls the "peculiar sensation" of double-consciousness, the ability to hold two seemingly contradictory realities simultaneously. What DuBois describes as a necessary adaptation for black folk living in a white racist society parallels what I witnessed and experienced as necessary for girls and women living in patriarchy. Sheila at fifteen sums up the predicament in a wry and witty image as she speaks of standing with her boyfriend in a relationship that is sinking. "It's like two people standing in a boat that they both know is sinking. I don't want to say anything to you because it will upset you, and you don't want to say anything to me because it will upset you. And we are both standing here in water up to about our ankles, watching it rise."

The Abolitionist Feminists of the antebellum period in America saw freedom to love as a fundamental freedom—as fundamental as freedom of conscience or freedom of association. To constrain love was a form of moral slavery, inflicted on black and white women and also black men without any sense of constitutional violation. Although the constraint took vastly different forms depending on race and social class, with blacks enslaved and privileged white women elevated to pedestals or placed in golden cages, it signified an overriding of voice in both cases. In his 1908 essay "Civilized Sexual Morality and Modern Nervous Illness," Freud observed that the suppression of a woman's sexuality leads to a more general inhibition of desire and curiosity, creating a restriction on wanting and knowing that spreads throughout her life.

In breaking through this restriction, the Abolitionist Feminists—Sarah and Angelina Grimké, Lydia Maria Child, Lucretia Mott, Harriet Jacobs, Sojourner Truth, and Elizabeth Cady Stanton, to name some of the more outspoken—saw the links between racism and patriarchy. "Ain't I a woman?" Sojourner Truth asked, counterposing her experience to the image of the white woman on the pedestal. In *Incidents in the Life of a Slave Girl, Written by Herself,* Harriet Jacobs, a fugitive slave, exposed the sexual underside of slavery. She recounted her experience of having been forcibly separated from the black man she loved and subjected on a daily basis to the sexual advances and threats of her white master—until she ran away. "The lamp of hope had gone out," she explained; "[he] made my life a desert." Having experienced closeness with white women who at various points in her life befriended her, Jacobs brilliantly analyzed the animosity that grows up between a slave owner's wife, who is stranded on her pedestal, and the black woman in her household whom her husband desires.

Like the civil rights movement of the twentieth century, Abolitionist Feminism witnessed cooperation between black and white women and also between women and men. But with the outbreak of the Civil War, the more radical agenda of ending racism and patriarchy gave way to the more immediate goal of ending slavery. As the war enlisted the support of traditional ideals of masculinity and femininity, it became unseemly for men and women to question the heroism of soldiers and mothers who were sacrificing themselves or their children to the struggle. In the Reconstruction Amendments that followed the war, the call of abolitionism was split from feminism: black men were given the vote, while black women, like all women, were denied full citizenship.

In the late nineteenth and early twentieth centuries, Victoria Woodhull, Ida B. Wells-Barnett, Emma Goldman, and Margaret Sanger took up the radical agenda of the Abolitionist Feminists, exposing the hypocrisies of the sexual and racial double standard and calling for free love among and between blacks and whites, women and men. It was an inflammatory call. Woodhull was imprisoned, Wells-Barnett was threatened with death, Goldman was deported, and Sanger left the country, returning subsequently to pursue the more limited agenda of birth control. Recounting this history in his book *Women, Gays, and the Constitution,* David Richards—a philosopher and constitutional-law scholar—concludes that "feminism was more controversial than abolitionism"; no criticism of slavery and racism "was more stinging to Americans than any discussion of underlying issues of sexuality." Although the battle against slavery was fought openly, pleasure, it seems, was the more incendiary issue in the new republic.

Walt Whitman had written a paean to "the body electric," celebrating the human capacity for love and pleasure in all its forms. But pleasure, and especially women's pleasure, evoked images of loss and betrayal. As my research with girls caught a moment when pleasure becomes linked with danger, I began to reflect on my experience as the mother of sons, a woman who loves and has lived intimately with boys and men. My work with girls was giving me language in places where I found myself inarticulate and suggested a paradigm for explaining some of the more puzzling findings of psychological research. For more than a hundred years, psychologists have observed that boys in general are more likely than girls to show signs of emotional distress in early childhood—more prone to depression, learning disorders, and various forms of out-of-control or out-of-touch behavior. Whereas girls, hardier in childhood, show a resiliency—an ability to bounce back in the face of stress—that is at risk at adolescence. The sudden high incidence of depression, eating disorders, problems in learning, and destructive behavior among girls at adolescence parallels the heightened risk to boys' resiliency in the late years of early childhood, roughly around the age of five—the time Freud marked as the Oedipal crisis.

Various reasons have been given for this disparity, ranging from biological differences to socialization, but my research directed my attention to a second observation, also repeatedly confirmed. One confiding relationship, meaning a relationship where one can speak one's heart and mind freely, has been found to be the best protection against most forms of psychological trouble, especially in times of stress. The evidence of my research identified the risk girls face in adolescence as a risk of losing a confiding relationship. In adolescence, girls often discover or fear that if they give voice to vital parts of themselves, their pleasure and their knowledge, they will endanger their connection with others and also the world at large. I wondered if a similar dynamic played out earlier in boys' lives.

With Judy Chu, then a graduate student at Harvard, I took my research into the province of four- and five-year-old boys and began to listen more intently to men's silences. Moved by the tenderness between boys and their fathers in an early morning pre-kindergarten class where fathers commonly brought their children to school, I was reminded of what the British psychiatrist Ian Suttie had called "the taboo on tenderness." I watched the play of light and shadow as this taboo passed across the faces of boys and men until there was scant evidence, little trace on the surface, of what I had seen. I became interested in boys' resistance to losses associated with masculinity and also in the consequences of this resistance.

"Mummy," four-year-old Jake says one morning to his mother, Rachel, "you have a happy voice, but I also hear a little worried voice." Listening to her voice, Jake registers her happiness and also her anxiety. Rachel knows that Jake knows her feelings. "He is my barometer," she says. Jake takes pride in accompanying his mother. "I am your knight," he tells her. But when Rachel speaks of the tension she was under at a time when she was still nursing Jake and her department at the university increased her teaching load and her administrative responsibilities, as if to test her allegiance to them; when she describes how Jake picked up her tension and the day-care workers complained that he was "off the wall," I feel my hesitation. I ask Rachel if she had tried to shield Jake from the anxiety she was feeling. "No," she says, and then, reminding me of the closeness between them, she explains, "To do so would have been to betray his love." If she did not want him to know what she was feeling, she would have had to place a shield between them. Instead, she sought to address the source of the tension, and she was fortunate in that she was able to find another job at a better university. With the help of her husband, she commuted for a time until they were able to move the family.

When Alex, Nick's father, expresses his remorse for having "lost it" and hit Nick the previous day, Nick, age five, says to his father: "You are afraid that if you hit me, when I grow up I'll hit my children." Alex, who had been hit by his father, had vowed to break the cycle. Nick, his son, articulates his fear.

Concerns about manhood can become an impediment to this closeness between boys and their parents. When parents feel bound to uphold idealized images of mothers or fathers, thus concealing parts of themselves; when a boy's expression of tenderness or vulnerability arouses fears about his ability to hold his own on the playground or anxiety about his masculinity, these concerns will threaten the possibility of a confiding relationship, just as concerns about womanhood can stand in the way of girls speaking freely. Masculinity often implies an ability to stand alone and forgo relationships, whereas femininity connotes a willingness to compromise oneself for the sake of relationships. But both strategies (forgoing relationships to maintain one's voice and muting one's voice to maintain relationships) entail a loss of voice and relationship. By holding voice and relationship together, a confiding relationship offers protection from this loss. Since the initiation of boys into the codes of masculinity intensifies around the age of five, while girls are given more leeway with respect to femininity until adolescence, girls are more likely to name and openly resist a loss that boys often suffer in silence.

When Terrence Real broke silence with his book *I Don't Want to Talk About It: Overcoming the Secret Legacy of Male Depression,* he quoted the Yiddish proverb "The son wishes to remember what the father wishes to forget." The memories are memories of love and its loss, often experienced as traumatic. Terry Real is an experienced therapist, and his work caught my eye because of his ability to speak with men truthfully and lovingly. Taking my study of couples in crisis into the intimate arena of couples therapy, I joined with Real in a search to discover ways of moving in the face of impasse. We were interested more specifically in the tensions between love and patriarchy as they play out within and between women and men generation after generation, and also in the challenges posed for couples by the changes brought about by women's liberation. Because I want to explore whether love in and of itself sets in motion a resistance to patriarchy, I have chosen to focus on heterosexual love, which is culturally sanctioned, rather than gay and lesbian relationships. Working for the most part with straight couples, Real and I came to an illumination that was unexpected.

From years of listening to people in therapy, Terry Real has an acute ear for the silences surrounding traumatic experience. To our work with couples, I brought an understanding of the resonances women seek if they are to speak freely, especially in the presence of men, and also a map of development drawn from my work with adolescent girls and young boys. My ear was tuned to the voice of pleasure—not the remembered voice but the actual voice from these times in development that often precede dissociation.

As Terry picked up the signs of trauma and I tracked the voice of pleasure, we charted a terrain of loss. At the far side of loss, after the loss, a tragic story is told, but on the near side of loss pleasure lives, and then often is buried. In the couples therapy, it was the voice of pleasure that created an opening in the tragic story. And with it, an exquisite vulnerability, because now loss was in front of them rather than behind them. Facing love had come to mean exposing oneself to what seemed its fated tragic ending. I came to see love as a courageous act and pleasure as its harbinger.

In the course of our work, Real and I were struck by the extent to which people know in some sense where they have sealed off love, the deals they have made and the compromises struck, always for good reason but often at enormous cost. The awareness of complicity is so shameful that it often seems easier to justify it than to experience and question what has been sacrificed. To do so means to go back and undo the process of initiation that sanctioned the sacrifice, typically for the sake of relationships and making one's way in the world. The very language of love and pleasure, like the meaning of the word "relationship," changes in the course of this initiation, shrouding the loss in confusion and making it difficult for people to speak and listen. To free love and pleasure from the trappings of a manhood or womanhood that holds them captive means to undo dissociation by risking association— knowing what one knows, feeling one's feelings, being naked in the presence of another by removing the protective clothes of masculinity and femininity, however they are culturally designed.

Thus I came to a psychology of love as it plays out on a familiar landscape, a cultural formation that has been built up over thousands of years. This landscape rests on a fracture of relationship, a psychological fault. The trauma that is inherent in patriarchy and that fuels its continuation is a break in relationship with women and boys on the part of both women and men. This is the story we tell over and over again, the tragic story of love. Because girls stand somewhat to the side of this drama until adolescence, they can serve as a chorus, observing and commenting on what is happening until they become women and are swept up in its plot. To hear tragic love as a story immediately suggests the existence of other stories and also the possibility of new stories. But to make it "a story" rather than "the story," one story rather than our story, means to question losses that have seemed fated, that we have deemed necessary or taken for granted. It means to imagine an escape from tragedy.

In this light, I came upon the tale of Psyche and Cupid and found it startling. It maps an intricately choreographed resistance to tragic stories of love, the love-death stories of high and low culture, by highlighting crucial moves at vital life junctures: adolescence, marriage, the conception and birth of a child. It also plays out the patterns of relationship that mark a patriarchal social order—the silent mother, envy among women, the son's dilemma, the law of the father—and then shows the radical nature of love between a woman and a man, caught by history behind the lines of patriarchy, and the high adventure of their efforts to escape into a new psychological territory. If passionate love, meaning a love driven more by chemistry than custom, has flourished for the most part on the edges of the existing social order, perhaps this says as much about that order as it says about love.

It was not surprising, then, to discover that the myth of Psyche and Cupid was written at a time when the hegemony of male gods was becoming unsettled, a time in this respect very much like our own. The place, North Africa in the second century, was a site where African, Greek, and Roman cultures were mixing, a site resonant with women's voices, given the growing popularity of the religion of Isis. The story appears at the center of Apuleius' novel *Metamorphoses, or The Golden Ass,* where it is presented as "an old wife's tale." I am interested in this voice, a story of love that a woman would tell after living for many years with a man and children. I am interested that Apuleius tells this story, that it lies in the province of both women and men.

The word "metamorphosis" literally means changing the shape or overcoming the form. Apuleius' novel follows the adventures of Lucius, a man whose curiosity leads him to be turned into a donkey. He is the supreme or golden ass. In this form he travels through a familiar landscape of millers and priests, highways and robbers, taverns and wenches, until, with the intervention of Isis and the coming of spring, he regains his human shape by eating roses. For a time he devotes himself to Isis before returning to his old life as a new man. Midway through this journey, the story of Psyche and Cupid bubbles up, seemingly from nowhere like an ancient spring. It too is a story about transformation, overcoming the traditional form of love between a woman and a man. Its central position in the novel suggests that only when Lucius has assimilated this change in the love story can he regain his male human body without assuming the old forms of manhood. The revolutionary insight in this comic novel lies in this realization: a change in the love story is key to a psychological and cultural transformation.

While Apuleius' novel ends with an ode to Isis, suggesting a change in shape from patriarchy to matriarchy (a change that retains the hierarchical form), the love story ends on a more radical note: as a just and lawful and equal relationship between a woman and a man signals the end of patriarchy, so the birth of pleasure carries the intimation of a new form.

The tale of Psyche and Cupid traveled from North Africa into the heart of Europe at the time of the Renaissance, becoming an inspiration to poets and painters and a prime source for Shakespeare—shaping his writing about love and the voices of the women characters in the comedies, tragedies, and romance plays just as Holinshed's *Chronicles* shaped the writing of the history plays. Tracing the extent of Shakespeare's borrowings from Apuleius, J. J. M. Tobin, a classics scholar, has dubbed *The Golden Ass* "Shakespeare's favorite novel." In this way, a radical map of love given by an old mother to a young woman, presented as a dream interpretation and called an old wife's tale, came into the center of high Western culture. Carried along on the cultural mainstream, the story itself undergoes transformation. We hear it repeated over and over again in a variety of forms. The old woman who tells the story in Apuleius' novel becomes the street woman in Virginia Woolf's *Mrs. Dalloway,* whose barely comprehensible raw syllables of love and ancient love story interrupt the stream of people's consciousness as they cross a busy street in London. And Psyche's voice becomes Katharine's voice in Michael Ondaatje's novel *The English Patient,* when she says to Almasy, "If you make love to me I won't lie about it. If I make love to you I won't lie about it."

THE MYTH is set in the following frame. The old woman is a servant. She cooks for robbers who have kidnapped a young woman named Charite from the house of her parents on the day of her seemingly perfect marriage. Taken into the forest and held for ransom, Charite becomes frightened by a dream. She dreams that her husband, in coming to rescue her, is waylaid and killed by the thieves.

"Cheer up," the old woman tells her; "don't be afraid." The logic of dreams is often contrary, and when it comes to love, to dream of a full belly and the pleasures of Venus "will foretell that one is going to be harassed by mental depression and physical weakness and every other sort of loss," whereas to dream of "weeping and being beaten and occasionally having your throat cut" may augur well. To illustrate this strange dream interpretation, she offers to tell Charite an old wives' tale, and she tells the story of Psyche and Cupid.

Read allegorically, it is a timeless myth about the relationship between love and the soul: Eros (or Amor) and Psyche. Read historically, it is a tale of cultural mixing, captured in the names of the lovers—Cupid, which is Latin, and Psyche, which is Greek—and also in their different lineages: Psyche is mortal and Cupid a god. I will read it as an encoded map of resistance, showing how to get out of the Oedipus tragedy—a way of breaking the patriarchal cycle. Marking a path leading to freedom, it is a radical geography of love. In the end, all these readings converge. The resistance story is a psychological story set in a historical and political landscape, and both love and the soul need to be placed in a cultural framework. Then we can see why we have loved tragic stories of love, or at least raise the question as to whether the tragic love story is the watermark of patriarchy, the imprint it leaves on the human soul. I will return to this question, but first the story.

PSYCHE IS the youngest and most beautiful of three daughters, the magical position in the folk tale tradition, the young woman slated to marry the prince. She was so beautiful, the story goes, that everyone honored her and called her "the new Venus," as if the goddess of love had returned to earth, now a young woman again. This fantasy of replacement, one woman seen as a replica of another, leads to envy among women and also to isolation. Venus, replaced, becomes old Venus. And Psyche, although worshiped by all, is loved by no one, because nobody sees her. Her beauty has become a blind, dazzling others who admire her as the ideal woman, an object of beauty, the goddess of love herself. Psyche is lonely, depressed, and confused by the fact that while everyone idolizes her, no one will marry her—nobody knows who she is. She hates in herself that beauty in which the world takes such pleasure.

Her father the king, distressed by his daughter's unhappiness and suspecting a god's intervention in her failure to marry, goes to consult the oracle of Apollo—a woman who speaks for the male god. She tells him that his daughter is destined for a funereal marriage to a wild and cruel and snaky monster. He is to take her to a lofty mountain crag and leave her to her fate.

Psyche's parents—active father, silent mother—are bereft at the news of their daughter's sad fate. With heavy hearts, they prepare to take her to the high hill. But Psyche, hearing them weep, tells them they are grieving at the wrong time: "When countries and peoples were giving me divine honours, when with a single voice they were all calling me a new Venus, that is when you should have grieved, that is when you should have wept, that is when you should have mourned me as if I were already dead." They had taken her honor as cause for celebration without seeing that, for Psyche, being renamed New Venus signified her erasure. This was her funeral, she says, showing the obduracy of adolescents but also revealing that, like the Fool in the Renaissance play, she is the truth-teller in this story about love. Buoyed by the truth and clear in her determination that she would rather die than continue to live her death-in-life existence as New Venus, she leads the procession to the mountain with a firm step. "Take me," she says, "and put me on the cliff appointed by the oracle. I hasten to enter into this happy marriage. I hasten to see this high-born husband of mine." Yet, left alone on the high ledge, Psyche waits in terror for the serpent monster.

Venus, shocked to discover that there is—that there could be—a new Venus, sends for her son, Cupid, and kissing him long and intensely with parted lips, she beseeches him in the name of the maternal bond to punish that "defiant beauty." He is to make Psyche fall in love with the most wretched of men. Cupid takes off for the high mountain ledge, but when he sees the beautiful and terrified young woman who looks like his mother, he predictably falls in love with her.

THE LOVE STORY begins with the wind. Summoned by Cupid, it brings the sensations of love, the feeling of being lifted and carried, stirring memory and desire, taking Psyche from the ledge of terror and carrying her gently into the pleasures of her own body. There came, the sensual story goes, a softly blowing zephyr, which lifted her garments up, causing them to billow. And with its tranquil breath it carried her, little by little, down the slopes of the high cliff and into a valley deep below, where she lay on a bed of moist and fragrant flowers. In the slow rhythm of this sensuous awakening ("Come slowly, Eden," Emily Dickinson will write), Psyche sleeps and then wakes, feeling calm. Now she finds herself in a grove of tall trees, next to a glistening stream. In the middle of the grove, she sees a magnificent palace, which she enters, and there her unknown husband visits her at night. And so, the sexual story continues, "that which was at first a novelty did by continual custom bring her great pleasure, and the sound of a mysterious voice gave comfort to her loneliness." But this is a love conducted in darkness and sealed by silence. Hidden from Venus, an illicit love.

Cupid tells Psyche that she must not try to see him, must never speak about their love. If she does, he will leave her. But while Psyche cannot see her lover, he is nonetheless sensible both to her hands and to her ears. She knows him through touch and by the sound of his voice, though she cannot see or say what she knows.

Soon the lyrical love story gives way to depression. Left alone all day with her needs attended to by disembodied voices, unable to see with whom she is living or who is speaking to her, deprived of human conversation and missing the company of her sisters, Psyche languishes in her magnificent palace. She spends her days weeping and refuses both food and bathing. Then Cupid, moved by her despair, agrees to bring her sisters to visit her.

It is easy to read the story of the evil sisters as yet another story of envy among women. The sisters are evil in their intention to spoil what they see as Psyche's pleasure and their wish to replace her in what they rightly suspect is a marriage to a god. But the evil sisters are also "evil" in that they are the ones who encourage Psyche to break the taboo on seeing and speaking, challenging her to move out of the stupor of her depression and to look at the monster who has imprisoned her. At first Psyche resists, moved perhaps by the tenderness of her lover and also their passion, unwilling or afraid to jeopardize this marriage.

Until she becomes pregnant. Her dissociation from her body is evident as Cupid announces the pregnancy to her, telling her that if she keeps her promise and does not try to see him or speak about their love, she will bear an immortal child. Otherwise, the child will be mortal as she is. As the pregnancy brings Psyche back into relationship with her body, she blossoms with happiness, "amazed at such a pretty swelling of her fertile womb." She counts the days and months as they pass, marveling as the promise grows. By the face and the shape of the child, she believes she will come to know the identity of her mysterious husband. Meanwhile, within her body, she is coming to know the child.

Her sisters come again to visit, and when they see that Psyche is pregnant, they remind her of the oracle's prophecy, telling her that she is married to a monster and warning her that he is waiting to devour both her and the child. They advise her to take a knife and a lamp and hide them by her side of the bed; then when the monster has fallen asleep, she can cut off his head.

Now Psyche is in terrible turmoil. Not knowing whom to believe or what stories are true, she sways between "haste and procrastination, daring and fear, despair and anger; and worst of all, in the same body she loathed the beast but loved the husband." In the end, she chooses not to risk herself and the child. Taking the lamp and the knife and concealing them next to the bed, she waits for the monster to fall asleep, prepared to cut off his head.

But when Psyche ignites the lamp and sees Cupid sleeping under the light, she discovers that her mysterious lover is a beautiful young man. In this moment, Psyche sees what in another sense she knows: the lover who brought her great pleasure, whose mysterious voice gave comfort to her loneliness, who was moved by her depression and brought her sisters to visit her. What she discovers is that her tender and passionate lover is Cupid, the god of love. But not Cupid of the stories about Cupid—the naughty boy with his arrows, flying around the world making trouble. She discovers a man she had known but had not been allowed to see or to speak of. And in the light of this discovery, she realizes that the stories told by the oracle, by her parents, and by her sisters are not true.

Now her curiosity becomes insatiable. Gazing at Cupid, she delights in his resplendent beauty—his arms, his shoulders with their feathery wings, his golden hair and milky neck. Marveling at and touching his magnificent body, she takes one of the arrows from his quiver and tests its point against the tip of her finger. But, her hands still trembling from excitement and fear, she pricks too hard and pushes too deeply until a drop of rosy-red blood moistens the surface of her skin. And so, "without knowing it Psyche of her own accord fell in love with Love." Acting unconsciously, Psyche chose love.

At this point Cupid, burned by a drop of hot oil that fell from the lamp onto his shoulder, wakes to discover that Psyche has seen him. Wounded by the oil and also by her betrayal, he jumps up and leaves "without a word." Psyche grasps his right leg in both of her hands, becoming "a pitiable appendage to his soaring flight and a trailing attachment in dangling companionship through the cloudy regions."

BOTH OF THESE scenes are repeatedly painted: Psyche looking at Cupid under the light, falling in love with him; Cupid taking off into the sky, Psyche trailing behind him. Their visual drama is irresistible, and together they tell a familiar story—love leading to loss, pleasure followed by the threat of impending death. But this ancient love story contains a deeper koan of love. Cupid leaves Psyche at the moment when she falls in love with him. And Psyche falls in love with Cupid only when she has broken his injunction against seeing him or speaking about their love.

"I AM LOOKING for a framework," Eileen tells me. The maps she has used to locate her situation suddenly seem out of date. Married for seventeen years and the mother of two sons, she finds herself "looking at separation in a way that I never had before." A woman in her late thirties of Celtic descent, tall, pale, and casually dressed in black slacks and a beige sweater, she sits facing me in a quiet room, the gold light of the late November sun picking out the reds in her hair. I am drawn to her quiet intensity as she begins the story that brought her to my study of couples in crisis.

The previous January, Rick, her husband, told her that their relationship was not close enough, they were not intimate enough, he was not happy, and he was thinking of "calling it all off again," just as Eileen was feeling that their relationship was healing, she was beginning to look forward, and Rick was becoming more open to the tender, passionate part of himself "that's extremely intimate," the part Eileen feels connected with and loves. "I'm uncomfortable," Eileen says, "because I don't know if he feels the same way."

I ask her, "And if he didn't, what would happen to you?" She says, "I'd be sad, because it would be wasting this feeling on someone who doesn't reciprocate it. That's one thing." Her other thought is more radical: "I also think I can't feel the way I feel without having somebody reciprocate it. I don't think it's in my head, and I don't know."

Rick was nearing his fortieth birthday when he told Eileen that their relationship lacked intimacy. It is easy to see this as a mid-life crisis, the Dantean moment in modern marriage. Eileen's questions are about chemistry: the fire that she feels between them. If Rick says their relationship lacks intensity while she picks up the vibrations of fire and chemistry, where is reality?

"I'm scared," Eileen says, and I understand her fear. Her life, like that of many women, depends for its continuation on her ability to read emotional cues, to know more or less where her children are psychologically, to keep track of her friends, her colleagues, her parents. To stay in touch with herself, with Rick, and with their relationship. To manage, in the lexicon of business, the dailiness of her busy life. Now all the balls threaten to fall to the ground as Rick's announcement leads Eileen to question the psychological foundation of her existence: her ability to know what is real in her relationships with people.

Philosophers and psychologists have said that we cannot know psychological reality: it is too complex, too hidden; the body is a blind. Or that reality does not exist. All we can know is our constructions, our fantasies, our projections. We can strive to know ourselves; we cannot read other minds. Like the lovers in *A Midsummer Night's Dream,* we wander in delusion, lost in a forest.

Eileen's quandary is that she thinks she knows. In this, she is supported by a quiet revolution in the human sciences. Studies of the immune system have revealed a profound connection between our minds and our bodies, suggesting ways of knowing that we are only beginning to take seriously in the West. Research on trauma has demonstrated the effects of traumatic experiences on memory, so that we remember these experiences differently, in fragments or dislocated images rather than as coherent narratives. But the simplest and perhaps most astonishing discoveries have to do with love.

Bringing mothers into the laboratory and filming them playing with their babies, researchers discovered how readily infants pick up and follow the rhythms and cadences of human connection, how quickly they learn the music of love. Infants, long considered incapable of relationship, were observed actively participating in relationship, initiating connection, responding, remembering the moves that had elicited response. The baby has a voice and thus the ability to communicate with other people. In their microanalysis of their films, the researchers caught the tidal rhythm of relationship: finding and losing and finding again, turning to, turning away, and turning back again, moving in and out of touch.

In the early seventeenth century, when Galileo looked through his telescope and saw the moons of Jupiter, he realized that the earth moves. It is not the still center of a turning world. The sense of stillness is an illusion—but one that upheld an orthodoxy dangerous to contest. If anyone could pick up a telescope and with some training see through the illusion, if people could see for themselves, then the orthodoxy depended for its continuation on people not looking or at least not seeing. Galileo was tried for heresy by the Inquisition, and he recanted to save his life. According to legend, in leaving the courtroom, he was overheard muttering *"Eppur si muove"*—but still it moves.

So in the late twentieth century, using video cameras and television monitors, researchers filmed mothers and babies playing and saw the movement of love. Their research was challenging an orthodoxy of separation (we are born alone, we die alone) by revealing a reality of relationship. Finding and losing and finding again. This is the rhythm of relationship, played over and over again in the games that delight babies and young children. It is the rhythm of love.

With Colwyn Trevarthen, one of the pioneers of the new infant research, Lynne Murray asked whether infants can tell the difference between the experience of relationship (being in sync with another person) and the appearance of relationship (smiling face, cooing voice, expressions of delight and pleasure). Designing a double closed-circuit television system, they filmed mothers and babies playing in real time, with each seeing a life-size video image of the other on a television monitor (like people talking on-screen from different cities). After a short interval, the researchers broke the synchrony of the relationship by quickly rewinding the mother's tape and playing it out of sequence with the baby. Instantly two-month-old infants picked up and responded to the loss of connection, showing puzzlement (nothing had signaled the sudden loss of connection; the mother hadn't turned away) and then distress. The visual image did not override their experience of losing relationship, finding themselves disconnected from their mother, suddenly out of touch.

Reversing the procedure and rewinding the tape of the baby so that the baby's responses were no longer in synchrony with the mother, the researchers discovered that the women reflected the loss of connection through a change in language. Instead of speaking *to* their babies, they began to speak *about* their babies, switching to a more objectified language in an effort to discover the source of the problem and typically locating it in themselves. Babies and also grown women can tell the difference between the appearance and the reality of relationship. And yet, as the women demonstrate, they may draw false inferences on the basis of their experience, in this case erroneously finding the fault in themselves.

When Edward Tronick and Katherine Weinberg studied the development of trust in relationships between mothers and babies, they found that trust grows when babies and mothers establish that they can find each other again after the inevitable moments of losing touch. It is not the goodness of the mother or the relationship per se that is the basis for trust; it is the ability of mother (or father or caretaker) and baby together to repair the breaks in their relationship that builds a safe house for love.

EILEEN AND RICK faced a shattering breach of trust five years ago when she discovered that he was having an affair with a colleague. At the time Eileen felt "totally down" on herself. Rick also was upset and in turmoil, and in marriage counseling they decided that they wanted to stay together and rebuild their relationship. This is the healing to which Eileen referred. When Cupid leaves Psyche and she grasps on to him, she is described as a pitiable appendage, a trailing attachment, a dangling companion—a pathetic creature, an object of pity if not contempt. Eileen had said that if Rick did not feel the same way she did, she would be wasting her love to stay with him. But she also had said, "I also think I can't feel the way I feel without having somebody reciprocate it. I don't think it's in my head, and I don't know."

I listen to her first-person voice in this passage, lifting its phrases ("I also think, I can't feel, I feel, I don't think, I don't know") out of the sentences. Strung together, they fall into a poetic cadence, composing an "I poem"—a sonogram of the psyche:

I also think
I can't feel

I feel
I don't think

I don't know.

The poem is an ode to dissociation. If she thinks, she can't feel; if she feels, she doesn't think. In this way, she heeds the injunction "don't" that stands between "I" and "know." But Eileen is moving out of dissociation, and in doing so, she is questioning the premise of separation—not the literal separation that Rick is considering, but the separation of her feelings from Rick's. Instead, she thinks that she could not be feeling the heat of love that she is feeling if he were not feeling the same way. It leads her to the radical suspicion that it is the connection between them that is precipitating his leaving, and in the face of this suspicion she has decided, for the moment, to stay. In this sense, she is looking at separation in a new way.

It is truly difficult to frame her experience, because it flies in the face of our usual ways of speaking as well as the codes of honor that surround relationships between women and men. Why would she stay with a man who is talking about leaving her? Why would she stay with a man who has had an affair? Why would Psyche hang on to Cupid, who, in leaving without saying a word, seems to have confirmed the monster story?

When Psyche cannnot see or speak about what she knows, she has no way to frame her experience. And without framing it, she cannot tell her story, or counter the stories that others have told her. Her sisters' motives are suspect because they are driven by envy, but their point is a real one. Psyche was asked to believe in Cupid's love while being kept in the dark about him. When she opened her eyes to what she thought she knew, given the stories she was told, he took it as a betrayal. Discovering that her experience was reliable, she fell in love with her lover. The tenderness and vulnerability she knew in Cupid were not part of the stories told about him.

The love between Psyche and Cupid is a love that takes place in a culture that is unraveling; the myth of the magical princess does not have its predicted happy ending. Instead, in this second-century old wife's tale, we are shown what happens to the psyche—soul, breath, and blood—when one becomes an object in the eyes of other people, what happens to love or desire when one is used as the instrument of another's revenge; we see the difficulty of choosing love in the midst of confusion; and finally, we see Psyche falling in love with love.

It is true that love is blind in the sense of being driven by emotion, not reason, and also being beyond our control. Love is also silent, like water finding its way through the ground. But the conception of love as blind in the sense of contingent on not seeing or knowing the other has its origins in the Oedipus tragedy.

In prophesying a funereal marriage for Psyche, the oracle of Apollo has forecast the Oedipus tragedy. Oedipus' incestuous marriage to his mother can only be carried on in darkness and silence. And Oedipus turns away from Jocasta once he discovers who she is, dismissing her as an "unspeakable mother." Because it was she who gave him to the herdsman—possibly as the only move under the circumstances that could save his life. Jocasta is a woman who cannot live with the truth, who cannot bear to have anyone know what she did to Oedipus when he was a child. The chorus comments on her silence: "How could that Queen whom Laius won be silent when that deed was done?" When Oedipus discovers that she abandoned him as an infant, she strangles herself, hanging herself with a curtain.

If Psyche is destined for the Oedipus tragedy, she walks out of its plot. She refuses to play the parts that women play in that drama. She will not be Antigone, Oedipus' good daughter, who accompanies her father in his blindness; instead she speaks to her father about his blindness, telling him what he does not see (that becoming New Venus was like death). She will not act the part of Jocasta, who chose to protect her husband by wounding and abandoning the child. Having to choose between husband and child, Psyche makes the choice Jocasta did not. In choosing to kill the monster and protect her child and herself, she discovers that the choice itself is based on false premises—Cupid in fact is not a monster, nor in the end does he leave her. Walking out of an old story, she is a woman for our time. She refuses to live as an object; she breaks the taboos on seeing and speaking about love; she will not risk her own life or that of the child for a promise of immortality.

So far the tale has followed the old woman's dream interpretation. Erotic pleasure and sensual delights have led to mental depression, physical weakness, and every other sort of loss. Eileen tells a similar story. When she and Rick fell in love, they were "insanely happy"; their sexual relationship was passionate, and they were also best friends. In the early years of their marriage, they lived like children in a world of grown-ups. Their pleasure with one another felt illicit, as if they were getting away with something. This phase of their marriage ended with the birth of their children; they began to live in separate worlds. Eileen was depressed, lonely, and unhappy; she felt herself becoming "grim and closed." Following her discovery of Rick's affair, she entered therapy and recovered the intensity of her feelings—her anger and eventually her love of life. In the process, she went back to school for a degree in business administration, earning an income, developing a close circle of colleagues and friends, enjoying spending time with herself. She had gained a foothold on independence, a basis of economic viability. The ground of her relationship with Rick was changing.

In the world of the Psyche and Cupid myth, love itself is in disarray. A gossipy seagull tells Venus that "there is no joy anymore, no grace, no charm. Everything is unkempt and boorish and harsh. Weddings and social intercourse and the love of children are gone, leaving only a monstrous mess and an unpleasant disregard for anything as squalid as the bonds of marriage." Similar things are said about the contemporary world. But disarray, the breaking apart of old forms, is part of the process of transformation, and Eileen has a keen eye for the rhythms of change.

"Last spring I cried a lot. I was extremely sad. [Rick] wanted to go into marriage counseling, and I was extremely sad for months. I felt a door slam, and it slammed behind me, and I can't go back. Not that I want to." The door that closed was the door that led her into "just persevering or keeping going, bringing him along with only 20 percent agreement." She needs to know whether the love she feels with Rick is real or whether "it is something that feels good to me and so I construct it." I ask her, "What's your hunch?" She says, "My hunch is that he really is connected with me and he's confused about that."

As the mother of sons, Eileen has watched her boys grow in the largely white and Protestant New England culture into which she married and in which she is raising her sons. Thinking about her sons, her eye is caught by "that piece of what a man has to be. I don't know," she trails off, and then picks up with what she knows, saying now that it is not what a man "has to be" but what "they think they are supposed to be." And this subtle shift in phrasing opens a way out of her situation. She speaks now, still talking about her sons, of "that tender piece of them that they sort of have to set aside to be what they think they are supposed to be." And then, making this distinction between what she thinks and what they think, between what is and what could be, she rushes in to close the space she has opened, saying, "It makes me care for them. It makes me affectionate with them particularly, and feel bad for them, for the battles." It is the image of the pietà, the mother holding her wounded son.

What Eileen loves in her sons is something else—qualities she knows in Rick and that she now sees coming to the fore, "that tender part of him that I feel I know and that I feel I am connected with and I have to be extremely careful of." The "I poem" in this passage highlights her clarity:

> *I feel*
> *I know*
>
> *I feel*
> *I am connected*
> *I have to be extremely careful.*

Rick is a successful man in the eyes of the world; "the competitive male part of him is highly developed." Eileen admires his abundant masculinity. He is "an aggressive businessman doing deals and excited about that. He is intense in his connecting with people." She too has gone to business school. But this is not the side of him that "keeps me with him." She loves his tenderness, his intensity, but to stay with him, "I need to be seen."

"What about love?" I ask Eileen, and without missing a beat, she says, "If we scrap everything else, we're crazy about each other." And then she adds, "I think." Sex is passionate between them, but they get so mad they can barely speak. "So love," Eileen says, "I don't know what love is."

Eileen and I met twice, and at the end of our second conversation, we returned to the question with which she came: how to frame the crisis in her relationship with Rick. Speaking to the dissonance between what she is saying and what Rick is saying, she begins by taking what has become the party line in such matters: "He is no more right than I am about it. . . . It's his reality, and then my reality."

I think of the infant research—the baby and also the mother knowing when they are and are not in touch, disregarding the images on the screen when they do not jibe with what they are experiencing. I think of girls at adolescence, reading the human world as a naturalist reads a forest, distinguishing the species of relationship (friend, best friend, love, not love), and holding the complexity of human feelings ("she's my best friend; I hate her"). For a time, Eileen had shut down this capacity in herself, becoming, as she says, "grim and closed." But living now more comfortably with the range of her thoughts and relishing the intensity of her emotions, she has regained her inner compass, her sense of true north. I wonder with Eileen whether her psychological presence is heightening Rick's vulnerability, whether it is the growing intensity of the connection between them that is leading him to think about leaving. She had said that she thought he might need to separate from her in order to grow a part of himself without her seeing or speaking about it. I say to Eileen, "If Rick is saying that your relationship lacks intensity and intimacy and you are picking up the vibes of fire and chemistry between you, then it's not his reality and your reality but reality and not reality."

"Right," Eileen says. I feel I have said "Rumpelstiltskin,"

the name nobody was supposed to guess. Suddenly the pale woman sitting in front of me looks vibrant. I see the fire and passion in her for the first time. Now she says simply that she does not believe Rick: "It's a crock of baloney." What she sees in Rick, she has observed in her boys. Her older son, now thirteen, has become interested in knowing her and her women friends. He approaches them shyly, "like a deer coming up to the porch." Exquisite in the beauty of new manhood, he is easily startled. Eileen finds him "a pleasure." Her ten-year-old son "right now is very traditional." A scout, an acolyte at church, he "likes Mom in an apron making apple pies. He doesn't like me very much. He likes me to be a mother." Just as she made a space between what a man is and what they think they are supposed to be, so too a space opens here between what a mother is and what a mother is supposed to be—between a person and an image. When she speaks of her younger son liking Mom in an apron making apple pies, when she says "he doesn't like me very much," she distinguishes between "me" and "me being a mother," between herself and her playing a role. And so it is with Rick. She feels he is crazy about her, and she also feels that he does not see her, that he is holding an image that blocks her out.

In saying that she does not believe what Rick is saying, Eileen is not questioning his hold on reality or his ability to represent himself. Rather, she does not believe what he is saying about their relationship because she does not hear in what he is saying any representation of herself. And without holding her experience as well as his own, he is out of touch with them. "I didn't not believe him," she explains, backtracking now, "it's just a lot to hold in reality. It was a lot for me to hold at the time. I think," she says, coming forward again, "that he was profoundly connected to me all that time. That's what I think, and you know . . . what was called into question was my reality."

Eileen asks if she is deceiving herself, and yet she holds to her experience—the empirical ground of what she knows. As she does so, she says, "It's how crazy I feel." We can ask with Eileen if she is maintaining a construction or holding on to a fantasy love in order not to face the pain and the shame of Rick's rejection or the sadness of this loss. We can also ask if Eileen is fighting dissociation, healing an old wound, resisting a path once taken that led her to split herself into two people: one passionate and lively, a woman of fire and chemistry, the other grim and closed.

As I listen to Eileen and she hears her voice resounded and amplified through my questions, as I learn from her what she knows, our conversation encourages her to go further out on a limb—to explore the edges of her knowing, her hunches, her sense of what's real and what's not real, what is and is not love. In doing so, she comes to a clear framing of what is at stake for her in this crisis. "It's a fight," she says, "at the foundation, in the arenas that are most important to me, my relationships with other people. And love, and how it's returned, and how I read people and how I read where we are in terms of intimacy. I value that more than anything . . . to fight there, I mean, it's fighting for your life."

WHEN PSYCHE lets go of Cupid's leg and falls, exhausted, to the ground, Cupid turns in his flight. Alighting on the top of a tall cypress, he speaks to her about what he had not wanted her to see: his relationship with his mother, his vulnerability. "My poor, naïve Psyche," he begins. She did not know what was happening, could not know except insofar as she felt his fear of being exposed, his fragility, and the urgency of his need for control. Now anger rushes to the surface as he begins to speak about his love. His voice is distant and supercilious: "I in fact disobeyed the orders of my mother Venus, who had commanded me to chain you with passion for some wretched and worthless man and sentence you to the lowest sort of marriage. Instead I flew to you myself as your lover." He had shot himself with his own arrow, falling in love with her and making her his wife, only to discover that she had thought him a wild beast, a monster, and had taken a knife to cut off his head, "the head that held a lover's eyes." It is hard to hear the love ("your lover, lover's eyes") through the veil of attack, which now picks up force. He had warned her not to listen to her sisters ("those excellent advisors of yours"). She had disobeyed him, she had betrayed him, she was not the woman he thought she was, she was not the woman he loved. He will take his revenge on her sisters. As for Psyche, he will punish her now "merely by leaving." With this, Cupid takes off into the sky, heading for his mother's chambers. By refusing to accompany her father in his blindness, by saving herself and her child instead of obeying her husband, by opening her eyes and seeing with whom she is living, Psyche has walked out of the Oedipus plot, but Cupid is heading into the heart of the tragedy.

ON A RAINY Saturday, Dan, a man in his forties and the father of three children, spent the day building a tree house in the backyard. Jude, his wife, was painting their son's room. At the end of the afternoon, as Dan was coming in to shower and Jude was going to prepare the dinner, they met unexpectedly in the archway to the dining room. Spontaneously they embraced and kissed, love welling up and desire taking them by surprise. Together they went out to look at the tree house and discovered that the rain had stopped. As they stood in the yard, the sun broke through the clouds, creating a brilliant orange-red slit in the otherwise gray October sky, framing the tree house and its ladder. It was magical, this sudden sun and the love between them after a long and difficult time.

Ten minutes later, when Jude called Dan and the children to dinner, the man who came to the table was "a different man." His face had closed, lost its color; his body was slack, no longer muscular; his eyes had no expression. He sat at the table in the midst of Jude and the children, eating his dinner in silence.

Jude is telling this story about "the two Dans." In a previous session, Terry Real and I had focused our attention on Jude and her fears, stemming from her childhood, that she was not a lovable person, that there was something wrong with her. Terry encouraged her to stay with these fears, to explore what felt so overwhelming to her. In the interim, she discovered that in fact she could stay with her feelings and know them, rather than running away. She began to keep track of her own experience. She realized that when she left the house on Sundays, preferring to go to work rather than stay at home, it was because she could not bear to be present in the face of Dan's emotional absence; when he closed himself off from her, she felt that he had slammed a door in her face, and she blamed herself, assuming that he had seen something in her that drove him away. Clocking her own experience, she became aware that she was living with two Dans.

Listening to Jude's experience of being with the open and loving Dan and then finding herself with a closed and distant man, I find myself wondering why pleasure had led Dan to disappear. "Why would pleasure be followed by absence?" I ask.

Dan says, "It rained, we went inside, and life continued. The picture closed. The chapter ended. It didn't last." And then he adds, "Maybe I didn't want it to last. I don't know. It wasn't planned, it wasn't expected. I didn't know what to do with it." A smile flickers across his face, like fleeting sun. I ask about the smile, and he says that he was pleased with the image. He has completely shut Jude out.

Pressed further, he explains that he withdrew into himself

when Jude turned her attention to the children and the dinner. It was as if he was accommodating himself to her, except that this was not what she wanted.

We are sitting in a consulting room at the Cambridge Family Institute. Dan and Jude sit next to each other, but there is little contact between them. Terry Real and I sit facing them. There is a feeling of static in the room. Jude wraps her athletic jacket around her as if she is cold; I notice her earrings—silver pendants and a sapphire stud. I sense she is a more spirited woman than she seems.

"What's that like," Terry asks Dan, "when it stops being about you and it starts being about them? Can we slow that down and look at it?"

After a long pause, Dan says, "I think it starts with a feeling of being left out somehow, and to deal with that, I just shift into thinking about things. There's always something I can think about, and the more remote it is from what's going on, the further away I am. . . . I didn't feel comfortable. I didn't feel—I don't know. I didn't feel that I belonged there. And I dealt with it by disappearing." It is hard to remember that he is describing feelings that followed an experience of intense pleasure. Dan volunteers that he is more comfortable feeling miserable than he is feeling happy; to feel happy and open, he says, "makes me feel vulnerable."

At this point, Dan starts to talk about his mother. He describes her as an intrusive and controlling woman who had tried to bind him to her by giving him what he wanted: the perfect gift, the perfect meal. I find myself feeling sympathetic with this woman who somehow was defeated no matter what she did. And then I am stunned to hear Dan say that he and his mother "were pals." "We were buddies," he explains, suddenly lively. When he was four or five, Dan would be at home with his mother in the afternoons; his older brother was still in school, his father away at work. Dan and his mother would spend the afternoons in the kitchen baking together.

In this time, Dan knew his mother; he saw "the face behind her face." He says, "The real Frances would blow through that veneer, and I would see it. She was very angry." Dan knew her anger and also her sadness. She had not married the man she wanted to marry; she felt unsure of herself, having grown up in a working-class family and living now among "respectable people." She was trying to do the right thing: the perfect gift, the perfect meal. Dan and his brother were to be perfect children. But Dan also knew her pleasure. They had fun in the kitchen together, eating doughnuts, being buddies, pals.

Dan's anger at his mother is on the surface; he tells her story with thinly veiled contempt. It is pleasure that he has hidden, alluding only briefly to the closeness between them. He is seemingly a man without curiosity. When Jude spoke of leaving on Sundays because she could not bear his absence, I asked if he was curious why she came back. All he said was "It's sad."

In his essay "Knowingness and Abandonment: An Oedipus for Our Time," Jonathan Lear, a philosopher and psychoanalyst, observes that we always read in the context of our own time. His Oedipus is a man who has imprisoned himself in reason, a man who abandons himself to thinking so as not to think about the fact of his abandonment. *Oedipus Tyrannus,* Sophocles' tragedy, is perhaps the most powerful dramatic rendering of dissociation: the determination at all costs not to see what in another sense one knows. Asked a riddle about feet (what walks on four feet in the morning, two at noon, three in the afternoon), Oedipus does not look at his feet, which contain the clue to his story. Going through life with a name meaning "swollen foot," he remains startlingly uncurious about his wounds. But the play also demonstrates the power of association, as Oedipus is inexorably drawn first to his father, whom he murders, then to his mother, whom he marries, and finally to the truth of who he is and what has happened to him. To Lear, Oedipus is a know-it-all, a man who is afraid to know, who "displays a stunning lack of curiosity"; his "knowingness" keeps him from feeling. In this, he is an Oedipus for our time.

Dan is angry about becoming the problem in this couples therapy; he was the problem when he was a child. The imperfect son of the perfect mother. His anger at her is intense. She took him to a round of doctors, subjecting him to humiliating and intrusive and painful procedures, ranging from psychological tests to unnecessary surgeries. Terry encourages Dan's memories of feeling helpless and powerless, ashamed and enraged, by this endless probing. At the time he could not protect himself from his mother's intrusions; now as an adult he can create boundaries. I find myself thinking about Dan's saying that he and his mother were pals.

Looking at the sullen man sitting across from me, I think of a child who feels unseen and unappreciated. He's holding out, I suspect, and I wonder why. Dan loved his mother as a young boy. He saw the human face behind the mask she wore, and also her wish not to be seen. I find myself wondering whether out of love for her, he moved away from her so as not to see her. Did he sacrifice his relationship with his mother out of his love for her? And was he waiting for someone to see his sacrifice and appreciate his love? He became the problem in his childhood family; now he was the problem in his adult family. He was a successful computer scientist and a budding poet, but he lived in his body like a swollen child.

In moving away from his mother, he was protecting himself from her abandonment of him (putting on her mask, hiding her face) and also from her anger and her sadness. But in closing himself off from her, he was also protecting her by not seeing what she did not want people to see (her anger, her sadness, her imperfection), distancing himself from her so as not to blow her cover. In this, he had been a loving son. I say this to Dan, and Jude's face changes, softens; she moves closer to him and starts to cry. Dan feels present for the first time.

Terry makes the connection. When Dan feels pleasure with Jude like he felt with his mother, perhaps the habit of covering takes over, so that he withdraws from her as he withdrew from his mother, as an act of protection, but this act leaves Jude feeling abandoned. Feeling blamed perhaps in the way that Dan may have blamed his mother for not wanting him to see her, for closing herself off from him. So that their closeness with each other and their pleasure became hidden and came to feel illicit, turning into a smoldering, angry, incestuous love.

The I poem from the passage where Dan speaks of feeling left out and dealing with it by disappearing sums up the impasse:

> *I think*
> *I just shift into thinking*
> *I can think*
> *I am.*
>
> *I didn't feel*
> *I didn't feel*
> *I don't know.*
>
> *I didn't feel*
> *I belonged there.*
> *I dealt with it*
> > *by disappearing.*

Like Oedipus, Dan abandons himself to thinking in order not to think about his abandonment; he is determined not to feel, in part because he feels so wounded and so alone. The Dan who disappears is the loving son, the wounded son, the loving man who, experiencing pleasure, deals with it by turning away. He had in effect married his mother; and it was, as he said, sad for Jude.

IN THE SECOND half of the Psyche and Cupid myth, Psyche sets out to find Cupid. I wonder why this story is told and retold, why Psyche is seen as heroic by feminist critics, why the love between Cupid and Psyche has been portrayed by Jungian analysts as ideal. The story itself is so violent that it belies any attempt at idealization. If this is a timeless myth about love and the soul, then we are all in trouble. Psyche is beaten by Venus and tortured by her servants, Trouble and Sadness. Repeatedly she moves to kill herself. I remember the old woman's dream interpretation: that this scenario may augur well. I remember that *Metamorphoses* is a novel about transformation, changing a shape or overcoming a form. And then I remember that this ancient story about love is presented as an old wife's tale, a story told by an old mother to a young woman on the eve of her seemingly perfect marriage, and that shortly after telling the story, the old woman is hanged—like a member of the Resistance. Suggesting that this is a dangerous story to tell, this tale that asks us to see and to say what we know about love.

Apuleius is writing in the tradition of comedy; his story about love is a story about knowing. Psyche is the main actor in this drama and the model for the women in Shakespeare's comedies who, with the help of the fools, the clowns, and the rustics, avert the unfolding of a tragic story by turning it into *Much Ado About Nothing,* by showing that you can have it *As You Like It,* and that *All's Well That Ends Well.* If feminism is understood not as a battle in the war between the sexes but rather a movement to transform a world in which both men and women suffer losses that constrain their ability to love, then the story of Psyche and Cupid is a feminist tale. In breaking the taboo on seeing Cupid and speaking about their love, Psyche reveals the world in which she has been living: a world where Cupid is hiding his love and where she cannot know what she knows.

WHEN CUPID flies off to his mother, Psyche throws herself into a river, but the river throws her right back on the bank. With this act, the natural world returns as a central actor in this drama, reminding us that we are creatures of nature as well as beings who live in culture and that when we violate our nature, just as when we break the taboos of culture, we find ourselves in trouble. Reminding Psyche that she has chosen love, the natural world refuses the pollution of her self-destructive act. Thus, Psyche takes "an unfamiliar road."

It will lead her through a wasteland of relationships among women, a landscape devastated by envy and fear. But the road she has taken is unfamiliar in part because, in exposing the costs to women of living in patriarchy, it will also lead her out of that territory. To leave patriarchy, she must cross its psychic terrain, and as the old woman foretells, the labor of love that leads to the birth of pleasure is a difficult psychological labor.

SONYA AND PHIL met at a large Midwestern university where they both played varsity sports and belonged to the same religious community. Their spiritual connection was matched by a powerful physical attraction. Phil says, "We had an unbelievable sexual relationship. We would stare at each other for an hour straight, lying on the bed or just sitting somewhere on a couch." Phil's pride is evident as he explains that Sonya at the time was studying to be ordained and that she became the first woman to take part in what historically had been an all-male service. It was a dramatic time, and also fun. They loved being together; they were part of a lively youth group at church and active in the community. Eventually they married and in time became the parents of four children. Phil worked long hours and felt enormous pressure to succeed in a highly competitive field. At home, he would periodically erupt in rages, occasionally hitting Sonya. She experienced him now as a possessive and controlling man. She began to second-guess everything she said, needing to anticipate how Phil would hear her and how he would respond. She felt that she was not being seen or respected, and these feelings came to a head one weekend when, in the presence of her mother, Phil refused to participate in a much-anticipated family celebration. Following this incident, Sonya resolved to leave the marriage and called a former colleague for help in reentering her profession. She was planning to leave Phil once she established her economic viability; in the interim, her friendship with her colleague deepened.

When Phil learned of Sonya's relationship with her colleague and realized that he was about to lose her, he did "a complete U-turn." He began coming home every night for dinner; on weekends, rather than going out to places that would affirm his sense of himself as a successful, cool guy, they would stay home, playing Monopoly with the children and then spending the rest of the evening together. This was the relationship Sonya had wanted; the intimacy and passion they had known with each other returned, and the physical and emotional bullying stopped.

When they came to consult with Terry Real and me, they spoke initially about pleasure. They were like children with a secret, and the secret was their delight in finding each other again. It was infectious; pleasure filled the room. Sonya was stunningly beautiful—a dark, passionate, intensely alive and intelligent woman. "There is so much hope," Phil says. But he adds, "I have this one little thing which is this—the truth." Sonya would not answer Phil's question: "Did she or didn't she sleep with the guy?" Phil had read an article in *Psychology*

Today that said that for a marriage to heal after the rupture of infidelity, there has to be a level playing field. The unfaithful partner must tell the other the truth and honestly answer the other's questions. And yet Sonya refused to answer his question.

It was striking how quickly pleasure gave way to this argument about truth, how quickly patriarchy rushed back into the room. No mention was made of Phil's hitting Sonya; it was her infidelity that was "the problem." As Phil insists that Sonya answer his question, I watch Sonya recede into silence.

In the film *Private Confessions*, Anna, a married woman, confesses to her uncle Jacob, a Lutheran pastor, that she has been unfaithful. She has fallen in love with a younger man, who is studying to enter the church. Jacob hears her confession and advises her that she must tell her husband the truth. He will mature, he tells her, and the truth will bring them closer together. In a scene that is quietly lit with the intensity and concentration of a Vermeer painting, Anna says that she knows her husband, she knows that what her uncle has said is not true. She also introduces a subtle shift, speaking not of "the truth" but of "what is called the Truth." There are other truths that she has spoken. And yet she gives in. In each of the five conversations that constitute the film, Anna throws away pleasure—for the sake of the truth, for the sake of her uncle, for one good reason or another. In the next-to-last scene, Jacob is dying of cancer. He has sent for Anna, worried about the advice that he gave her; he wants to know how things worked out. One look at her tells him, and he is stricken. Anna seeks to reassure him, saying that she "did as you advised me" and lying about her husband's response. A colleague with whom Jacob was ordained comes in to give communion, and then, in a dramatic convulsion, Jacob throws up the wafer. The film, directed by Liv Ullman, was written by Ingmar Bergman, who based it on his parents' marriage. In the final scene, we see Anna at eighteen, in the bloom of new womanhood, intensely alive, and radiant in her new hat. It is the eve of her confirmation, and she confesses to Jacob, her uncle and pastor, that she cannot go to communion, saying that it would be "a deceit," "a lie," that she would be acting a part. She senses his displeasure, his disapproval of her new hat. And as they stand on one of the seven bridges crossing the river, we watch Anna throw her hat in.

Sitting with Phil and Sonya, I am moved by his honesty in looking at himself. He reflects on his blindness in the marriage: he had thought he was giving Sonya everything. In giving her all the accoutrements of life with a successful man—a house, an expensive car, an au pair, dinners at good restaurants—he says, "I thought that I was going to be okay. And the one thing I wasn't giving her, which was the most significant thing, was—she wanted me. I just—I felt like I couldn't give me . . . and then she'd say even though you're home on weekends, you're not fully present."

"Why couldn't you give you?" I ask.

"I was just—I was just so overwhelmed and stressed with the company," Phil says.

"What would it mean to give you?" I wonder.

"I felt that somehow—I don't know—maybe it would soften me, or maybe it would take the focus off my business. I mean I was always thinking about business. Most of our discussions, I mean she has been a great listener. She listened to me about the business a lot."

"What did she want?"

"Excuse me?" Phil asks.

I rephrase my question: "What did you think she wanted?"

"I don't really know, because I don't think we ever had it."

"Do you know?" I ask, turning to Sonya, and she says, "I wanted the you that is now. Everything that you are now is what I wanted back then." Asked if she can describe that "you," she says, "Being present, caring about what's going on with the family and with me, and I mean there's so much. It's just the shift in attitude. . . . I really wish we could be best friends. That's what I think a marriage—a happy marriage—should be. . . . And a friendship to me is a mutual thing, so if one person starts acting weird, then the other person can say, you know, 'What's wrong with you? What's going on?' Or whatever, and then you could readjust. But if that doesn't happen, then I can see that I could start walling off."

Sonya has described the process of repair, the grounds for trust, the way people can find each other when they have lost touch. It is the basis for a happy marriage, for being best friends, for any enduring relationship. Phil's view of trust is more static; it has to do with telling the truth. In the face of his jealousy and his suspicions, his anxiety about himself and his business, he had tried to do the right thing. As he said, "I thought that I was going to be okay." He was trying to do his best for Sonya while at the same time holding himself apart from her—"I felt like I couldn't give me." It was this that defeated Sonya. "He'd stonewall," she says; and she—feeling that she could not speak and be heard, that "everything I said had to be sold"—began to wall herself off as well.

Taking down these walls, they have come to a place of pleasure. "It's sublime," Phil says. But they have also come to a seeming roadblock that stands in the way of love: Phil's insistence on knowing what Sonya now calls "the truth, what-ever that is," thus alluding to the way that the truth was being framed. If you frame the choices in a certain way, then you never have to step outside the framework.

"Let's talk about the truth," I say. "What's the truth?"

Phil says that he's "wrestling with this whole principle; do I—if I know the truth—I know that she slept with him." His incoherence catches his struggle with his own question: whether he can live with what he knows, on principle.

Terry speaks of the pain that comes with knowing that somebody is having an affair, the discovery that you have been lied to, and the need "to sort of make sense of it all and get out there on ground zero and share reality with each other." Looking Sonya in the eye, Phil knows that she is lying. Phil has been untrusting and jealous of Sonya for years. Her beauty, her independence of spirit, her vibrancy, which drew him to her in the first place, now threaten him because of their power to draw other men as well. The very life in her that led him to fall in love with her has become a threat to their marriage, since it raises the specter of loss, the possibility of betrayal. What Phil most loved in Sonya, he tried to squelch, hitting her, trying to beat the life out of her, in a paradoxical effort to keep her for himself.

"I just want to say that there is a frame around this discussion," I say. "And you set the frame for me when you spoke about the church. Sonya was the first woman to be ordained?" I ask.

Phil answers with pride. "She was the first." Sonya elaborates, saying that she was the first noncelibate woman allowed on the altar in any official sense of the word. "So I could probably be the only noncelibate woman"—the only woman in the full sense of the word—to have participated in the religious service.

Sonya's sexuality is part of her vibrancy; it challenged the patriarchal structure of the church and also of her marriage. Could she stay in her body, in touch with her sensuality, and also stay in the church and with Phil? Initially it seemed possible; both she and Phil were committed to equality between them; they were both invested in the process of change. So that when Sonya found herself living with a jealous and possessive and violent man, she was shocked; and not wanting to know what she knew, at least for a time, she dissociated herself from the life she was living, "walking in a confused fog."

I wonder what each of them makes of the fact that it was only when Sonya became involved with another man that Phil came into her presence and stopped withholding himself. "What's that about?" I ask them.

Phil says, "I don't know. Maturity, growth, the ultimate nightmare." His ultimate nightmare is "her in the arms of another man." The stage is set for the Trojan War, with Sonya a modern-day Helen. Historically it has been the ultimate nightmare—one's woman in the arms of another man. It was the reason that Atreus felt justified in killing his brother's children and feeding them to him; it was the reason that Agamemnon felt compelled to sail to Troy, sacrificing his daughter Iphigenia for the sake of restoring honor to Greece, after Helen had slighted Greek manhood by running off with Paris, a barbarian. What is it about this loss that makes it so incendiary?

"Why is this the ultimate nightmare?" I press Phil. And he lets the patriarchal mantle fall from his shoulders. Instead of speaking about honor, he speaks about love. "I guess the ultimate nightmare really for me was to never have the opportunity to show her how I really feel and to be a family man, to open my heart and to love her."

THE SIMPLICITY of this moment is exquisite. Phil's openhearted expression of love. And for a moment, history falls away. Life comes into the room. Showing how he really feels, Phil becomes "a family man." But this places his manhood at risk, or what he has thought of as manhood. It is not surprising then that at this moment of turn in every possible respect, he returns to his question: he wants a guarantee that if he opens his heart to Sonya, she will open herself to him. He wants to know that if he asks her again about the affair, she won't "look me in the eyes and tell me any lies." I can feel his anger mounting, overtaking his love.

"I don't get it," I say, thinking of Sonya. "I don't get what Sonya is supposed to do."

Phil says, "She says she didn't and I know she did."

"But if you know, then why ask her?" I wonder. "There's no

point in it. I mean, if I know that today is Thursday, there's no point in my asking Terry, 'What day is this?' To see if he's going to lie to me? If I know, I don't ask. So if I'm asking, there's something else going on. At the very moment when something new is starting between you, when you are doing something so quintessentially human, which for you is unfamiliar, opening yourselves to one another in love, you don't know what is going to happen if you open your heart and stay present and she doesn't second-guess herself. So what is it you want? Is there a real question you have?"

Terry says, "I think the real question is, will you leave me?"

Phil begins to cry.

THE REAL question is about love: if I love you, will you leave me? It is a child's question: will you leave me, how will I survive? It is every lover's question—the question at the heart of this triangle. Does Sonya love Phil, will she leave him again for another man? The two men in this triangle are in competition with each other, and Sonya holds the key. The answer to Phil's question is that she loves him, and she is choosing him over the other man. "If I loved you": it is the conditional question of the old song. "If" I loved you, what would happen? It is about how hard it is to speak one's love.

> *If I loved you,*
> *Time and again I would try to say*
> *All I'd want you to know.*
> *If I loved you,*
> *Words wouldn't come in an easy way—*
> *Round in circles I'd go.*
> *Longin' to tell you, but afraid and shy,*
> *I'd let my golden chances pass me by.*
> *Soon you'd leave me,*

Off you would go in the mist of day,
Never, never to know
How I loved you—
If I loved you.

Sonya's question is if he loves her, if he can see her and delight in her without starting "to act weird." I want to tell her that I understand her second-guessing herself; I want to encourage her to know what she knows. "This isn't happening nowhere," I say. I talk about the church that they both know, and Sonya's courage in overcoming its patriarchal form by her participation. What if Phil were to break that form as well by dropping his question and staying in the present, by remembering what his true nightmare is.

"How would you feel?" Terry asks him.

Phil says, "Very scared."

THE SESSION is ending. Phil has said that stepping into the river at a different place or into a different river would mean more joy, more harmony, more love, more communication, more connection, more hope, more pleasure. Sonya says that she will not go back into the patriarchal form their marriage had taken or live like a person walking through a fog; if Phil wants to go back, she will leave him. When they moved to the South and the local church would not recognize Sonya's ordination, neither of them attended services. Sonya knows that change is possible, having succeeded in transforming the church, at least in one place and for a time. "It's one of the major reasons I fell in love with her," Phil says.

Terry says, "You were attracted to a woman who could stand up to the system that was burying both of you. . . . And when it turned out that you were burying her, she broke out and you woke up. Good choice, Phil."

"Good move, Sonya," I say.

Like Psyche, Sonya intended to end her marriage. Setting out to protect herself and her children, she sought to regain her economic freedom. In the process, she freed her love. This became the incendiary act, burning Phil and waking him from his relational slumber. Seeing that he is about to lose the relationship he wanted—a relationship he knew because they once had it—Phil makes, as he says, "a complete U-turn." And Sonya turns back as Psyche turned back, when she saw the man with whom she had fallen in love, a man who had virtually disappeared from sight.

Perhaps it is necessary to go into the heart of tragedy in order to find a path that leads back to pleasure. Sonya has walked into the emotional epicenter of patriarchy, the place where love and honor collide. For the moment, she and Phil have chosen love, stepping into a river that is leading, as Phil says, to more joy, more harmony, more hope, more possibilities. What is the truth that shadows this ending? Freeing her love, Sonya wounded Phil's manhood. She challenged the hierarchy of man over woman by breaking out of a marriage with a man who had hit her, by seeing and saying, as she says one would in a friendship, that something was weird and wrong. In turning to another man, she placed herself at the center of a competition between men, setting up an explosive triangle. Phil says that for him to feel what he feels is to be a family man. To do so means to struggle with the meaning of manhood: whether manhood and the courage of manhood require him to defend his honor and uphold the hierarchy, or whether being a man means having the courage to open his heart and express his love.

II

Regions of Light

Love merely as the best
There is, and one would make the best of that
By saying how it grows and in what climates . . .
To say at the end, however we find it, good,
Bad, or indifferent, it helps us, and the air
Is sweetest there. The air is very sweet.

—JAMES MERRILL

IT IS EIGHT o'clock on Thursday morning, and I am sitting on a small chair in a sunny pre-kindergarten room. Next to me, an Egyptian spiny mouse runs, spinning its wheel against the wall of its glass cage. The four-year-old boys begin to drift in. Gabe comes in, carried by his father, his face buried in his father's neck. Slowly, this large man lowers himself onto the floor with his son, takes out a plastic container of toys, and begins to arrange the small figures of people and horses into a scene. Curious, Gabe unwraps his arms from around his father's neck, turning to see, his face flushed, his blond hair tousled. Soon, father and son are playing together, quietly absorbed. After a time, when Gabe has settled, his father gently takes his leave.

Jake strides in alongside his father, who brings a generous, warm energy into the room. A sensuous and gregarious man, he stops to talk with Lucia and Jen, the teachers, while Jake wanders off into the room. After a while, I notice Jake's father on the floor on all fours with Jake on his back, Jake's arms wrapped around his father's neck, his face reaching around like a turtle's, kissing his father tenderly on the cheek. I am moved by this father's ease in receiving the love of his small son, his steadiness, his unhurried presence, his open affection as Tony, walking behind them, tugs at the back of Jake's father's shirt until he too is swept up in an embrace, Jake's father kneeling now, holding one boy in each arm.

Gradually the parents take their leave, and the morning free-play period begins. Suddenly I notice that in this classroom where guns are forbidden, each boy is carrying something that looks suspiciously like a weapon, a gunlike object made out of brightly colored large pieces of Lego. When Jen comes over to Nick and asks what he is carrying, Nick turns the Lego construction up vertically and, peering through an imagined lens, explains to Jen that it is "an old-fashioned camera."

The boys congregate in the dress-up corner, casually armed. Jake picks up a piece of pink lace. "Look at," he says to Tony, peering through the gauzy cloth. Tony picks up his Lego gun: "Come on, you guys," he says to the group, "help me bring these animals to the hideout. We're blowing things up, we're the bad guys." Jake takes his Lego gun: "We're going to blow up the police."

Lucia comes over to talk with the boys, aware that I am recording this scene. "Are you the good guys or the bad guys?" she asks in her easy, offhand manner, radiating a spirit of good humor.

"We're the good guys," Justin explains.

The following Thursday, I listen attentively as this good-guy, bad-guy play resumes. "Hey," Nick says, taking the lead, "let's go, partner, let's go." Gabe holds his stuffed bunny by one ear, his Lego gun in the other hand. Nick puts on a cape:

"I'm a bank robber too, in disguise." Jake says, "I'm gonna shoot, shoot the bad guys." "No," Nick counters, "we're the bad guys."

Listening to this conversation, I hear the boys' voices take on a voice-over quality. They are repeating a script, speaking in the voices of its familiar characters: the good guy, the bad guy, the partner, the robber, the cowboy, the outlaw, the police. I remember the tenderness, the sweetness between these boys and their fathers, the lace and the bunny, the love that is evident among these boys along with the guns and the disguises. They are taking on the role of protectors, splitting themselves into good and bad guys, still holding the lace and the bunny.

I ask the fathers if they would meet with me and speak about their experiences in raising young sons. I want to know how their sons are affecting them, at this moment of turn in boys' lives and also historically in men's. With the exception of Tony's father, each of them comes, gathering in the library of the school in the first of a series of meetings that continue through the spring. Repeatedly, I hear these men speak about the opening their sons have created, an opening within themselves to which they have a complicated response. Alex takes the lead in our first meeting, the winter sky dark outside the windows as he speaks of Nick being "out there"—emotionally open, vulnerable, exposed. The room becomes quiet as he continues; I feel the attentiveness of the men. "He's out there, he needs to really be out there, and I always feel, it's always tricky how much you want to clamp down on him. And clamp down in the sense that he was getting into all sorts of trouble at school. . . . I always think about it, there's spunk there . . . he's very spunky, and I hate for that to be squeezed out of him. As I believe it was squeezed out of me, you know, I was exactly like that."

"And you remember losing your spunk?" I ask him, wondering about the word, its sexual overtones, its evocation of life and joy. "Yeah," he says. "How did you lose it?" I wonder. Alex hesitates: "I think I just got into trouble so much in school. . . . I remember, I think it took me until about tenth grade to figure that out." It is as if he is fighting with memory as he speaks of having been good enough in school, getting good grades, "but every now and then I would remember, you know"—and then he breaks the sentence, picking it up by saying, "There'd be a parent-teacher conference where, you know, 'This kid is out of control, there's too much energy here,' or something like that." He remembers the words of his parents and teachers, but for himself, this otherwise very articulate man seems to be at a loss for words or to have no words for what he remembers, a sensation perhaps, a spirit rising, a liveliness that became linked with being "out of control" or having "too much energy." "I just became good," Alex says, "and decided, you know, to study hard and blend into the crowd, and go to track practice, that was it." Tom interjects, "That sucked up the energy." But Alex continues on his train of thought: "And it was, it's sad."

I have opened a conversation about boys with fathers and come very quickly to sadness. The invocation of pleasure—Alex's delight in Nick's spunk—reminds these men of a loss that they can't quite name but that they remember. With their young sons, they face a dilemma in the real meaning of the word: a conflict to which there is no easy resolution, no road without a cost. "I really don't want that to happen to him," Alex says, speaking about Nick. "So what's the negative," Michael asks, "what did you lose?" Alex says matter-of-factly, illustrating his point with his manner, "I think I lost my spunk."

Alex is a professor, tenured at an early age at a prestigious university. He was hit by his father; he has vowed not to repeat the pattern. He has separated from his wife; he is trying to become more connected with his children. He is a man struggling with issues that many men struggle with—how to be a good man, a father; how not to repeat his father's patterns; how to live with himself and with women; how to raise a son and a daughter. And doing so from a position of advantage: he is high up on the patriarchal ladder, and he wants the best for his children.

Which is where the quandary enters: Alex fears that Nick will walk the same path that he has, and also that Nick will fall off that path.

"My experience was very different," Tom says, and then adds quietly, "but sort of the same." The wild one in his family was his brother. "I was a very quiet child. . . . And everybody always perceived me as 'Oh, he's fine,' you know, 'don't worry about him.'" He was the good boy, his brother bad, except that it wasn't that simple, because his brother, the one who was "very fired up," was also "very smart. That guy had tons of energy to do stuff, always the big deal and always real smart and always doing really well and always totally on the edge of being thrown out of wherever he was." He was afraid to take the risk of failing, "so rather than risking that situation, he would just not do things, or not finish them, or whatever."

The good-guy, bad-guy script, however simplistic, imposes a clear form—higher and lower—and links it with the split between good and bad. It is the basic script of patriarchy. The fight is over which guy is on top, the good guy or the bad guy, God or the devil. Any hierarchy creates tension, competition, and splits that keep people from feeling free to love. It is destructive to love between and among women and men, to any kind of love. In their play, the four-year-old boys are taking on the role of protectors, entering the protection racket, becoming the law, challenging the law—playing with the stuff of patriarchy, the world of fathers, gods, godfathers, and the like. And their fathers, tasting a love that they savor, picking up in their boys a spirit they find enlivening, wonder how to protect them. When I ask the fathers what they see in their boys that leads them to say, "I hope he doesn't lose that," they speak of their spunk, their energy, their wide-openness, their sensitivity, their delight, their "real joy."

I ask Alex for an example of Nick's spunk. He begins, "It was incredible." Nick and his sister were in a children's chorus; his sister was in a musical, and Nick had memorized all the songs. At a school assembly, he told his teacher that he wanted to be on the stage and sing and do the Russian dance, and when she forgot to put him on the program, he "just got up on stage, picked up the microphone," and after at first being nervous and acting silly, "he did it: he got up, he sang, he did a little dance. Applause. And even today people say, the teacher said to me that someone asked him, 'You speak Russian, don't you?' That's the kind of spunk, or that he's so friendly to people, strangers. Imaginative, in every play that they do. There's this sort of joy about it, and if he can keep that, he would be a very happy person."

"Spunk" connotes a primal energy associated with joy, spontaneity, and pleasure, knowing and following one's heart's desire. But this very quality of being out there in the world, curious, spirited, and wide open, also means taking in the world—the voices of its characters, the plots of its scripts (the good guy, the bad guy, the police, the robber). Alex speaks about Nick's vulnerability, "the softer, more sensitive part." He is moved by the sweetness, the tenderness of his son. "I think for boys it's not just that the spunk gets channeled, at best, but that it's this other side," Alex explains. "They're very sensitive, they're emotional, they seem to like each other very much. There's this soft side, and it's very interesting to figure out what strategies they learn, these boys in this classroom. Somehow they can't show this; I feel they have to hide it, and they've learned so fast how to hide it, except for those moments; with my kids it's usually in the car and we're driving, or at nighttime after the read, after reading to them, sort of lying with them a little bit, and then there are these incredible questions and it opens up." The "it" is the separation, or maybe Alex's heart that opens, surprisingly and painfully, to his four-year-old son's questions about love. At bottom, Nick wants to know if his father will be with him.

I turn to Tom and ask what he sees in Jake that leads him to think, "I hope he keeps that." Tom says, "His energy level. I mean I hope he can manage to keep his energy level and not squish it out of him for one reason or another. Because there's lots of forces to do that. You know, sitting in a classroom is a rough thing. And for Jake, and I assume it's similar for me, sitting in a classroom is asking a lot of him. If he's really into something, he'll definitely sit and pay attention, and he similarly has an unbelievable memory where, you know, he'll hear a song or see something and especially visual, if he sees something he remembers every little detail. . . . He'll think about things and say things and make connections that are just very wide open . . . and I'd hate to see that go. He checks out all the edges of everything, and finds out where it all ends up. For him, the world is really a much more interactive place than for you and me. Everything is there to be touched, to taste, to smell, to mess around with, just, just experienced. We don't do that so much anymore. And it's always a blast to go cruising around with him, 'cause it's like so, sort of eye-opening."

Speaking of Gabe, Michael doesn't want him to lose "his sensitivity," his "real joy," the "delight he has in his friends." "It's just so sweet, the sort of excitement they feel and the warmth they feel, even if it doesn't translate into always being, getting along together, I think they're delighted to have that connection," and, Michael adds, "they just make me feel so good." Michael is a musician; the four-year-olds touch his sensibility. Gabe has artistic talent; he is in love with shape and with color—poring over his brightly colored drawings. Michael worries that Gabe "hides his sensitivity."

It is difficult for young boys to read the world around them and show the sensitive, soft sides of themselves. The fathers love their boys' being "out there," but they also see that this openness carries with it a vulnerability that they, the fathers, want to protect. The pleasure they know with their sons evokes memories of themselves at a time before a loss they experienced. Men's conflicts around intimacy are tied to a history that these fathers are coming to remember as they see it repeating in front of their eyes, being played over again from the beginning. An often unrecognized and mutilated history, interrupted by gaps in memory, a loss of language—the signs of dissociation. Closeness and tenderness with their sons will bring them back into association with parts of themselves that they have hidden. The pain of remembering is that it brings them face-to-face with a loss that was behind them but now is in front of them as they step into the river again with their sons.

With Nick, Alex retraces a history that he is coming to remember, finding again "the softer, sensitive part" that also gets channeled, at best, like the spunk, or more commonly, hidden—this "very sensitive," "emotional" side of boys, their open affection for one another, "this soft side," which "somehow they can't show." Alex sees the consequences of this playing out in his adult life, in what he hides in himself and is now struggling to bring out, as he sees Nick and the other boys in his class somehow compelled "to hide it, and they've learned so fast how to hide it."

Nick is the leader of the "mean team" at school, the secret society of the boys in the class, formed for the purpose of chasing the girls. As the leader of the mean team, Nick is intimidating—loud, gruff, seemingly inaccessible. He is in trouble at school, often angry, sullen, getting into fights, hitting people; his parents are working with him to change his behavior, guided by a behavior therapist. At the same time, he has very close friends among the boys; the following year, in kindergarten, he will be the boy whom the girls want to be with. Alex knows all this and worries about Nick, his spunk, which is already linked with trouble; he also knows Nick's softness, his tenderness, and "these incredible questions," his curiosity. For Alex to stay with Nick means to become more open himself, more curious about what he is doing and feeling.

With Jake, Tom loves "getting close and getting quiet and hearing and talking on sort of a personal, very personal level. Those are the things we do together . . . and have these great conversations and be really physical and have this very sweet time, so unselfconsciously." I ask Tom for an example, and he tells me about an evening when Jake was in the bathtub, fooling around with bubbles, and they were just "hanging out and you know, very calm and comfortable and very relaxed and we're talking about his buddies actually, same thing, talking about buddies, and he was telling me some stories about his buddies and how much he likes his buddies and then he was asking me about my buddies and, you know, who they are, 'How about Mom? Is she a buddy?' "

The boys are talking with their fathers about love—what love is, what friendship means to them. Tom, whose warmth and gregariousness suggest that he has many friends, says, "I don't have very many close relationships outside my family as it is now. . . . The world can be an indifferent place. . . . Those qualities can easily get lost as you grow up. . . . Men are at risk if they look too vulnerable."

Tom's experience of the world includes working as a carpenter, a contractor, teaching at a university, staying home with children, and at the moment, starting a computer business. "There are certain situations in the world you sort of feel like you'd be better off if you were much tougher, rougher," he says. He resists this. But I will see Tom change visibly the following year, in a way that startles me; for a moment I don't recognize him as we meet unexpectedly in the school hallway. Jake is now five and in kindergarten. He has been referred to a specialist for testing; his teachers are concerned that he may have an attention deficit disorder or a learning disability. Tom has become much tougher and rougher looking, more masculine in the conventional manner—a little more of an edge, more swagger, his hair brushed back; he has grown a mustache. We talk about Jake. Tom now sees that the qualities he treasured and nurtured in Jake may be getting in his way, distracting him from paying attention to what he needs to focus on in school, drawing his attention away from the center and to the edges, away from the lesson and to what is happening emotionally in the room. Jake is tracking the relationships, Tom says, rather than paying attention to what he needs to do in school. It is separating him from the other boys, and he is losing his position in the group. I see Tom's concern, his fear really, that maybe he was leading Jake down a wrong path. I try to make emotional contact, but I have the impression that Tom is not open for the conversation I want to have, or at least not at that moment. He is focused on helping Jake make the adjustment to school. I feel I am in the presence of a different man.

Michael also seems different to me the following year. He tells me proudly that Gabe, now five and in kindergarten, is into soccer and coin collecting. "What about his drawing?" I ask. I could be speaking a foreign language. Michael brushes off the question and repeats that Gabe is now playing soccer and collecting coins.

THE PREVIOUS year in the fathers group, I ask the men how well their sons read them. Alex says, "Very well, too well. Just everything, I mean, he's too clued in to reading people's facial expressions, tone of voice." Nick picked up Alex's fear when Alex hit him, his worry that now Nick would grow up to hit his children. Alex says, "I just thought and I just said, 'Yeah, you're right. I am worried about that.'" Nick asked him one day, "Why did you make Mommy cry?" Alex did not remember, but when he asked Sharon, she reminded him of a phone call between them. She had been in the bedroom, Nick was outside the closed door; he had picked up the sounds of her crying and figured out to whom she was speaking. "They pick up everything even if they pretend that they don't pick it up, and they're in touch or, you know, it's bad. I mean, it's not bad, it's sad," Alex says.

Tom speaks of his sons "reading this stuff, they're sucking in all my anxieties about things." He worries about anger, he has "set up this logic . . . I'm not gonna hit." His anger is so strong, and he is so strong; he talks with Jake about how strong anger is, how it feels, and also how sometimes you hit people when you're angry, and about how that feels. These fathers are trying not to intimidate their sons. They all know what they call "the voice." "The Dad voice." "Do the voice," I say. Steve explains how you do it: "You lower your voice, speak loud, and—" Tom adds, "Clearly and loud." "Forceful," Steve says. "Speak in your Dad voice," I say. Tom says, "No, I can't. I feel bad ordering them around."

I recall the voices of the boys in their play—the partner, the good guy, the bad guy, the robber. They were practicing "the voice," ordering each other around, taking on the power that their fathers were questioning as they heard the detachment in the voice that spoke so clearly and loudly, as they thought about their own sadness and anger.

"How can we help preserve our sons' vulnerability without putting them at risk for teasing and being beaten up?" Alex asks. The question hangs over the group. "You don't want to put them in a situation where, you know, out in the 'real world' they will get . . ." The sentence dangles, unfinished. I ask, "Can you tell them something of what you know about how to navigate this?" Alex says, "I don't know." I hear these phrases: "you know," "I mean," "I don't know"—in my work with adolescent girls they were the marker of a struggle to know and also to be in relationship. "You know" was a question: do you know? what do you know? It stood on the edge of dissociation. The struggle for meaning was often a struggle with language: how to say what you mean and be heard and understood. "I don't know" often signaled the onset of dissociation—the way in which psychically we separate ourselves from knowing what we cannot bear to know.

I am hearing the same interruptions, loss of language, with these fathers as they speak about themselves in relation to their sons. The sons are so full of life and relationship, so adept at reading the human world. The fathers wonder, how am I going to protect them? Alex says, "I don't know. It's a delicate balance." He pauses and then, "I mean, just trying to make them sort of true to themselves, it seems to be the only way to do it, so they can read the world in a way that makes sense to them, but . . ."

"I don't know . . . I mean . . ." the sentence picks up, and then it falls off. To be true to themselves means to be truly in relationship.

I say, "If you are going to be open and in relationship, you are vulnerable. I mean, that's just it. The only way to stop, not be vulnerable, is to close yourself off. At that point, you're vulnerable to a whole set of other things. But in terms of the openness, the vulnerability, if you have that, then you can make some choices around it. Otherwise, if you lose that, you have no choice."

Tom thinks this is too easy. He has seen what happens to high-energy boys. His brother and also Jake and Nick—both of whom have been referred by the school for assessment or special help, Nick for hitting and Jake for his wandering attention. With these high-energy boys, "things come out." Tom sees that the very openness of the boys makes it easier to stop them, "just to say, 'That's an inappropriate thing,' or

'Don't do that' . . . they reach a point of being sort of slapped down. Because of their openness, that hurts more, and that's part of the containment."

Speaking of Nick, Alex says, "Suddenly you see his face, and it's not a happy face. But sometimes, I guess, I worry that with these kind of more active boys, that it's almost a shield, all this activity, being out there, stuff like that, they have this other feeling, but it's the stuff that comes out either, sort of, it seeps out sometimes, so that it gets slapped down or it only gets expressed when they're, you know, in the back of the car feeling totally safe or in some sort of quiet moments . . . then he's incredibly sweet." It's hard to follow the sentence because he is saying two things simultaneously: the high activity level can be a shield against feeling, and the very out-there quality of these boys may mean that all their feelings get exposed, seep out, and then are slapped down, so that they learn to hide their vulnerability, except in places where they feel safe. Like Cupid hides his love for Psyche.

The most riveting conversation I have with the fathers is about voice. I tell them of a film I have seen called *Inside Out*, about children's imaginary worlds. Joanna Lipper filmed boys and girls between the ages of five and twelve who were referred to her project by teachers, selected for their rich imaginative lives. The imaginary worlds of all the children were inventive, riveting, at times startlingly beautiful— breathtaking in the depth of feeling and the artistry of expression. I had been asked to discuss the film at a local screening. I made the observation that the voices of the boys and the girls differed: the girls' voices were like singing, going up and down the scale of emotions and thoughts, while the boys' voices were monotonic, with the sole exception of the one five-year-old boy. People in the audience heard it. Just as the fathers, now that they think about it, hear the difference between their voices, the one- or two-note range, and their sons' voices, which are "out there"—all over the scale. The sadness that has hedged our conversation comes into the center of the room. The loss is audible; they can hear it. The room becomes very still; the fathers are listening, hearing the difference between their own voices and their sons', the constraint and the control in their speaking, the freedom they hear in their boys.

"MUMMY, I'm in love with you," four-year-old Hyun says to his mother, Clara. Clara is in love with Hyun. She loves what happens when they are together, the "intensity" she feels in his presence. Clara is a clinical psychologist, reflective about her relationship with her son: "I think what I really appreciate about this age, and in my case, Hyun is still, he can be completely whatever he is in the moment. And that's what he allows, like a different kind of intensity. He and I in our own interactions can be, I guess that's what I allow myself to be with him, which is sort of completely whatever he is feeling in the moment, in relation to him, whatever he generates in me and whatever he is with me." Clara struggles with the constraints of a language that does not give much room for expressing the way people affect and change one another by being with one another—like breathing out and breathing in. With Hyun, Clara feels permission ("that's what he allows") to be with him in the moment, to take in his feelings, and gives herself permission ("I guess that's what I allow myself") to be with him. With Hyun, she feels permitted to be in relationship, to bring herself into the moment with him and to feel the intensity of her feelings. "And so I think I am much more aware than ever, being intensely angry, really rageful, having rageful moments and also with him having the most intense love, just no-holds-barred kind of love."

Clara's face is alive, vibrant, open. I am meeting with the mothers of the boys, also in the library of the school. They had requested the meeting after hearing about the fathers group. They joke at first, wanting to know what the men said. I say I didn't think I had heard anything they didn't know. Actually, they want to talk about their relationships with their sons. All of them will talk about anger—not anger at their sons or with their sons. They will talk about the freedom they feel with their sons to feel their feelings, a freedom often signaled by a mother's discovery that her son can know her anger without turning on her or leaving her, know it as an emotion in the way they know her love. For a woman, for any woman living in patriarchy, it is extraordinarily freeing to go back or forward into a time when love is not split from anger, when the universe of emotion returns as a world in which she can move freely, where she is not bedeviled by a split between good and bad women, one loving, the other angry—images of women that are surreal, that come from the unconscious of men. Which may be why these mothers' experiences with their sons are so powerful—why Clara speaks of such intensity of feeling, real rage and also the most intense love—because it signifies such release. There is no way to love freely, to experience freedom in loving, when you cannot feel your feelings, and anger is just that, a feeling.

I wonder about the "Oedipus complex," the forbidden love between mother and son that becomes the rationale for separation. What exactly is this love that threatens a son's masculinity? Once Clara has spoken of herself as "being intensely angry, really rageful, having rageful moments and also with him having the most intense love," she hears within herself a censorious voice; she has been trained as a psychologist, she is a Korean-American woman. Displacing that voice, or rather replacing it with her own, her own sense of her relationship with her son, she says, "It's so wonderful you don't have to be self-conscious about these external-like values or the sort of perceived aspect of it." In allowing herself to be with Hyun and enjoying the intensity of relationship, Clara is turning away from values she experiences as external to her, and also from the way mother-son intimacy is generally perceived. In essence, in turning toward her son, she is turning away from the values and the judgments of patriarchy. Freeing herself to be in relationship with him, she discovers the pleasure of living without the self-consciousness she usually feels, and she holds her experience apart from the intimations that her love and her anger are dangerous to Hyun. In the Oedipus tragedy, the murderous anger and incestuous love follow rather than precede the parents' abandonment and sacrifice of their son.

Rachel speaks about Tom and his relationship with Jake: "It's so much of an echo of what his dad did with him. His dad worked a lot but was very connected with his sons, and I see that being repeated a lot in terms of what Tom has as a role model and what the kids have for their role model in terms of being aware of nuances." That morning, Jake had picked up the happiness in Rachel's voice and also her worry. She said to him, "I'm happy that it's a beautiful day, but you are right, I'm worried because it's going to be a really busy day today." Jake said, "Well, have a really nice day." It seemed a simple exchange until Rachel added: "Just that nobody pays attention to me like that. Jake is just, like, clued in. It's like, 'Mom, why did you kind of use that angry voice with me?' "

I am hearing mothers describe their four- and five-year-old sons as emotionally present and clued in to them in a way that their husbands are not. I am hearing fathers speak of their closeness with their sons, the sweetness and spiritedness of the boys, and also about sadness and a loss they remember. The sacrifice of relationship is the ritual of initiation into patriarchy. It is enacted in the Hebrew Bible and in the New Testament. Abraham's willingness to sacrifice Isaac, God's sacrifice of his only son. In these father-son dramas the mothers are absent or silent. But here mothers are actively resisting these old stories of abandonment and child-sacrifice that leave love split from anger, that divide good from bad women, and that definitively end the subversive potential of the mother-son couple or father-son intimacy in favor of establishing a clear hierarchy (father over sons, men over women). In their own ways, with greater or lesser degrees of conviction and fear, these parents of sons are coming to the discovery that love erodes patriarchy.

SHARON SAYS, "It's almost half-conscious to me that I'm feeling tense or stressed and distracted, and Nick will say, 'Mom, why are you sounding angry? Are you tired, Mom?'"

Rachel continues her train of thought, about Jake paying attention to her feelings and being clued in, as it leads her back to thinking about Jake's relationship with Tom: "I don't find that he does that as much with Tom. He doesn't have to do that decoding with Tom. He knows perfectly well why Tom is angry, 'cause he threw the ball into the neighbor's yard. 'Dad, why do you sound upset?' He doesn't say that. So there doesn't seem to be that same decoding. Or maybe it's the same attention."

I wonder about Rachel's observation; Tom described such intimate conversations with Jake, Jake asking him about his buddies, his relationship with Rachel, talking together about what friendship means, how anger feels. I wonder how the opening these parents are finding with their boys is affecting their relationships with each other, whether the mothers' experience of their sons' emotional presence intensifies the rivalry between father and son, challenging the husbands in these couples to become more emotionally open and heightening their sense of vulnerability. And I wonder whether the men in these heterosexual couples are opening themselves in ways that may make their wives feel uneasy, what stake the women may have in perpetuating this split between father and son with respect to manhood.

The women talk about the men not remembering: they are talking about dissociation. Rachel says that Tom did not remember that he was very much like Jake as a child. "No, I wasn't like that," he said. "Yeah, you were. Yeah, I have heard your parents' stories," Rachel tells him. Tom does not remember; he compares Jake with his brother, as if he has dissociated himself from that wild part of himself. Sharon says, "Alex didn't remember what he was like as a little boy—he didn't remember that he used to get really rough and really active as a young boy—until he experienced Nick being that way. 'I don't remember that,' he said, and it feels so different from now, 'cause he is so not like that. . . . Alex's worst fear is that he doesn't want Nick to get squashed like he was. . . . It's hard for Alex to be spirited, to feel spirited. Very important to us, but we are sliding a slippery slope, that spirit . . . such a gleam . . . that's the greatest thing about Nick, I see this real pizzazz and spunk."

Nan brings up the inevitable subject: separation. The separation between mothers and sons is mandated in patriarchy. This is what the Oedipus complex is about: sexualizing the intimacy, placing it under taboo, linking freedom with leaving women and going off with men, and making any woman who resists this separation a virtual Jocasta, Oedipus' "unspeakable mother." Except of course Jocasta didn't resist. She joined Laius, her husband, in wounding and abandoning her son.

PROUST WATCHES this drama as a child in his family; he forgets it, and then much later recalls it, recording it in his novel *In Search of Lost Time*—a novel he first conceived as a letter to his mother. In the long opening passage of *Swann's Way*, the first volume, the narrator takes us into a young boy's awareness of his mother's sacrifice of herself—a sacrifice that renders her ultimately untrustworthy in love. It is exquisitely observed, with all the nuance we have come to expect from four-year-old boys. The narrator telling the story is a grown man; going to bed early one night and finding himself unable to fall asleep, he remembers a night in his childhood when he was sent to bed early and refused to go to sleep. Monsieur Swann was invited for dinner, and since dinner was to be late and the boy looked tired, his father and grandfather sent him off to bed early—before he had kissed his mother good night. The boy protests; he won't go without his mother's kiss. "No, no, leave your mother alone," his father says. "You've said good night to one another, that's enough. These exhibitions are absurd. Go on upstairs."

Mounting the stairs "against [his] heart," the boy vows that he will not sleep until his mother comes and kisses him. "I had formed a resolution to abandon all attempts to go to sleep without seeing Mamma, had made up my mind to kiss her at all costs, even though this meant the certainty of being in disgrace with her for long afterwards—when she herself came up to bed." Opening his window so as to stay awake, he watches Monsieur Swann arrive; he sends a message to his mother via the maid, begging her to come upstairs; he suffers "the anguish that comes from knowing that the creature one adores is in some place of enjoyment where oneself is not and cannot follow"; and then he hears his parents' footsteps as they accompany Swann to the gate and the clanging of the bell that signals his leaving. Finally, hearing his mother mounting the stairs, he goes out into the passage. "My heart was beating so violently that I could hardly move, but at least it was throbbing no longer with anxiety, but with terror and joy. . . . Then I saw Mamma herself and I threw myself upon her. For an instant she looked at me in astonishment," but then, hearing her husband's footsteps, she said, "Off you go at once. Do you want your father to see you waiting there like an idiot?" Again he implores her, "Come and say good night to me." But now his father is upon them. "I'm done for!" he thinks, and then discovers:

> I was not, however. My father used constantly to refuse to let me do things which were quite clearly allowed by the more liberal charters granted me by my mother and grandmother, because he paid no heed to "principles," and because for him there was no such thing as the "rule of law." . . . He looked at me for a moment with an air of surprise and annoyance, and then when Mamma had told him, not without some embarrassment, what had happened, said to her: "Go along with him, then. You said just now that you didn't feel very sleepy, so stay in his room for a little. I don't need anything."
>
> "But, my dear," my mother answered timidly, "whether or not I feel sleepy is not the point; we mustn't let the child get into the habit—"
>
> "There's no question of getting into a habit," said my father, with a shrug of the shoulders; "you can see quite well that the child is unhappy. After all, we aren't gaolers. You'll end by making him ill, and a lot of good that will do. There are two beds in his room; tell Françoise to make up the big one for you, and stay with him for the rest of the night. Anyhow, I'm off to bed; I'm not so nervy as you. Good night."

Because the father is the law, he can change the law at will. Mother and son live under the father's law, but the son's resistance to that law—his insistence on kissing his mother good night—leads him to see into the core of relationships in this patriarchal household.

In Search of Lost Time—the meaning of the novel's title becomes clear. The lost time is a time of pleasure and also of a heroic resistance to its loss. The boy's victory is pyrrhic, and the failure of his resistance becomes the engine of the search, fueled implicitly by the question "Why?" What happened to his mother's love?

What the young boy in Proust's novel discovers, what many boys discover at a similar age, is that his mother has bound herself to the law of the father, which the father himself enforces sporadically, depending more or less on how tuned in he is to his son. Bound herself in part for the sake of her son, to strengthen his will and encourage his manhood. When the boy realizes that he cannot count on his mother's love because she is acting on his father's wishes rather than her own, her love becomes untrustworthy. Up until this time, he had suffered her absences but he had not questioned her love—the love that made his own feelings for her make sense. The rift is huge (within himself as well as with her), and the loss inconsolable:

> Of late I have been increasingly able to catch, if I listen attentively, the sound of the sobs which I had the strength to control in my father's presence, and which broke out only when I found myself alone with Mamma. In reality their echo has never ceased.

The boy begins to reconstruct his world:

> Perhaps even what I called [my father's] severity, when he sent me off to bed, deserved that title less than my mother's or my grandmother's attitude, for his nature, which in some respects differed more than theirs from my own, had probably prevented him from realising until then how wretched I was every evening, something which my mother and grandmother knew well; but they loved me enough to be unwilling to spare me that suffering, which they hoped to teach me to overcome, so as to reduce my nervous sensibility and to strengthen my will.

Whereas my father, whose affection for me was of another kind, would not, I suspect, have had the same courage, for as soon as he had grasped the fact that I was unhappy, he had said to my mother: "Go and comfort him."

Now love is tied to sacrifice, to a loss of relationship that strengthens the will and reduces nervous sensibility. His mother out of love for him subjects him to suffering by breaking relationship with him—withholding her kisses as the father demanded, in the hope of strengthening her son to become a man. It is an initiation designed to help him overcome his suffering, reduce his nervous sensibility, strengthen his will. His mother and also her mother become agents of his initiation into patriarchy. Breaking relationship at the command of the father, they encourage the boy to become like the father, withholding themselves for his own good. So that in time, he will become more sporadically in touch with people's feelings, more quixotic in his relationships, able to make and to break the law, to act on his will. "It's not bad, it's sad"— Alex's mantra hangs over this scene.

The boy's nature will become more like his father's, his sensibility less like that of his mother and his grandmother. He will become the father, not the son, in the story; the one who is more emotionally distant, less attentive to relationship, but also less severe and more generous, able to follow his own impulses—or at least that is the plan. Proust, of course, is a resister; he locked himself into a cork-lined room to write. He had to shut out the sounds of the world around him in order to hear again these voices from his childhood and recapture the moment when he came to see his mother and his father differently—the moment of his initiation into the way of seeing that aligned his perception with that of the world around him. To write the novel, he had to break this alignment, to come back into a love whose language had come to seem incredible—so that his wanting, what he had wanted so desperately and adamantly as a boy, made sense.

Like a fossil in amber, this process of initiation is caught in the diary of Anne Frank. For Proust, the lost time is a time in early childhood; for Anne Frank, it is the edge of adolescence. Her diary is an extraordinary record of a girl's adolescence because, like Proust, she is a gifted writer, and also because she rewrites her diary, so that we can see the process of initiation as a process of self-editing, an eclipse of a self that has come into full light.

"Gorgeous" is the opening word of the diary, as Anne initially writes it. "Gorgeous photograph isn't it!!!!" She has pasted a photograph of herself on the inside front cover—the now famous photograph of Anne smiling, the dimples in her cheeks showing as well as the raised eyebrows and bright eyes of an intensely alive and spirited child. Her four exclamation points carry her exuberance, her delight in herself. She lists the "7 or 12 beautiful features (not mine, mind you!)" of a woman, and then, throwing modesty to the winds, opts instead for honest scrutiny, proceeding to fill in "which ones I have and which ones I don't!" The list ("drawn up by myself") reads:

1. blue eyes, black hair (no.)
2. dimples in cheeks (yes.)
3. dimple in chin (yes.)
4. widow's peak (no.)
5. white skin (yes.)
6. straight teeth (no.)
7. small mouth (no.)
8. curly eyelashes (no.)
9. straight nose (yes.) (at least so far.)
10. nice clothes (sometimes.) (not nearly enough in my opinion.)
11. nice fingernails (sometimes.)
12. intelligent (sometimes.)

A story commonly told about Anne Frank is that her father edited the diary. The actual story is far more interesting. For the most part, Anne edited the diary herself. On March 28, Gerrit Bolkestein, the minister of education, art, and science, in the Dutch government in exile, speaking on Radio Free Orange, which was broadcasting from London into the Netherlands, had announced the government's plans to create a war museum after the war. They were interested in ordinary documents—diaries, letters, collections of sermons—that would show how the Dutch people carried on their lives under the extreme conditions of the war. Anne's dream was to become a famous writer, and she seized her chance, beginning to rewrite the diary in May of 1944 and completing 324 pages of the revision—reaching March 1944 in her edited version—in the short time between May and the beginning of August, when the Gestapo raided the Secret Annex. With some notable exceptions, her father followed her editing, presenting his daughter to the world as she wished to be seen.

The opening voice of the actual diary—"Gorgeous photograph isn't it" and the list of the "7 or 12 beautiful features"—this openhearted, joyous, exuberant voice disappeared into prehistory. Anne's revision begins more soberly:

> It's an odd idea for someone like me to keep a diary; not only because I have never done so before, but because it seems to me that neither I—nor for that matter anyone else—will be interested in the unbosomings of a thirteen-year-old schoolgirl. Still, what does that matter? I want to write but more than that, I want to bring out all kinds of things that lie buried deep in my heart.

Her father's edition, meaning the diary as first published, opens with a voice that fits its title, *Diary of a Young Girl:* "On Friday, June 12, I woke up at six o'clock and no wonder, it was my birthday"—a voice taken from Anne's June 14 diary entry.

The "Definitive Edition," published in 1995, begins with the sentence written on the front endpaper (underneath "Gorgeous photograph"), where Anne states her intention in keeping the diary: "I hope I will be able to confide everything in you, as I have never been able to confide in anyone, and I hope you will be a great source of comfort and support."

Only in the Critical Edition, compiled by the War Museum, now called the Netherlands Institute for War Documentation, can we read the actual diary as Anne wrote it—and also compare the three versions of the diary: Anne's original entries (the A version); Anne's edited version, the diary as she rewrote and edited it (the B version); and the diary as edited by her father and as first published (the C version). In comparing the three versions, we can trace the evolution of what becomes Anne Frank's "voice."

Lawrence Langer, who has written extensively about the Holocaust, has made the observation—has insisted, really—that Anne Frank's diary is not a war document, or a record of the Holocaust. In Barnes and Noble, looking for the diary, I am directed first to history, then to Holocaust studies, then to Jewish studies, before I learn that the diary is out of stock. Like the opening voice of the original diary, the diary itself is displaced. Elevated, rendered more serious by being made part of history, or by its association with the Holocaust and Jewish studies. I suspect it has been read so extensively and become an international best-seller because it captures the voice of a girl whose considerable powers of observation and expression may ironically have been heightened by her confinement. It is not "the diary of a young girl" but, rather, the diary of a girl becoming a young woman, who records a passage that is at once remembered and forgotten. It contains a voice from a dissociated time, familiar and surprising, moving in its emotional clarity, startling in its freshness and depth of perception, delightful in its openhearted embrace of pleasure, and in the end, sad. The death of Anne Frank in

Bergen-Belsen—naked and starving and covered with lice—just weeks before the camp's liberation is horrifying.

As in any tragedy, we play out in our minds over and over again the possibility of averting the tragic ending. We try to find the place where it could have gone differently, to learn from history. We are gripped by the realization, almost too painful to consider, that if the camp had been liberated only a few weeks earlier, Anne Frank would have lived. We are transfixed by these moments in life and literature before the accident happens, before the letter is misdelivered. But as Anne Frank's diary is swept up in a historical tragedy, it also holds in suspension a moment in life history: the passage from girl into woman. And as the diary in its original and its edited versions illuminates this passage with unequaled clarity, we can ask whether parts of our history that we have taken as natural or fated are in fact an artifact of history: the psyche's response to a tragic conflict between human nature, in all its complexity and variation, and a human condition that we have created. The historical tragedy that surrounds and ultimately engulfs Anne Frank overshadows the diary as the diary of an adolescent girl whose diary writing itself is an act of resistance.

Living an enforced hermetic existence, Anne Frank turns a writer's eye and ear on a small patch of a strained human landscape. Driven by the Holocaust into the equivalent of Proust's cork-lined room, she will record in real time rather than as recaptured memory the process of her initiation. In her diary, she will describe her experience of becoming "two Annes": a vibrant, sensual, pleasure-loving Anne, who becomes the bad Anne, or at least "not good"; and the good Anne, quiet, pure, deep like still water, an Anne who never appears in public. The writer, the "I" who keeps the diary, observes the process that she describes—of hiding herself within herself, writing down all her joys, her sorrows, and her contempt in her diary, and then editing the diary to keep this joyful, sorrowful, contemptuous self out of the public eye. Ironically, the edited diary reads like a young girl's diary; it was Anne's way of protecting herself.

The voice she mutes or takes out completely is the voice of pleasure—the exuberant, unfettered voice of Anne, whose desire and curiosity lead her to explore her own changing body, the psychology of the world in which she is living, and also its politics: the realities of position and power. The voice of the original diary is astonishing in its freedom—joyous, delighted, serious, prosaic, funny, earnest, and sad. Anne will look at and see her own changing body; she will record her discovery of intense sensual, sexual pleasure, which comes over her first in a dream; she will become fascinated by the psychology of the world, the logic that governs the flow of daily living; she will be angered by the war, frightened and saddened by the news of the Holocaust that reaches her, concerned for the safety of people who are in danger, and also contemptuous of patriarchy.

"Open me carefully—" Emily Dickinson writes on the letter she sends to her friend Susan Huntington Gilbert in June of 1852. They were in their early twenties at the time, separated because Susan was away teaching at a girls' school in Baltimore. The recent publication of Emily's letters to Susan changes the public image of Emily Dickinson. The inaccessible, ethereal recluse, dressed in white, virginal and living in seclusion, turns out to have been an invented image. In fact, Emily was involved for over four decades in an intense correspondence and passionate relationship with Susan, her friend, her writing companion, eventually her sister-in-law, her confidante, perhaps her lover, and her next-door neighbor. For long periods, they exchanged notes and probably saw each other daily. But Emily's instruction that she placed for Susan to see when she first unfolded the letter—"Open me carefully"—extends to our reading of the "intimate letters" that she intended for Susan and also to our reading the diary that Anne Frank intended only for her imagined friend, Kitty. Entering the A version of the diary, we enter an illuminated world.

For every girl and woman who reads the passages where Anne describes looking at and seeing her own changing body, the question becomes: did you look? And what did you see? Anne discovers her new woman's body, its sensations, its "sweet secrets" and pleasures, and her own astonishment at her discoveries:

"My vagina is getting wider"; she could be imagining this, she says, but "when I'm on the w.c. I sometimes look then I can see." Her ignorance amuses her—"The funniest thing of all was that I thought that the urine came out of the clitoris"—but it mirrors an ignorance on the part of her mother that she can only take as insincere: "When I asked Mummy once what that stub of a thing was for, she said that she didn't know, she still pretends to be ignorant even now!"

Anne chooses not to be ignorant; she chooses to know for herself. With Peter, the son of the van Pels family, with whom the Franks share their hideout, Anne confronts the question of whether she will rely on him to tell her about her body or whether she will see for herself. "When I was with Peter yesterday we ended up, I honestly don't remember how, by discussing sex." Anne writes that Peter "knows everything"—by which she means that he knows how contraceptives work, how boys can tell if they are grown up, and also about girls. Except, as she discovers, he doesn't know. "I would like to ask him whether he knows what a girl really looks like there." She knows what men look like—from art books and from the museums, from photographs of naked men, where "you can see exactly what a naked man looks like." But with women, "the sexual parts or whatever they are called are further between the legs." Anne suspects that Peter "probably hasn't seen a girl from so close to, to be honest I haven't either. He was talking about 'the mouth of the womb' but that's right inside, you can't see anything of that."

As we see Anne choosing to see for herself we also see the power of an injunction against seeing and speaking that would keep her from knowing or in any case revealing what she now comes to know: her body, what it looks like "down there," her sexual parts. Anne brushes aside the injunction as she writes, speaking now of her relationship with Peter, "When the subject [of sex] comes up again how in heaven's name will you be able to explain what things are like without using examples? Shall I just try it out here in the meantime? Well then get on with it!" In its precise, naturalistic rendering, Anne's description of her body resembles the exquisite botanical drawings of the nineteenth century:

From the front when you stand up you can see nothing but hair, between your legs there are things like little cushions, soft, with hair on them too, which press together when you stand up so that you can't see what's inside. When you sit down they divide and inside it looks very red and ugly and fleshy. At the very top, between the big outer lips there is a little fold of skin which turns out to be a kind of little bladder on closer inspection, that is the clitoris. Then come the small inner lips, they are also pressed against each other just like a little pleat. When they open, there is a fleshy little stump inside, no bigger than the top of my thumb. The top of it is porous, there are different little holes in it and that's where the urine comes out. The lower part looks as if it's nothing but skin, but that is where the vagina is. There are little folds of skin all over the place, you can hardly find it. The little hole underneath is so terribly small that I simply can't imagine how a man can get in there, let alone how a whole baby can get out. The hole is so small you can't even put your index finger in, not easily anyway. That's all it is and yet it plays such an important role!

Robert LeVine, a psychological anthropologist, writes that culture appears in the unspoken; it is the way of seeing and speaking that is so much part of everyone's living that it never has to be articulated. Culture is revealed in those moments when someone does not know how they are supposed to see or to speak, or when the tacit rules are broken. Anne Frank's depiction of her body should strike us as ordinary: a lively, curious girl, whose body is changing, decides to look and see for herself what's happening, so that she can speak for herself about herself rather than relying on Peter to tell her "everything."

Anne turns the same keen eye and ear on the world around her; her delight in knowing is apparent as she records the daily life of the Secret Annex. Like Clara with Hyun, Anne Frank with Kitty lives in the full weather of her emotions. She knows the intensity of anger, really rageful moments, and also the most intense love. "Mummy, Margot and I are as thick as thieves again. It's really much better. I get into Margot's bed now almost every evening." This entry, written on 14 October 1942, follows an entry written on 27 September, where Anne writes:

Today I had a so-called "discussion" with Mummy, but the boring thing was that I burst into tears straight away. I can't help it. Daddy is always so nice to me, and he understands me so much better too. Oh, I can't stand Mummy at such times, and I am a stranger as far as she is concerned as well, for you see, she doesn't even know how I think about the most ordinary things. We were talking about servants, that you should call them the "household help," and will most definitely have to after the war, but I had hardly brought out the words when she said that I'm always carrying on about "later" and that just like Peter, I make myself out to be a grand lady, but that is absolutely not true, and surely I can build castles in the air, that's not so bad, one doesn't have to take everything so seriously. Daddy at least defends me, without him I would honestly be almost unable to stand it here.

Intense love, intense anger, an impassioned seeing and speaking of what is happening in the moment: "Everyone here is getting on well together. There's no quarreling, but it won't last long, we haven't had such peace in the home for at least half a year." This is 22 December 1943. The next day, longing for freedom ("Cycling again, dancing, flirting and what-have-you, how I would love that; if only I were free again!"), having been "shut up for 1½ years," she writes, "sometimes I even think, will anybody understand me, will anybody overlook my ingratitude, overlook Jew or non-Jew, and just see the young girl in me who is badly in need of some rollicking fun? I don't know and I couldn't talk about it to anybody, because then I know I should cry. Crying can bring such relief, but only if you can cry on someone's shoulder and despite everything, in spite of all of my theories, and however much trouble I take, each day I miss having a real mother who understands me."

Writing to Kitty, Anne describes the problems with her mother with which all the readers of the diary are familiar. In the actual diary, Anne tends to contrast her relationship with her mother with her relationship with her father and also to describe her problems with her mother as problems of relationship: finding herself unable to cry on her mother's shoulder, feeling misheard, not seen, not understood, not taken seriously. Anne also observes that her mother does not reveal herself, or at least not in the way Anne desires; she claims not to know about her body, she withholds herself from their relationship. The pleasure Anne seeks with her mother is the pleasure of relationship, and it is palpable when she finds it, as when she says that they are "thick as thieves."

In revising her diary, Anne omits this description of closeness (although her father restores it in the C version, the diary as first published). In her edited version, Anne is less likely to name the problem with her mother as arising from misunderstanding or not listening, breaks in relationship that are amenable to repair, and more likely to name the problem as her mother's problem, citing her "untidiness, her sarcasm, and her lack of sweetness," which then justifies Anne's "contempt." And these revisions are carried forward from the B to the C version and into the 1995 edition that reflects the editorial hand of Mirjam Pressler as well as that of Otto Frank. They have become part of the lore of Anne Frank, buttressing a familiar image that is contested by reading the actual diary, as the image of Emily Dickinson is challenged by her letters to Susan.

It is puzzling initially to observe Anne concealing her love, since the idealized image of the good woman, which Anne both resists and buys into, is that of a loving person. But Anne's love is palpably linked with pleasure, and once pleasure becomes explicitly associated with sexuality, Anne begins to divide herself from her body and from herself. The power of the image of the woman on the pedestal lies in forcing this division. Rewriting her diary, Anne hides or at least shadows her joy in herself, her delight in her changing body, the intensity of her desires, her sorrow at the distance she feels between herself and her mother, her longing for a closeness that eludes her, and also her contempt for adult hypocrisy around sexual matters and for the patriarchal nature of the world she inhabits. Her voice in the revision becomes more analytical and also more political as she steps back from and examines the relationships in her family and in the world outside the Secret

Annex—a world she knows from her reading, from the radio broadcasts, and from the stories that the helpers bring in. She decries the suffering caused by the war at the same time as she cheers the Allies' invasion and even dares to hope of returning to school in the fall; she observes with wry humor that parents and people in general are reluctant to talk with children about sexual matters because "they believe that children will stop looking on marriage as something sacred and pure when it dawns on them that in most cases the purity is nothing more than eyewash." She asks penetrating questions about women's silence with respect to patriarchy and observes that the more centuries it lasts, the more deeply entrenched it becomes. ("It is stupid enough of women to have borne it all in silence for such a long time, since the more centuries this arrangement lasts, the more deeply rooted it becomes.")

In the constricted space of her living, Anne Frank finds pleasure in writing, in her relationship with her father, with Peter, with the Peter of her dreams, in life and with herself. Her openness is astonishing, and as with the young boys I observed, it exposes her to being slapped down, told that she is being inappropriate, hearing herself called "unpleasant" and "insufferable"—words that she will use to describe herself and that explain why psychologically she goes into hiding. Because in contrast to the four-year-old boys who cannot name what they are doing, Anne, like other adolescent girls, describes the process of closing herself.

Judy Chu, writing about the year she spent with the boys in the pre-kindergarten class, describes the changes she observed in the boys over the course of the year. At the beginning of the year, she found the boys to be remarkably direct, attentive, articulate, and authentic. When she first approached them, wanting to observe their play, Jake asked the others: "Should we trust her?" Nick said, "No." They had no relationship with her; no basis for trust. Some weeks later, when they had become familiar with her and her project of learning about boys from them, Nick draped a piece of lace over her head as she joined the boys in the blocks corner and, aptly summing up her purpose, said, "We're just going to pretend that you're not here."

This accurate reading of relationship, like the range of young boys' voices and their emotional freedom, reflects the openness or out-there quality of the boys, which leads them to pick up the emotional vibrations and thought waves of other people. The qualities in the boys that Chu found so impressive are the same qualities that their parents comment on: aspects of a natural, in the sense of unlabored, knowing of the human world. As they picked up their parents' love, their anger, their happiness, and their worries, so they tuned in to Chu's project and her feelings, responding to her with a directness that she found bracing. As they were direct in speaking to her, so she was in her interactions with them.

And it was the shift in her experience of relationship with them that alerted her to the meaning of the changes she observed among the boys as they turned five and prepared to enter kindergarten. They were separating themselves from their relationships, and in the process they were becoming less direct, less attentive, less articulate, and less authentic. They were becoming more like "boys." Inattentive, indirect, inarticulate, inauthentic—words that captured the boys' response to a crisis of relationship; to become one of the boys, they had to cover parts of themselves.

The changes Chu observed and experienced with boys around the age of five are analogous to the changes girls experience at adolescence when they speak of themselves as becoming more indirect, more inauthentic in their relationships, not saying what they are feeling and thinking. Both of these times—the end of early childhood and the beginning of adolescence—are times of developmental transition, marked by physiological maturation, the advent of new cognitive and emotional capabilities, and also new experiences. But they are also times of initiation. Boys at around the age of five, if they are to become one of the boys, must conceal those parts of themselves that are not considered to be manly or heroic. The cultural force driving this initiation surfaces in the often brutal teasing and shaming of boys who resist or do not fit cultural codes of masculinity. Girls, given more leeway until adolescence, experience a similar initiation into womanhood at that time, manifest in the often vicious games of inclusion and exclusion among girls that adults find so disturbing. The helplessness and powerlessness that women so often feel in witnessing these informal initiation rites, which regularly involve acts of cruelty, suggest the scars they carry and also the force of the cultural hand behind these practices. For boys and for girls, to resist the initiation is to risk one's claim to manhood or womanhood.

Elizabeth Debold, a researcher exploring this terrain, considers the implications of boys' and girls' taking on the attributes of manhood or womanhood at very different points in their development. At age five, children are learning about the world as it is; it is the era of the naturalist. At adolescence, they are learning to know the world as it is said to be; it is the age of the hypothetical, the ability to envision possibility. Debold notes that boys at five take on the attributes of masculinity as a matter of fact, whereas girls at adolescence are more likely to notice a gap between the way things are and the way things are said to be. The good-guy/bad-guy play of four- and five-year-old boys sets the stage for the division of girls at adolescence into the good and bad girls; but by stepping into this river at a later point in time, and also because in some ways it is not their river, girls who stop and ask themselves what they are seeing will often record their sense of shock.

"Dearest Kit," Anne writes at the end of January 1944, "I wonder whether you could tell me why it is that people always try so hard to hide their real feelings? How is it that I am always quite different from what I should be in other people's company and also quite different from what I am inside? Why do people trust one another so little? Oh, I do know there must be a reason, but things are bad, very bad indeed!" She had an intensely erotic dream about a boy from school named Peter Schiff, the boy she refers to as "Petel," and since the dream, which left an aching sense of desire, a longing to be touched, to be seen and loved, she experiences herself differently. "I have changed, have grown up a lot, have become more of an independent being." Overcome with happiness, Anne longs for life and liberty; but the pursuit of happiness leads to confusion.

> The sun is shining, the sky is deep blue, there is a lovely breeze and I'm longing—so longing—for everything.— To talk, for freedom, for friends, to be alone. And I do so long—to cry! I feel as if I'm going to burst, and I know that it would get better with crying, but I can't. I'm restless. I go from one room to the other, breathe at the bottom of a window, feel my heart beating, as if it is saying, "Can't you satisfy my longings at last?" . . . I believe that it's spring within me. I feel that spring is awakening, I feel it in my whole body and soul. I have to keep myself under control—time and again, I long for my Petel, I long for every boy, even for Peter—here. I want to shout at him: "Oh say something to me, don't just smile all the time, touch me, so that I can again get that delicious feeling inside me that I first had in my dream of Petel's cheek!" I feel completely confused. I don't know what to read, what to write, what to do, I only know that I am longing.

In the late winter and spring of 1944, Anne records an inner struggle between her longing for love and pleasure and her efforts to control herself. Love and pleasure, now associated with "that delicious feeling inside me," carry with them the threat of loss. "I made a special effort not to look at him too much because whenever I did, he kept on looking too and then—yes, then—it gave me a lovely feeling inside, but which I mustn't feel too often." Although Anne censors this passage, her father restores it. It is the romance story with which we are familiar: Anne, confined to the attic, drawn to Peter, three years older than herself.

Peter begins to "[unburden] himself a little" to her, he admires her facility with words, her outspokenness ("that's why I admire you so. You are never at a loss for a word, you say exactly what you want to say to people and are not so shy"). Anne confesses her self-doubts to him ("'Just listen,' I said, generally I say things quite differently from the way I wanted to say them, I talk too much and that's no good either!"). She can tell from "his words, his gestures, his voice and his eyes" that "something was burning inside him just as it burns in me." "Dearest Kitty," she writes, "It's lovely weather again and I've quite perked up since yesterday. My writing, the finest thing I have, is making good progress . . . all I want is to be left in peace."

Anne omits several entries about herself and Peter when she rewrites her diary ("Whenever I go upstairs now, I keep hoping that I shall see 'him.'"), and her father restores them, along with a familiar complaint about grown-ups, the "know-alls" who don't know what they don't know. But this seemingly innocent teenage romance is tied to reflections on love that are far more disturbing, at least to the conventional eye. Anne edits out her reflections on love, and this time her father sustains her editing:

Love, what is love? I believe love is something that can't really be put into words. Love is understanding someone, caring for someone, sharing their ups and downs. And in the long run that also means physical love, you have shared something, given something away and received something, no matter whether you are married or unmarried, or whether you are with child or not. It doesn't matter in the least if you've lost your honor, as long as you know that someone will stand by you, will understand you for the rest of your life, someone you won't have to share with anyone else! (2 March 1944)

Anne is fourteen; she has not yet fallen in love in the full sense of that experience. But in sorting out what she knows (love is understanding, caring, sharing—opening yourself to another, taking another into yourself), she comes upon the tension between love and the code of honor and chastity that ensures the continuation of patrilineal descent, the passing down of fathers' names and property through the institution of marriage. Recklessly, Anne erases the line separating the soul from the body. She frees love from marriage and concerns about honor and chastity. Writing in the second person about a "you" who would risk losing your honor, she fends off the threat of isolation by linking love with knowing: knowing that somebody will stand by you, will understand you, will be with you rather than somebody else. What makes love risky is the threat of abandonment.

Anne observes Peter closely, seeing how he "clings to his manliness, to his solitude and to his affected indifference, but it's only an act, so as never, never to show his real feelings." "Poor Peter," she writes, "how long will he be able to go on playing this role, surely a terrible outburst must follow as a result of this superhuman effort? Oh, Peter, if only I could help you, if only you would let me! Together we could drive away your loneliness and mine" (6 March 1944).

But as Anne sees manliness as a role that poses an impediment to closeness, so womanhood comes to stand between her and her desire to show her real feelings to Peter. She too begins to enact a part: that of the good, not sexual girl. "Thank goodness they can't tell downstairs what my inward feelings are. . . . I'm completely closed up." Within her, "war still reigns incessantly . . . between desire and common sense." Her desires include a wish to be seen; she wonders if Peter could "be the first and only one to have looked through my concrete armor." As she closes herself off from her parents and from Peter, she finds an outlet for herself in her writing: "At least I can write down my thoughts and feelings, otherwise I would be completely stifled."

On 28 April 1944, Anne describes "two Annes": an "ordinary Anne" and a new arrival. She has never forgotten her dream about Peter Schiff—the feel of his cheek against hers in the dream, and within herself "that lovely feeling that made everything good." Now she has this feeling at times with Peter van Pels; and in the face of erotic desire and pleasure, a new Anne appears. "Suddenly the ordinary Anne slipped away and a 2nd Anne took her place, a second Anne who is not reckless and jocular, but one who just wants to love and be gentle." The familiar Anne has been displaced by an image, a girl who wants only to love and be gentle. She wonders if Peter notices her sadness, if he is aware of the split; but this is a question that remains unasked:

I sat pressed closely against him and felt a wave of emotion come over me, tears sprang into my eyes, the left one trickled onto his dungarees, the right one ran down my nose and also fell onto his dungarees. Did he notice? He made no move or sign to show that he did. I wonder if he feels the same as I do? He hardly said a word. Does he know that he has two Annes before him? These questions must remain unanswered. At half past 8 . . . I was still Anne No. 2. He came towards me, I flung my arms around his neck and gave him a kiss on his left cheek, and was about to kiss the other cheek, when my lips met his and we just pressed them together. In a whirl we were clasped in each other's arms, again and again, never to leave off. . . . Once more there is a question that gives me no peace: "Is it right?" Is it right that I should have yielded so soon, that I am so ardent, just as ardent and eager as Peter himself? May I, a girl, let myself go to this extent? There is but *one* answer: "I have longed so much and for so long—I am so lonely—and now I have found consolation."

Starting to write herself into the familiar romance story— "Peter has taken possession of me and turned me inside out"—Anne stops herself, bringing herself up short with the injunction, "be honest!" She longs to be with Peter, but she does not want to marry him or to give herself away:

> If I were older and he should ask me to marry him, what should I answer. Anne, be honest! You would not be able to marry him, but yet, it would be hard to let him go. Peter hasn't enough character yet, not enough will power, too little courage and strength. He is still a child in his heart of hearts. . . . I am afraid of myself, I am afraid that in my longing I'm giving myself too quickly.

Anne now holds in suspension her newfound sense of herself as a woman and desires that seem incompatible with womanhood, like the boys at four, armed and playing with lace and bunnies. She also has taken in the conventions of womanhood, linking love and sexual pleasure with marriage at the same time as she observes that Peter is not up to the challenge of being with her; he is still too much of a child, he hasn't yet developed sufficient character, courage, willpower, and strength for the kind of love that Anne wants. "I soon closed up my inner self from him, if he wants to force the lock again he'll have to work a good deal harder than before!"

For the moment, Anne turns to her writing, but there too she faces a similar dilemma: can she open her inner self to the world, and if she does so, how will she be judged? Thus she begins to experiment with her writing, turning to fiction, writing a fictionalized version of the diary (*"Het Achterhuis,"* The Secret Annex) and also creating a voice for her diary that is a fiction, writing in the spring of '44 diary entries that she dates as if they were written earlier—a voice that sounds more acceptable to her than the voice of her actual diary writing. On 13 June, well into her rewriting, Anne, just turned fifteen, writes to Kitty:

Peter loves me not as a lover but as a friend, and grows more affectionate every day. But what is the mysterious something that holds us both back? I don't understand it myself . . . he tries most persistently to remove the blots from his copybook and to keep his innermost self to himself and why am I never allowed there? By nature he is more closed-up than I am, I agree, but I know and from my own experience that at some time or other even uncommunicative people long just as much, if not more, to find someone in whom they can confide. . . . I still seem to miss the real thing and yet I know it's there!

Listening to the "I," the first-person voice in this passage, we hear Anne, like Psyche, wanting to break through the barrier that blocks her access to Peter and to say and see what she knows about love.

> *I don't understand*
> *I am not allowed*
>
> *I am*
> *I agree*
> *I know*
> *I seem to miss the real thing*
> *I know it's there.*

In what becomes the final entry in her diary, Anne writes about contradiction. "Little bundle of contradiction," she begins—that's what she has been called, and she finds that it fits, but, she asks, "Can you tell me exactly what it is. What does contradiction mean? Like so many words it can mean two things, contradiction from without and contradiction from within." The first is "the ordinary, not giving in easily, always knowing best, getting in the last word, *enfin,* all the unpleasant qualities for which I am renowned." What Anne describes as ordinary is her integrity, but it has taken on the coloration of unpleasantness, so that the very essence of relationship, being oneself with another person, has come into contradiction with having relationships. This is what she calls contradiction from without.

Contradiction from within is internal conflict, and this Anne reveals only to Kitty: "The second nobody knows about, that's my own secret. . . . I have, as it were, a dual personality." Comparable to her rendering of the secrets of her body, Anne now gives an exquisitely detailed description of her split personality and thus records the route into dissociation. The two Annes have become characters in an internal drama: "One half embodies my exuberant cheerfulness, making fun of everything, vivacity and above all the way I take everything lightly. This includes not minding flirtation, a kiss, an embrace, a dirty joke. This side is usually lying in wait and pushes away the other, which is much better, deeper and purer. You must realize that nobody knows Anne's better side and that's why most people find me so insufferable . . . a giddy clown . . . a diversion . . . not bad, but certainly not good."

Anne observes these two sides of herself, the exuberant Anne of the original diary, the irrepressible friend of Kitty's, and the good Anne, who never appears in public—whose goodness, in fact, depends on keeping herself out of the public eye. One Anne can't appear without becoming "insufferable" or at the very least "unpleasant"; the other cannot show herself because, as Anne writes, she cannot bear what she knows to be the world's response to her: she will not be taken seriously, they will "laugh at me, think I'm ridiculous, sentimental, not take me in earnest." The Anne who does not take herself seriously, who is "a frolicsome little goat who's breaking loose," can bear the world's dismissive eye, but not the Anne who has "a happy nature within," the Anne whose pleasure encompasses both her soul and her body, the Anne who knows what she knows. This is the Anne who goes into hiding, the Anne whose voice is irresistible, the Anne who continues to write to Kitty, and yet who is caught in a contradiction that folds in upon itself, because in opening herself to herself, to the people around her and to the world at large, she takes in a reality that she cannot ingest and still stay open in the world.

Anne wants to be "a great writer," she wants to be seen as having "real talent." Submitting her writing to the eyes of the world, she anticipates disappointment: "and if I haven't any talent . . . I can always write for myself." She "wants to get on" with her writing so as not to find herself in the "same sort of life as Mummy and Mrs. V. P. and all the women who do their work and are then forgotten. I must have something besides a husband and children, something that I can devote myself to." She wants to be a published writer, to become part of history.

But turning her fourteen-year-old eye to history, she sees the patriarchal structure of the world in which she is living and also the role that women and men play in perpetuating this arrangement:

A question that has been raised more than once and that gives me no inner peace is why did so many nations in the past, and often still now, treat women as inferior to men? Everyone can agree how unjust this is, but that is not enough for me, I would also like to know the cause of the great injustice! . . . It is stupid enough of women to have borne it all in silence for such a long time, since the more centuries this arrangement lasts, the more deeply rooted it becomes . . . many people, particularly women, but also men, now realize for how long this state of affairs has been wrong, and modern women demand the right of complete independence! But that's not all, respect for women, that's going to have to come as well. . . . Soldiers and war heroes are honored and celebrated, explorers acquire immortal fame, martyrs are revered, but how many will look upon a woman as they would upon a soldier?

There is something in the book "The Fight for Life" that has affected me deeply, along the lines that women suffer more pain, more illness and more misery than any war hero just from giving birth to children. And what reward does woman reap for coming successfully through all this pain? She is pushed to one side should she lose her figure through giving birth, her children soon leave her, her beauty passes. Women are much braver, much more courageous soldiers, struggling and enduring pain for the continuance of mankind, than all the freedom-fighting heroes with their big mouths.

Soldiers and mothers—the sacrificial couple: brave, courageous, struggling, and enduring pain to ensure the continuation of mankind, but while soldiers are elevated and honored, mothers are left or pushed aside. This diary entry, written in June 1944, lies beyond the hand of Anne's editing. It was omitted by her father and restored in the 1995 edition of the diary, when the issues she raises about the injustices of patriarchy, the lack of respect for women's courage and suffering, and the complicity of women and men in perpetuating this situation, had become part of an open conversation along with the more open discussion of women's bodies, women's sexuality, and relationships between women and men.

The naturalistic eye of Anne Frank had taken in realities that have repeatedly been seen and then hidden. In her editing of the diary we see this process at the same time as, in the actual diary entries as Anne continues to write them, we see the effects on Anne of coming to hide herself. She is enacting within herself or upon herself the very process of withholding and becoming "closed up" that she finds so frustrating and inauthentic in her mother and also in Peter—that leads her to turn away from these relationships and from the plot of the romance story in order to follow the writer's, the artist's, injunction: "be honest!" Writing to Kitty, Anne says what she knows, and thus we see her resisting as she records the process of her dissociation.

The story of Anne's relationship with her mother is more complicated. Ironically, while much of the controversy over the diary and the main reason given for her father's editing has to do with Anne's harshness toward her mother, her harshness is for the most part the voice of the B version. It is not the original diary-writing voice nearly to the extent that it is the voice of Anne's revision, and it signals her disassociation of herself from her mother. Anne's anger at her mother is acceptable; she can say most anything against her mother in public; it becomes part of what is in effect a class-action suit. The portrait of Anne's mother in the diary as Anne rewrites it is oddly tailored. For example, Anne not only omits the passage "Mummy, Margot and I are as thick as thieves again. It's really much better. I get into Margot's bed now almost every evening," but she also changes the entry where she wrote,

today I had a so-called "discussion" with Mummy, but the boring thing was that I burst into tears straight away. I can't help it. Daddy is always so nice to me, and he understands me so much better too. Oh, I can't stand

Mummy at such times, and I am a stranger as far as she is concerned as well, for you see, she doesn't even know how I think about the most ordinary things,

to a much more distant and categorical dismissal of her mother as a complete stranger:

Just had a big bust-up with Mummy for the umpteenth time, we simply don't get on together these days, and Margot and I don't hit it off any too well either. As a rule we don't go in for such outbursts as this in our family. Still, it's by no means always pleasant for me. Margot's and Mummy's natures are completely strange to me. I can understand my friends better than my own mother—too bad, isn't it!

The voice of Anne's rewriting is stilted. Her phrasing, at least in translation, edges toward cliché ("big bust-up," "the umpteenth time"), veers toward the norm ("As a rule we don't go in for such outbursts as this in our family"), and then opts for the extreme ("Margot's and Mummy's natures are completely strange to me"). Anne distances herself from the actual feel of the incident—the "discussion" that was not really a discussion at all but that led her instantly to burst into tears because she felt that her mother was not listening and only her father understood her. Anne is closely observing her parents at this time, when she is thirteen, in the fall of 1942, and she takes in her father's sadness: "His eyes look so sad again— poor soul." But in the spring of '44, when she edits the diary, she deletes this observation.

A straightforward voice ("My father Otto Heinrich Frank") becomes an embellished voice ("My father, the dearest darling of a father I have ever seen"); a funny, metaphorical description of the German invasion of the Netherlands ("Now that the Germans rule the roost here we are in real trouble") becomes a more ponderous voice ("After May, 1940, good times rapidly fled, first the war, then the capitulation, followed by the German invasion which is when the sufferings of us Jews really began"). Anne is clearly concerned with her reader—now imagined as a visitor to the war museum, or a critic or judge of good writing, perhaps Gerrit Bolkestein himself. She fears that her diary will be read as "the unbosomings of a thirteen-year-old school girl" rather than as reflecting a writer's sensibility; she knows that it is fathers who will judge her writing, and she writes in a voice that is now so familiar that we take it as the voice of the real diary. What becomes most puzzling is why the editors who felt free to select from her actual diary entries and thus to override the hand of her editing—her father initially and later also Mirjam Pressler—chose so often to go with the voice of the edited version.

In part, they had no choice. Miep Geis, the courageous and openhearted friend who sustained the Frank family in hiding and who was especially devoted to Anne, swept up the notebooks and loose sheets of paper that the Gestapo had dumped out of a briefcase and kept them until Otto Frank returned from Auschwitz after the war, the sole survivor among the inhabitants of the Secret Annex. But one of the diary notebooks was missing, spanning the period from mid-November of 1942 to late December of 1943, the year in which Anne turns fourteen. During this period, only her edited version survives. We don't know what Anne originally wrote, but these entries, rewritten in the late spring and early summer of 1944, contain the harshest, most cutting comments about her mother and also about Anne's difficulties with her mother, many of which are carried forward without change from the B to the C version of the diary. Anne refuses her mother's offer to say her prayers with her at bedtime; she writes of feeling sorry for Mummy, "very, very sorry," as she notices that her mother minds her coldness toward her:

Just as I shrink at her hard words so did her heart when she realized that the love between us was gone. . . . Everyone expects me to apologize, but this is something I can't apologize for because I spoke the truth, and Mummy will have to know it sooner or later anyway. I am and seem indifferent both to Mummy's tears and Daddy's looks because for the first time they are both aware of something which I have always felt. I can only feel sorry for Mummy, who has now had to discover that I have adopted her own attitude. For myself, I remain silent and aloof. I shall not shrink from the truth any longer, since the longer it is put off, the more difficult it will be for them when they do hear it.

This is the same voice—arch, distant, somewhat supercilious—as that of the earlier revisions, a voice very different from the voice of the actual diary entries that Anne was revising.

In creating Kitty, Anne creates a resonance that encourages and allows her to open herself completely. In rewriting her diary for an audience of strangers and anticipating a critical response, Anne hides herself and also divides herself from the public who will see her showing her anger, her contempt for her mother, and withholding her love. Perhaps she is angry at her mother in part because her mother has modeled this withholding for her, showing her an example that she does not want to follow and yet finds herself copying as she moves out of relationship—the full weather of human connection—in her desire to have relationships in the world. "I never utter my real feelings, " she writes.

ON SEPTEMBER 10, 1998, a front-page *New York Times* article reports that five more pages of the diary have come to light. In these pages Anne writes what she knows about her parents' marriage and explores the reasons for her mother's coldness. "I am unable to talk with her, I cannot look lovingly into those cold eyes. I cannot, never" is the diary excerpt that the *Times* runs under its headline. The article continues with the familiar stress on Anne's "difficulties with her mother," yet these are the pages where Anne explores the reasons for the difficulty—it is the passage most sympathetic to her mother, offering an explanation for the emotional distance that Anne struggles against repeatedly. Anne writes: "For a woman in love it cannot be easy to know that she will never occupy the first place in her husband's heart, and Mother knew." She goes on to observe that "Father appreciates Mother and loves her, but not with the kind of love that I envisage for a marriage." As for her diary, the *Times* article continues, "which became one of the world's best-known books, published in 56 languages," Anne says, "I shall also take care that nobody can lay hands on it."

Anne's anger toward her mother, her difficulties with her mother, are typically seen as part of an adolescent girl's struggle to separate herself from her mother, to free herself from a love that feels potentially engulfing, to distinguish herself from her mother and become her own person. Yet whatever tendencies we may have to brush aside or question the validity of Anne's observations, they are brought up short by the evidence presented by Melissa Muller in her recent biography of Anne Frank. According to Muller, Otto Frank had fallen in love with a wealthy young woman in Frankfurt, but her parents had ruled out marriage on financial grounds, leaving him "heartbroken and ultimately devoid of passion for Edith."

In a diary entry, written on blue sheets of paper and dated February 8, 1944, Anne addresses her fictional friend Kitty and talks about going through a period of reflection centering on her parents' marriage, always presented to her as "ideal." Otto Frank removed these pages when he turned over the diary to the Netherlands Institute, going to some lengths to conceal their existence by giving them to a friend so that he could say when asked that he had no more of the diary in his possession. The Critical Edition marks the omission in the A version of the diary, an asterisk directing the reader to a footnote that says, "In the 47 lines omitted here, Anne Frank gave an extremely unkind and partly unfair picture of her parents' marriage. At the request of the Frank family this passage has been deleted."

Anne says she knows "a thing or two" about her father's past and, joining this knowledge with her observation of her parents' marriage, concludes that her father married her mother because "he deemed her the right person to be his wife." She goes on: "I must say that I admire my mother for the way she has filled that position without a murmur and without jealousy, as far as I can tell. . . . Father is not in love, he gives her a kiss the way he kisses us." As for her mother, Anne writes:

> Quite possibly because of her great sacrifice Mother has grown hard and disagreeable toward her surroundings and consequently, she will drift further and further away from the path of love, will gain less and less admiration and, no doubt, Father will eventually come to realize that because externally she has never claimed his full love, she has crumbled away bit by bit internally. She loves him more than anybody else and it is hard to see this kind of love unanswered time and again.

Her insight is stunning. It combines a child's sensibility ("Mummy, you have a happy voice, but I also hear a little worried voice") with the razor-sharp intelligence of adolescence. Anne sees the difference between being in relationship and filling a role or playing a part in relationships ("he deemed her the right person to be his wife"). It is like the boys' fathers hearing the difference between the "Dad voice" and their real voice.

Anne's father had told her his tragic love story, but she is gripped less by the tragic story than by the cost of the sacrifice her mother has made. It is a sacrifice that she explicitly rejects for herself, and in doing so, she identifies herself as a resister. Her ability, even fleetingly, to see her mother as a complete person—as another woman rather than the other woman—brings to the fore again our difficulty in knowing a story between women that does not put them in competition with each other. Proust in recapturing a lost time in his early childhood and Anne in writing in the real time of her adolescence focus our attention on a sacrifice they see their mothers making—a sacrifice of love in the name of love, a giving up of pleasure. Asking herself, "Should I help her? Or my father?" Anne answers "No," and then turns on her mother in anger.

In my research with girls, I saw girls resisting self-sacrifice over and over again, but resisting it for the sake of relationship. The resistance story was a love story; they were in love with themselves ("Gorgeous photograph, isn't it!"), and they wanted to be with others and live in the world. I noticed how quickly a tragic story came in like a tide, washing over the resistance, so that research showing girls *resisting* losing their voices and losing relationship was repeatedly recast as showing girls losing their voices and losing relationship, as if to preempt the ending. I had seen a healthy resistance in girls, the psyche's resistance to losing voice and thereby losing relationship. Like the T cells of the body, the healthy psyche fights off infection, rejecting false voice and false relationships.

But this healthy resistance, when it threatens to upset the established order of relationships by exposing truths that are commonly hidden under homilies about love or equality or democracy or marriage, readily turns into a political resistance, girls speaking truth to power and jeopardizing their access to power in the process. Thus the great sacrifice begins: the giving up of relationship in order to have relationships, girls burying what they know about love and pleasure and taking into themselves an image of themselves that makes it seem impossible for them to say or even to know what they are really feeling and thinking. And yet in witnessing girls splitting themselves off from vital parts of themselves and moving into dissociation, I also saw them planting the seeds of transformation: an honest voice, a desire for relationship.

THE ANGER between mothers and daughters is legendary; the love often is held in silence. In the Psyche and Cupid myth, Venus' anger is center stage; Psyche's mother is completely silent. The conflict between Venus and Psyche runs through the story, becoming the focus of attention once Cupid leaves Psyche for his mother's chambers. But Psyche is also becoming a mother; she will become the mother of a daughter named Pleasure. The myth, the old wife's tale, suggests that the envy and anger between women must come to some resolution before such a birth can be imagined. But in setting the conflict between Venus and Psyche, the son's mother and his lover, the old wife has upended the Oedipal triangle. In place of a world that revolves around fathers, we see a constellation of two women and a young man, the lines of love and authority becoming more fluid. As Psyche resists the cast of New Venus, as she breaks the taboo on seeing and speaking about love, this triangle spins out of the orbit of tragedy and into a trajectory leading to Pleasure.

Rachel, the mother of four-year-old Jake, follows this trajectory in refusing to betray his love or deny the closeness between them. Clara holds to a similar path in embracing her no-holds-barred kind of love with Hyun. I notice in my responses to these women that it is the closeness or pleasure of these relationships, which I also knew with my sons, that sets off signals of danger. In my conversations with the fathers of four- and five-year-old boys, I am struck by how boys' exuberance and their questions about love and relationships ("Is Mom your buddy?") can awaken men to a knowing and an energy that they feel they have lost but that they remember—and they too associate this love and pleasure with their sons with danger.

It is not surprising to discover that young boys can teach us about knowing and loving; we remember what children see before they are taught how to see—we repeat the tale of the emperor's new clothes. Adolescent girls enlarge this picture, because in addition to the child's eye for truth and the adolescent's eye for hypocrisy, they bring an awareness of how we come not to see. When Anne Frank says that she misses having a "real mother," she is missing a woman she knows, and it is the absence of this woman that she finds so unsettling. When she reads her father's love story in a way he had not intended—in a way he deems harsh and partly unfair—she was writing only for Kitty; when she edited her diary, she omitted this entry, perhaps anticipating her father's response, or possibly aligning her perception with his way of seeing and agreeing with his judgment. Anne can express her anger at her mother; it is her sympathy with her mother that remains hidden.

FOR A LONG time, I forget my memories of pleasure with my mother, and also her encouragement of my pleasure, her delight in my sensuality, my voice, and my writing. I have come to see her as something of a duenna, shrouded in black, a guardian of patriarchy, and yet she dressed in bright colors and had a subversive edge. It was she who let me drive under conditions forbidden by my learner's permit ("I know she's a safe driver," she told my father, a lawyer, who found this reasoning unconvincing). It was she who encouraged me to trust myself: "Darling, you know," she would say. I carry this voice with me. But also a voice that is haughty and removed, the voice of the woman who is my mother but who does not look or sound like my mother, her fierce, grim expression terrifying as she suddenly withholds her approval: "What do you know?" she says, reminding me of my inexperience. That is the voice I remember from the fights of adolescence, when I challenged my mother, when I wanted to speak honestly with her about love. I learned to say I was sorry when I was not; I thought my mother was teaching me to lie. My mother, who had a sharp eye for truth but also a pragmatic take on reality. Inviting me to confide in her but holding her approval and disapproval as a wedge in a relationship that became so confusing in its alternations of presence and absence, closeness and distance, that for years it seemed easier to tell stories about betrayal (for which I found a ready ear and quick affirmation) than to sort out for myself what was going on between us.

I find myself in the midst of what seems a trauma landscape (dislocated memories, gaps in time, sudden flashbacks accompanied by waves of unexpectedly strong emotions), and yet nothing traumatic seems to have happened. I was not sexually abused, I did not suffer incest or violence. While I grew up in the wake of the Great Depression and also during the time of the Holocaust, while I remember climbing under my desk at school during air-raid drills and blackout shades in our New York apartment and the cantatas we sang in Hebrew school about Jews hiding in the forests of Poland and the refugees whom my parents helped, and while I faced quotas on Jews in applying to college, I did not directly experience poverty or the full force of anti-Semitism, or war or rape or the kinds of terror that we commonly associate with trauma.

But I did experience a shocking break in my relationship with my mother when I came home from camp at the age of twelve and discovered that my grandfather was no longer living in our house and that my mother had pressed him to find his own apartment. Popsy, my father's father, was the love of my childhood. A playful man, a man seemingly free from the burdens of manhood, whose unclouded love was so steady a feature of daily living that I never imagined his moving away. But since his new apartment was only a few blocks from ours and I would go there and he came every Friday night for dinner, I have come to suspect that the hole that opened in my life after that summer had more to do with what I felt as my mother's betrayal. Her reasons for wanting Popsy to leave had to do with my becoming a young woman: our rooms were too close, and it was no longer appropriate for me and my grandfather to share a bathroom. A chasm opened between me and my mother; I felt we were living in different worlds.

And perhaps my confusion was compounded by the fact that on my own at camp that summer I had stepped into the world my mother was preparing me to enter, in a seamless joining of my ongoing life with my girlfriends and counselors and the new experience of falling in love with a sixteen-year-old boy, a counselor in training with dark curly hair and blue eyes and an irresistible smile. He was something of a star at camp—the kind of boyfriend my mother envisioned me having—but to me he was a gentle and playful soul, like Popsy. We sat together wrapped in green blankets at the Sunday night campfire, and afterward, we would walk through the woods to the edge of the girls' campsite, kissing under tall pines. The sixteen-year-old girls whom I saw as goddesses, sunning themselves on the dock and shaving their legs, began to talk to me in the girls' bathroom at night, sharing their secrets, telling me not to use the brown paper towels to dry my face because they would clog my pores. But for the most part I was oblivious to this change in my status—too inside my life to look from the outside—until my mother shocked me out of relationship by pulling the ground of relationship out from under me, so that suddenly I became self-conscious about the moves I was making, aware of their implications in a universe of relationships that I had innocently entered, a world where pleasure became Act I in a play that ended badly.

My mother was an identical twin; her twin had died of a wasting disease (myasthenia gravis) when they were thirteen. My grandmother tells me the story of the twins, the "heavenly twins," and of Mildred dying, the family gathered around her. I find the story horrifying; my heart goes out to my mother, but for the most part she does not want to talk about it. Late in life, she will say, "It is a terrible thing to lose a twin." I can readily explain the turbulence that entered my relationship with my mother as I was approaching thirteen. My mother was terrified, remembering the loss, trying to keep me safely out of her twin story and distancing me from her in the process. Or simply overwhelmed with grief. And all this was true, but it leaves unexplained why similar experiences of sudden loss, shocking betrayal, and serious rifts in relationship occur so frequently between mothers and daughters at this time, suggesting the traumas that other mothers may have experienced or perhaps some common story that mothers and daughters find themselves enacting at the threshold where a mother sees her daughter crossing into the room of womanhood. Perhaps because my mother had literally lived, with her twin, the sense of inner division and the loss of a part of herself that many women experience in adolescence, it was easier for me to see it.

At a point early on in my research with girls, I become aware that I am asking girls questions I was taught as a researcher never to ask ("Do you really feel this way?" "Is that true?"). I discover that in response to my questions I am told the story under the story. Sheila, who has said that she did not like herself enough to look out for herself, tells me exactly how she looks out for herself (by never being herself in her relationships) and at what cost ("honesty in relationship"). Gail, who led off our interview in the second year of a four-year study by saying that "adolescent girls don't know what they think," tells me precisely what she thinks; anticipating our conversation, she came to realize that the block standing in the way of her achieving anywhere near her potential was held in place by her reluctance to know what she thinks about her mother, who stood by impassively when Gail's stepfather verbally lashed out at her. Gail had held on to an image of her mother as loving by becoming, as she says, "a sponge"—a creature unaware of thoughts and feelings, who merely soaks things in.

I puzzle over the truth of my relationship with my mother: how it was, what it really was like. Was it as painful as I remember? I encounter within myself a surprising reluctance to unravel what I am coming to suspect is an edited version of my own story. In coming-of-age novels written by women whose lives are otherwise very different from mine, I follow the path of an eclipse: one mother disappearing behind another, or a girl, coming of age and gaining a vantage point from which it becomes difficult for her to see a woman she knew intimately in childhood. What I had thought of as just my difficulty in coming to grips with my relationship with my mother seemed part of a more general struggle on the part of women to undo a rewriting of history.

In Jamaica Kincaid's novel *Annie John,* set in the Antigua of her childhood, Annie, age twelve, is shocked to discover that her mother, unbeknownst to her, is arranging a separation between them that Annie never imagined. It is part of a process of initiation, her mother preparing her to become a young lady. On the face of it, it seems unproblematic—a move toward independence and freedom. Her mother tells her that they can no longer wear dresses cut from the same cloth, that one day she will have her own house and she can choose her own way. And yet the voice of the novel—or, more precisely, the voice of the girl who opens the novel—describes a shattering sense of betrayal: "To say that I felt the earth swept away from under me would not be going too far. It wasn't just what she said, it was the way she said it. No accompanying little laugh. No bending over and kissing my little wet forehead (for suddenly I turned hot, then cold, and all my pores must have opened up, for fluids just flowed out of me)." What follows is the by-now familiar split of girls into the good and the bad, Annie choosing a bad girl ("the red girl") as her new best friend, experimenting with badness while maintaining an appearance of goodness, and finally succumbing to madness when it becomes impossible for her to see what she is seeing and also to listen to what people are saying, or to find a way of saying or even knowing what she wants or what she is feeling and thinking when words themselves, like "love" and "truth," have become so confused. In the end, Annie solves the problem by leaving. Summing up her childhood, she rewrites her history, making the betrayal she found so shocking seem ordinary—a familiar story about love and its loss. No longer fighting to stay in relationship with her mother, she has come instead to identify with her mother: to wear two faces and tell two stories about herself, a resistance story and a conventional story, the tragic story of love. "So now I, too, have hypocrisy, and breasts (small ones), and hair growing in the appropriate places, and sharp eyes, and I have made a vow never to be fooled again."

In *The Bluest Eye,* Toni Morrison asks how is it possible for a girl to see what she sees and love in the way she is supposed to love. Her narrator, Claudia, is ten years old, an African-American girl. Like Charlotte Brontë's Jane Eyre, who is white and English, like so many ten- and eleven- and twelve-year-old girls who appear in novels and plays and poems and films written or directed by women, Claudia resists lying about love. Attuned to her body, she knows what she desires. Tuned to the people around her, she knows what they want her to want. "It had begun with Christmas and the gift of dolls. The big, the special, the loving gift was always a big, blue-eyed Baby Doll. From the clucking sounds of adults I knew that the doll represented what they thought was my fondest wish . . . [it was] supposed to bring me great pleasure." If anyone had asked her what she wanted for Christmas,

had any adult with the power to fulfill my desires taken me seriously and asked me what I wanted, they would have known that I did not want to have anything to own, or to possess any object. I wanted rather to feel something on Christmas day. The real question would have been, "Dear Claudia, what experience would you like on Christmas?" I could have spoken up. "I want to sit on the low stool in Big Mama's kitchen with my lap full of lilacs and listen to Big Papa play his violin for me alone." The lowness of the stool made for my body, the security and warmth of Big Mama's kitchen, the smell of the lilacs, the sound of the music, and since it would be good to have all my senses engaged, the taste of a peach perhaps, afterward.

Claudia knew what she wanted: she wanted pleasure, all her senses engaged and the experience of relationship that comes with the awareness of being seen, being offered what gives her pleasure, being known, being loved. Seeing the grown-ups, the black folk who had fallen in love with Shirley Temple, wanting her to want the "big, blue-eyed Baby Doll" for Christmas, she realizes that "the best hiding place was love." "Fraudulent love," as she will discover, is "the best hiding place for cruelty. . . . It was a small step to Shirley Temple. I learned much later to worship her, just as I learned to delight in cleanliness, knowing, even as I learned, that the change was adjustment without improvement."

It is Claudia at the beginning of the novel, recalling the pain of her childhood—the house was old and cold, her mother so overburdened, distracted, impatient that Claudia's throwing up in her bed became the last straw—who stops herself, interrupting herself with the question: "But was it really like that? As painful as I remember?" A sensation returns like a flashback: "Love, thick and dark as Alaga syrup . . . I could smell it—taste it . . . everywhere in that house." The bad-mother story gives way to a memory of her mother as a woman with hands, busy, irascible, and loving her child: "And in the night when my coughing was dry and tough, feet padded into the room, hands repinned the flannel, readjusted the quilt, and rested a moment on my forehead. So when I think of autumn, I think of somebody with hands who does not want me to die."

With the publication of Anne Frank's actual diary and the discovery of the five missing pages, with the outpouring of novels, plays, stories, poems, memoirs, and diaries written by women, evidence is amassing to dispel an illusion so powerful and so emotionally compelling that it is readily taken for reality—like our sense of the earth as still. A view of mothers and of relationships between mothers and daughters, so fixed and seemingly convincing that it seems a mirror of nature, or the anger at mothers that sets in like a fog, turns out to be something of an overlay, a palimpsest—a script written over another. I pick up the key to my memories of pleasure with my mother; seemingly inaccessible, they turn out to be readily at hand.

MY MOTHER had two names. Her maiden name, now called her "real name," and the name she took when she married my father. I see her in her wedding photograph, stunning, with a sense of style. She is wearing not a formal bridal gown but a dress with a flapper's hem, her hair bobbed, hugging her face, her eyes bright, her face flooded with light. She stands next to my father, his collar pinned, his striped tie knotted, a serious expression on his face. Their marriage was always presented as ideal. I see my parents at various times in their long marriage dancing with each other, singing together in the car, laughing in a secret language, falling into the rhythm of their love. It was my mother's dream, her life with my father. She was Mabel Friedman, she was a wife and a mother; eventually she became a nursery school teacher and a therapist helping emotionally disturbed children to form relationships. Mabel Friedman, Mrs. Friedman—these were the names I heard her called, over and over again, in my childhood and adult life.

But recently I have found myself thinking about Mabel Caminez, a name she also used. As a young woman she worked as a decorator, and she kept that name on her accounts. I see her signing it at the bottom of order slips when she took me with her into decorators' showrooms to buy fabrics or lamps or furniture, for her house and then later for mine. When I think of Mabel Caminez, I think of the woman with an eye for light and color and pattern, the woman who had worked for an oriental-rug dealer and also for the *Menorah Journal*, a Jewish literary magazine. Her father, Jacob Caminez, had been a furniture dealer, a "millionaire," my grandmother said, speaking with pride about the heyday of her husband, who came to this country alone at sixteen from the village of Kamenets-Podolski in Ukraine and started out as a peddler on New York's Lower East Side. My grandmother Bertha came with her family from Hamburg via Palestine when she was eighteen. In the full bloom of their marriage, my grandparents lived in a large house near Prospect Park in Brooklyn with six children, my grandmother's mother and brother, maids and governesses, carriages and horses, until my grandfather lost his fortune in a fire, or to his relatives whom he brought over, depending on who was telling the story and when. The family survived because my grandmother had shrewdly put away money in a time of plenty. My grandfather was something of a religious mystic, a generous man who lived with God; "God will provide," he would always say. In fact, it was my grandmother.

My mother tells me about herself and her twin, how they played with their twinship, one twin collecting two allowances, one staying after school for the other, how their best friend was an only child like me.

Perhaps she kept the name Caminez in part to stay with her sister. In photographs of the twins, I can always pick out my mother. She was the livelier of the two. A spirited woman, shadowed by loss, shrewd like her mother, generous and optimistic like her father, Mabel Caminez was fun to be with. I remember bicycling with my mother one summer when we rented a house near the Long Island Sound; I was five, and gas was rationed because of the war. In a photograph from that time, we are wearing our mother-daughter dresses, our bodies in sync as when we were cycling. I remember the lean-to in the Adirondacks, overlooking a lake, where we would sit and sew balsam pillows—the smell of the balsam, the light on the water, the quiet of early afternoon. My mother often preferred the company of children.

When I was a small child, she sang to me in German and French as well as in English, teaching me the magic of words; later we sang together in the synagogue choir. She would take me with her on trips to visit her friends—eccentric women who lived in brown houses whom my father did not much care for, and also friends who lived in distant cities: Buffalo and Philadelphia. On winter afternoons in New York, she would sometimes take me to visit an artist friend who painted in a studio under the Fifty-Ninth Street Bridge. When we traveled alone together, she was Mabel Caminez, and I adored her.

Mrs. Friedman was another matter. She was my father's wife, she was Mother, she worked with young children and ran her household. I see her giving parties, singing around the piano, having company for dinner. She made a beautiful home. Oriental rugs in deep reds and blues. She was in love with my father, her handsome husband, and together they lived the American dream. But watching her face as she sat at one end of her exquisitely set table, my father at the other, I often sensed that she was not there. She would set the scene and then observe what happened. I often felt I was a character in a play she was directing; she would give me my lines, and I would say them ("Tell Auntie Bess that you loved her present," "Say 'My mother says I have to be home by midnight'") until I had learned them by heart.

But I have superimposed one image over another, a voice from one time running into a voice from another, as I will forget Mabel Caminez and superimpose Mrs. Friedman. The exquisitely set table is from later in my parents' marriage; it covers the simpler table of my early adolescence, as I will cover my voice from that time. At the simple oak table pushed up against one wall of the living room, my father sits at one end, my mother at the other, and I on the long bench between them. I have eaten my meat and my vegetables and finished my milk; I ask to be excused, drawn by the sounds coming in through the window of my friends playing outside on the street. "Eat your potatoes," my mother says, eyeing my plate. I refuse. "Potatoes are filled with vitamin C," she says, and then, the hysteria in her voice rising, "The British navy always took potatoes with them when they went on long sea voyages; that's why they didn't get scurvy." The logic swirls like a snowstorm. I am not going on a long sea voyage, and anyway, I have eaten my vegetables. I trump her. "They are called 'limeys,'" I say, riding over her, glancing at my father, the soul of rationality, knowing that I am loosening a seawall by picking at the absurdity of her argument, that I will be engulfed by rage and madness. It is too easy, this fight with my mother, this alignment with my father, this Oedipal story. I see a part of my mother watching, taking it in. I feel my heart break as I see her seeing me leave her, following a path she had laid out before me. My anger at her hardens.

My father and I take the dog to the park on Sundays; we let her run without her leash. In the summer, we swim far out into the lake, the dog standing on the dock barking until, all four paws splaying, she dives into the water and swims out to join us.

The clothes my parents wore at their wedding—my mother in her flapper's dress, my father tall, dark, and handsome in his wedding suit—capture a tension within and between them. Studies of marriage repeatedly trace a path leading from enchantment to disillusionment and then to what is called mature love, but this is not what I see. Perhaps because the love between my parents is so palpable, because my mother—the woman I think of as Mabel Caminez, the woman my father also fell in love with—has taken me with her into the world of her pleasure, and because I know my father's father as a man who turned his back on patriarchy, I see an ongoing tension between romantic images of love and marriage and a world of enchantment that resists the tragic love story, even in the face of loss. As I will resist my mother's efforts to teach me the games of love she thinks I need to play in order to succeed in the world that she sees me entering. And her image of me playing the guitar, surrounded by suitors, withholding my favors. As I will hear her in the same breath encouraging my freedom and imposing restraint, her voice splintering until it divides into what I have come to hear as the counterpoint between Mabel Caminez, the woman with the soul of an artist, and Mrs. Friedman, the mother raising her daughter in patriarchy. My resistance strengthened as I watch my father's face in the years after his father left our house periodically sink into the lineaments of depression and my mother's lightness take on an anxious cast, knowing as I see this that I am seeing what I am not supposed to be seeing.

The Indigo Girls, two women who are among the many contemporary popular women singers, sing a song about Galileo:

> *galileo's head was on the block*
> *the crime was looking up for truth*
> *and as the bombshells of my daily fears explode*
> *I try to trace them to my youth*
>
> *and then you had to bring up reincarnation*
> *over a couple of beers the other night*
> *and now I'm serving time for mistakes*
> *made by another in another lifetime*
>
> *how long till my soul gets it right*
> *can any human being ever reach that kind of light*
> *I call on the resting soul of galileo*
> *king of night vision, king of insight.*

I dream that I am with my friend Tina. She is a theater director, a stand-in no doubt for my mother as well as herself in the dream. We are in the kitchen of the apartment my family lived in until I went to college. We go down the hall into the room that was my grandfather's. A window looks out through the courtyard to the west, and in front of the window there is a yellow wicker sofa, gold-yellow, the color of the bed in van Gogh's painting of his room. I remember looking at that painting along with the sunflowers in the large gray portfolio of van Gogh reproductions that my mother kept closed up against the wall of her bedroom. In the dream, the sofa is light and airy, and Tina and I are busy arranging a bright red cushion along its length, trying to thread it through the armrest in the middle, looking for a way to anchor it. The wicker is scratchy, and without the cushion the sofa is not comfortable to sit on. But we never sit down. The mood of the dream is light and airy like summer and filled with motion, a flurry of activity.

Except for the stillness at one end of the sofa, next to the wall, where a birdcage sits under a cover. In the cage is Lizzie Ingram; I know she is there although I cannot see her. But I see her in my mind's eye. She is the actor whose performance I found riveting in the production of *Coriolanus* that Tina directed. She played Volumnia, Coriolanus' mother—Shakespeare's harsh and searing depiction of a mother in patriarchy, a woman aligned with the values of imperial Rome.

A bird does not sing when its cage is covered, and Volumnia is silenced in my dream. She sits in her covered cage, her face set in anger, the fierce, grim expression I remember seeing on my mother's face. I take this in seemingly without registering her presence, like keeping track of someone out of the corner of my eye. I worry that if, in arranging the cushion, Tina and I jostle the sofa, the cage will fall to the floor and Lizzie will get out.

As it is, Tina and I pay no attention to her; it is as if she isn't there, and yet I am tensely aware of her presence. As we start to leave, I reach into a jumble of old toys and clothes in a basket on the floor and retrieve two small stuffed birds, one red and one blue—the red and the blue of van Gogh's room and my mother's Persian carpets. The stuffing is coming out of the birds, but the colors are bright and clear. Without looking, I reach behind me and push the birds through the bars of the cage to Lizzie. Then, as we are crossing the threshold, leaving the room, I say to Tina: "She will go mad." I am stricken as I realize that Lizzie can hear me. I think now she will go mad because I have said it. I wish I had waited to speak until I was alone with Tina.

I never spoke with my mother about the doubleness that riddled our relationship; it was a silence between us that lasted to the end of her long life. And I am left with regret and also with guilt, the feelings at the end of the dream as I walk out of the room, wondering whether I, in my sensitivity to light and color and words and music, all of which I associate with my mother, in my love for her artist friends and the artist in her, and in my no doubt irritating challenges throughout my adolescence to what I then called her values, meaning her complicity in accommodating patriarchy and the premium she placed on *bella figura,* I wondered whether in loving Mabel Caminez, I was endangering Mrs. Friedman.

My memories of pleasure with my mother have the same rhythm of activity and clarity of light that energize the dream. I am leaving with Tina, the stand-in for my mother, the artist and the decorator, the theater director. I am leaving the caged woman, the patriarchal matron, and changing the direction of the play, leaving her with remnants of pleasure and sadness—twin birds, one red and one blue. "She will go mad," I say. I had watched my mother cover herself, stiffen herself, corset herself. And like many readers of Anne Frank's diary, I found a strong resonance in Anne's anger at her mother, Anne's preference for her father, and her determination to live a different life. But now I realize that what I had heard as the voice of the diary was not the actual voice of the diary but a voice Anne created for herself, voicing over her closely observed descriptions of a girl and her mother losing touch with each other as the girl becomes a young woman.

And I begin to understand why it was that the breaks in my relationship with my mother that we had managed to repair during my childhood came to seem irreparable in the course of my adolescence. When I was a child, when I was entering adolescence, I fought with my mother for relationship; but after a time I found myself turning away, because I felt that I was confronting not my mother or, as Anne Frank says, not my "real mother," but a woman who had aligned herself with "a mysterious something," a more powerful enemy. Like Venus in the myth of Psyche and Cupid.

The truths that remained unspoken between us were truths about love, mine and hers—not the protestations of love we repeatedly exchanged, but the depths of our feeling for each other and also our knowing of each other. My mother was a twin, a girl twin who knew a rare language of intimacy, who knew intuitively in a way that has resisted description but that we are now coming more to appreciate and understand. At the same time, the loss of her twin engraved on her psyche the association between closeness and danger; in this she embodied the cultural story: love leading to loss, pleasure to death.

With Mabel Caminez and Mrs. Friedman, I became an expert in double consciousness. The peculiar sensation that DuBois describes was for me an experience of living simultaneously with two seemingly contradictory people. And perhaps what Freud called "the family romance," the child's fantasy of having been born to better parents, reflects a reality many children experience, of being in relationship with one parent (one's "real" mother, or father) and then finding oneself suddenly in the presence of another, who seems unreal, a fabrication, someone playing a part in a play. I had watched my mother directing the lives of others, leaving herself to one side. The lithe, spirited woman whose face shone out of her wedding photograph had become more of an observer. It was when I picked up parts of myself that I had also put to one side that I found myself coming into a new relationship with my mother. But it was also a time when I was leaving the world she taught me to navigate so brilliantly, as she initiated me into being a woman in patriarchy.

The meaning of dreams spirals out like a shell, but in the innermost recess of a dream, there is often a place where it vanishes into mystery—sometimes called the navel of the dream—where associations break off and a connection is knotted. At the end of the dream, I say "She will go mad" and am immediately overcome with regret. For a long time the connection eludes me, until I remember my father standing in the kitchen, the same kitchen where the dream begins, and saying, his face flaring in anger: "Don't ever speak about your mother that way. Don't ever call her 'she.'" It was the time when my mother and I were fighting with a passion that seemingly brooked no restraint, the year my grandfather left and I turned thirteen. It was the year I thought my mother was going mad.

In the night vision of the dream, I undo the prohibition—my father's injunction against seeing and speaking. Overriding a voice I carried inside me, I am dismantling the internal structure of patriarchy. Popsy's room has been refurnished, Tina and I are putting the finishing touches in place. Volumnia, the patriarchal mother, has been caged; her cage is covered, her voice is silent. I pass the birds through the bars to Lizzie, the actor who is playing Volumnia. And I wonder if the insight of the dream, dreamed some years after my mother's death, is contained in this gesture, with its reminder of color and song and the possibility of flight. Imagined at a time when the view of the universe was shifting, when the lines of love and authority between men and women, parents and children, were becoming less hierarchical and more fluid. And the tragedy, perhaps, lies precisely in the vision enacted in the dream of how the story might have gone differently, might go differently now if pleasure and also the sympathy between women are no longer hidden but set in a room that was a father's room, their loss no longer outside but part of his story.

The child grows still, sensing something of importance.
The woman settles and begins her story.

Believe it, what we lost is here in this room
on this veiled evening . . . .

                    —EAVEN BOLAND

*J*OY WAS the most difficult emotion for women to stay with
in the workshops that Kristin Linklater and I offered under
the title "In Our Own Voices" as an outreach of The Company of Women, the all-women theater troupe we co-directed
from 1990 to 1996. We held weekend theater camps for girls
nine to thirteen and weekend workshops for women with the
intention of supporting the strength and clarity of girls' voices
and leading women through a combination of voice, theater,
and writing exercises, including some autobiographical story-
telling, to rediscover that strength in themselves. The "In Our
Own Voices" workshops opened women to the inspiration of
girls, encouraging women to find in themselves a resilience, a
sense of adventure, a directness of expression, an energy, and a
voice that they had forgotten or had not heard with such clarity for years. The girls built sound-houses for the women to
recall themselves in, and we found that training women actors
by bringing them into the company of girls led to a release of
voice and energy that inspired fresh and original and at times
brilliant work.

In these workshops I noticed how much easier it is for
women to tell a tragic story. Joy took the women to the near
side of a loss they remembered, so that the loss was palpably
in front of them rather than safely behind them. To taste a

pleasure that had once seemed ordinary but that over time had become extraordinary meant to risk losing joy again. As the weekend workshops opened a vocal road back into what was for many women a lost time, it was surprising how readily they followed it. And also how little it took. We began with the rudiments of Linklater's voice work, exercises connecting the impulse to speak with breath and sound; from the voice work, which brought women into relationship with their bodies, we went to writing exercises designed to bring them back into relationship with a part of their history, and more specifically, with the girls they were before becoming women. Since this was a journey that typically took women back through a time of dissociation, an associative process was necessary. In our workshops, it took the form of "free-writing": a line was given ("I am going back to find her . . ."), and the women were asked to write for three minutes without lifting pen from paper, recording the stream of their associations, including any blocks or impediments they encountered. Frequently women discovered a girl whom they knew but had not remembered—like Anne Frank of the original diary. A woman who came to the workshop depressed and angry, a dour expression on her face, brightened unexpectedly when she recalled herself as a fifth grader, standing up in the class show and singing "I'm Gonna Wash That Man Right Outta My Hair."

The journey continued with visualization: see yourself, draw yourself as you were when you were nine or ten or eleven, and then imagine your girl-self saying to you, "I want to take you on an adventure." We go with her, eyes closed, wherever she takes us and then record the journey for her. One participant, Patricia Delorey, writes:

With my new orange bike really big orange bike leaving the camp site going faster and faster along the river on the pavement but there down by the river warm but the

wind cold blowing in my face my hair behind faster &
faster no fear pedaling with power my body's power the
bike big & bright & orange & me big on the bike & the
river big & the river faster & me faster & orange &
bright & wild & alone me & the river & the orange
bike.

Following the adventure, we listened for her voice. "And she
came to tell me . . ." became the first line of a free-writing
exercise that, following the free fall of association, often fell
into the cadence of a poem:

And she came to tell me
a diamond of truth, my legacy
I held it in my small child's hand
put it up to the light, peered
and stepped through to the other side

she beckoned me to speak
but after so much silence, my tongue lay in my mouth
as though I were still
somehow asleep

I put my hands inside my mouth
and holding my tongue
thanked it for its labor of silence

My tongue suddenly flew above me then
Suddenly light and limitless
I turned my eyes toward it
astonished at its ambition
I never intended it to say that much!
But it sang, on and on
I put the diamond in my ear
Closed my eyes

And embraced the arias my tongue sang and sang
Above my head, free, unbound and tireless.
—ELIZABETH AUSTEN

The final free-write was an exercise in resonance: the woman's response to her girl-self, telling her what she heard her saying. "And I heard you say" started the writing.

And I heard you say,
Let me be wild and tangled and free
Let me run and yell and catch things
And come back dirty and shining, with thistles in my hair.
I am tired of being timid, you said.
I am tired of being quietly, perfectly creative.
I want to leave my closet door open at night
I want to climb out of the window of who I am expected to be
And leap into the reality of wishes, landing in a cascade of
*   cherry blossoms.*
—MIRIAM RUBINOW

"A Poem to My Voice" ended the workshop exercises.

If the depth of my feelings
matched the depth of my voice
If I remember the knowledge
of sound pure and full,
If I stay connected to
my breath and stand tall
If I keep my channels open,
will I still be a woman?
—ADRIENNE CUGINI

Freeing one's voice means freeing oneself, and with this freedom it becomes possible to make choices about speaking and silence. The "natural voice," meaning the voice we are born with, is "transparent" in Linklater's description, "revealing, not describing, inner impulses of emotion and thought, directly and spontaneously. The person is heard, not the person's voice."

Stephanie Levine, a graduate student at Harvard studying "the inner worlds and daily lives of Hasidic adolescent girls" in the Lubavitch community in Crown Heights, Brooklyn, asked if girls raised in orthodoxy have what might be called an independent voice, the ability to speak for themselves. Spending a year living in Crown Heights, she found a strength and variety of voice in these girls who were living within what Hawthorne's narrator in *The Scarlet Letter* refers to as "the iron framework."

The title of her dissertation, "Mystics, Mavericks, and Merrymakers," conveys the essence of her findings: some girls were extremely pious, young religious mystics; some were good-time girls within the bounds of the Hasidic community, wearing high-top sneakers under their long skirts, having fun within the limits of what was acceptable; and others were mavericks, breaking taboos, exploring for themselves, wanderers who gathered at an apartment just outside the community, girls and boys mingling, reading Nietzsche, listening to music, eating Chinese food.

Pressed to explain her findings, Levine begins by discussing her use of the Listening Guide method. Following a counterpoint of inner voices, she had traced the relationship between the "I" and the orthodoxy. And then she realized that her method, by directing her attention to inner voices, converged with the girls' practice of cultivating an inner voice, the voice of their *neshama,* or soul. Raised in orthodoxy, the girls had been schooled to listen to a voice within them, conceived within this religious community as a divine spark, a piece of the divine soul. Like Quaker women, many of whom were among the leading Abolitionist Feminists, they listened for a wellspring of truth within themselves. It is simplistic, as

Levine points out, to characterize human beings as prisoners of either nurture or nature, socially engineered or genetically determined; "we are more than our genetic makeup, more than our life histories, more than our cultural baggage." The Tanya, the book that Lubavitch girls study, teaches them to cultivate their *neshama*. Thus girls have some leeway within the orthodoxy: some become pious, some become merry, and some become mavericks, questioning the framework. They are not yet living as women with men, nor do they face the dilemma that Tova Hartman-Halbertal explores in her study of mothering in orthodoxy: the dilemma of being mothers who are raising daughters in patriarchy.

In *The Scarlet Letter,* Hawthorne's romance, Hester Prynne's pregnancy reveals her "lawless passion," her secret love affair with the Reverend Arthur Dimmesdale. Throughout the novel, Hawthorne contrasts Hester with the "goodwives" of Puritanism. But the contrast turns radical: Hester is more a woman in the eyes of many people. "Such helpfulness was found in her—so much power to do, and power to sympathize—that many people refused to interpret the scarlet A by its original signification. They said that it meant Able, so strong was Hester Prynne, with a woman's strength."

Living outside the framework of Puritanism, Hester sees the frame. "Is the world then so narrow?" she asks the anguished Dimmesdale, a man whose "genuine impulse" was to adore the truth, yet who was living a lie. "Doth the universe lie within the compass of yonder town, which only a little time ago was but a leaf-strewn desert?" It was an age "in which the human intellect, newly emancipated, had taken a more active and a wider range than for many centuries before. Men of the sword had overthrown nobles and kings. Men bolder than these had overthrown and rearranged—not actually, but within the sphere of theory . . . the whole system of ancient prejudice, wherewith was linked much of ancient principle." As Hester roams the forest on the edge of the settlement, her mind runs free, and in the spirit of her age, she questions "the whole system of ancient prejudice": the principles governing relationships between men and women, dividing her from Dimmesdale and Dimmesdale from himself, and also restricting her ability to cultivate in their daughter "the germ and blossom of womanhood." Color defines the distance between Hester and the goodwives of Puritanism; she is radiant, her hair dark and abundant, the scarlet letter embroidered brilliantly in red and gold thread; they are gray and pale. Hester sees that "the whole race of womanhood" and "the very nature of the opposite sex, or its long hereditary habit, which has become like nature," are in reality part of a "system of society" that, built up in one way, could be "torn down and built up anew." Such speculations, the narrator tells us, would have been considered by our forefathers "a deadlier crime than that stigmatized by the scarlet letter." Freeing her sexuality, Hester placed herself outside the iron framework of Puritanism; from this vantage point, she sees "the foundations of the Puritan establishment" as a human construction, neither divinely ordained nor natural.

We begin to understand why sexual freedom or freedom to love becomes so out-of-proportion incendiary.

THE WORD "patriarchy" runs through "The Custom-House," the introductory sketch Hawthorne appends to his romance: "patriarchal body of veterans"; "the father of the Custom-House—the patriarch"; "this patriarchal personage . . . [who] was, in truth, a rare phenomenon; so perfect, in one point of view; so shallow, so delusive, so impalpable, such an absolute nonentity, in every other." The word returns when Dimmesdale ("the minister in a maze") considers telling the truth: "patriarchal privilege," "the sanctified old patriarchal deacon." It is clear what is at stake. And Hester protects Dimmesdale's position, not only at her own expense but at the expense of her relationship with her daughter, the luminous and unruly Pearl. Pearl's "remarkable precocity and acuteness" encourage Hester to see her as someone whom she could entrust "with as much of her mother's sorrows as could be imparted, without irreverence either to the parent or the child." And yet when Pearl's searching questions open the way to such a relationship, Hester holds back. She sees emerging in Pearl's strong emotions and character the "sterling attributes" of "a noble woman" ("the stedfast principles of an unflinching courage,—an uncontrollable will,—a sturdy pride, which might be disciplined into self-respect,—and a bitter scorn of many things which, when examined, might be found to have the taint of falsehood in them"). And yet paradoxically to keep Pearl with her, she must distance herself from Pearl and educate her daughter to live within the bounds of a puritanical order.

"Mother," Pearl asks, "what does the scarlet letter mean?" "Mother!—Mother!—Why does the minister keep his hand over his heart?"

"What shall I say?" Hester asks herself.

"Silly Pearl," she says, "what questions are these? There are many things in this world that a child must not ask about. What know I of the minister's heart? And as for the scarlet letter, I wear it for the sake of its gold thread!" She cannot tell Pearl what Pearl in some sense knows, cannot allow her to know it: "Hold thy tongue, naughty child! . . . Do not tease me; else I shall shut thee into the dark closet."

Hawthorne—a boy raised by his mother, who was scorned by the more aristocratic family of his father (a sea captain who died when Nathaniel was four); a man who married Sophia Peabody, whose sister Elizabeth was one of the Abolitionist Feminists; a New Englander who lived for a time at Brook Farm and entertained the vision of a utopian community—wrote *The Scarlet Letter* in a rush of intensity and passion in the year following his mother's death. "I think I have never overcome my own adamant in any other instance," he subsequently reflected in his journal. The narrator describes the story as "a tale of human frailty and sorrow," a tragic story of romance and passion. But the story Hawthorne tells is far more radical.

Hester is introduced at the beginning of the novel as a sensual and spirited young woman, tall, "with a figure of perfect elegance, on a large scale"; the scarlet letter that she had embroidered "so fantastically" illuminated her, "taking her out of the ordinary relations with humanity, and inclosing her in a sphere by herself." By the end of the novel, she is the woman to whom other women come for comfort or counsel in love, "demanding why they were so wretched, and what the remedy!" She assures them "of her firm belief, that, at some brighter period, when the world should have grown ripe for it, in Heaven's own time, a new truth would be revealed, in order to establish the whole relation between man and woman on a surer ground of mutual happiness." For a time, she imagined that she herself might be the "prophetess" of this revelation, bringing a truth that would establish a new order of living, but she "had long since recognized the impossibility."

Hawthorne's insight into Hester's predicament is brilliant. With the economy of the single letter "A," he captures how the very qualities that enable a woman to free herself from the iron framework of patriarchy also disable her by causing her to be labeled an impure woman, a woman who has been adulterated. "A" means adultery, "A" means able, "A" means angel, "A" means abominable; the novel floats all these possibilities, and then draws its somber conclusion: "The angel and apostle of the coming revelation must be a woman, indeed, but lofty, pure, and beautiful; and wise, moreover, not through dusky grief, but the ethereal medium of joy." The very possibility turns out to be impossible, at least within the world of the novel. Aristocracy had yielded to democracy in the new world founded by the Puritans, but the chain of patriarchy could not be broken. The feminist project imagined in this 1850 romance and fueled by Hawthorne's love for his mother gives way in the end to the tragic love story.

WHEN PSYCHE breaks the taboo on seeing Cupid and speaking about love, when she falls in love with love and Cupid leaves her, she first tries to kill herself, but then she takes an unfamiliar road. It leads her through a wasteland of relationships among women, a landscape devastated by envy and fear. She will see her sisters, confront each of them with the story of what happened, lie to each sister, saying that Cupid now wants to marry her, and discover that, however helpful they have been to her in breaking through the lethargy of her depression and urging her not to sacrifice herself or her child, they will jump at the chance to marry Cupid, to take her place in his palace. Discouraged, Psyche continues to search for love. She finds that the goddesses who warn her that Venus is after her also turn their backs on her when she asks them to help her, saying that Venus is "a good woman" and calling Psyche a runaway slave. Finally, Psyche realizes that she must confront Venus directly. Summoning her courage, she wends her way to the goddess's door. There she is punished and tortured by Venus' servants, Habit, Trouble, and Sadness, until, weeping and beaten and unable to speak, Psyche finds herself face-to-face with Venus.

As the mother of sons, I am intrigued that the goddess and the god of love are mother and son. Within a patriarchal society and culture, mother and son are a potentially revolutionary couple. If a mother resists sacrificing her relationship with her son for the sake of his initiation into patriarchy, the patriarchal plot cannot go forward. If a son stays emotionally connected with his mother and picks up her love and her anger, he will learn to decode the world in the way that she does.

This became abundantly clear in my research with young boys and also with couples in crisis.

In the myth of Psyche and Cupid, Venus and Cupid, at least at the beginning, border on caricatures of a patriarchal mother and son. Venus, the goddess of love, is a captive of her own image, playing a role, a part in a story, in relationship with nobody. Cupid fits the bad-boy image, flying around, shooting his arrows. But even more pointedly, Venus relies on her son's power to accomplish her purposes of punishing Psyche; kissing her son intensely with open mouth, she tries to seduce him into doing her bidding, but he resists her effort to own him. Instead, he falls in love with Psyche and then panics when she sees him.

WE ARE entering the heart of the trauma: the break in relationship that is commonly blacked out. Venus, once she becomes "old Venus," begins to crumble away internally, because she discovers with the coming of "New Venus" that it was not she whom people had worshiped and loved. She was filling a role, playing a part in a story that was not her story. When the goddess of love discovers that she was not loved, or at least not loved for herself, she turns initially on the woman who replaces her, who takes her part, rather than on the people who named Psyche New Venus. The anger and the envy among women are inescapable in a world where one woman is seen as replacing another. If one woman can replace another, then neither woman is loved. It was not Venus or New Venus whom the people adored, but an image of Venus that they had created. Our investment in the fight among women keeps us from finding a way out of this tragic love story. Venus, having tried to seduce her son into punishing Psyche, having tried to beat Psyche into submission, will in the end become the goddess of love, not the image but the woman, as she strengthens Psyche, the younger woman, by teaching her a complicated lesson in love: how to get out of a seemingly impossible situation.

It is Tuesday, it is raining, and I am going to the Fine Arts Museum with eight eleven-year-old girls, members of the sixth grade at an elementary school in Watertown, Massachusetts. We meet at the school, climb into a van, and begin to make our way through the rain-dark streets into the city. It is June. School is over for the year. The sixth grade has graduated, and the girls in the class have returned for a week of writing and theater games designed to strengthen their voices and their courage. They gather in the coatroom of the museum, shedding backpacks and raincoats, retrieving notebooks; they are ready. "Today," I explain, "we are going to be investigative reporters. Our assignment is to find out how women and girls appear in this museum."

"Naked," Emma says without hesitation. A current of recognition runs silently, swiftly through the group. Like Dora, one of Freud's early patients, who remembers standing in the Dresden Art Gallery for two hours in front of the Sistine Madonna, Emma will be transfixed by these images of women, by their nakedness in this cool marble building. Later, when asked to write a conversation with one of the women, she chooses a headless, armless Greek statue, weaving into the conventions of polite conversation her two burning questions: "Are you cold?" and "Do you want some clothes?"

Emma's questions are a lover's questions: How are you feeling—are you cold? What do you want—do you want some clothes? She wants to know if the woman wants to be in the museum. The statue's response—"I have no money"—to the question about whether she wants some clothes turns the conversation from the issue of what she wants to the matter of whether she can have what she wants. Emma wants her to have it. She tells the statue that she knows a place where they give away clothes; "it is right around the corner." The conversation ends with Emma and the statue leaving the museum.

"One conclusion," Emma writes, starting a new page in her journal, "one of the conclusions I have come to is that many/most of the paintings/statues/artwork of women I have seen are of women naked. A lot of the art of women that I saw was done by men. Maybe because the women posed. None of the girls I saw were naked. Maybe because artists like to have people pose naked, and they think women are better because they have more growth."

Soon Emma's body will be a woman's body. Will she want to pose for artists? Or be an artist herself? A poster made by the Guerrilla Girls, women in the art world, echoes her query. This masked group of resisters sees the same world that Emma sees. Above a reproduction of an oil painting of a nude on whom they have placed their trademark gorilla mask, they float the question: "Do women have to be naked to get into the Met. Museum?" Below the nude, the poster conveys the information, "Less than 5% of the artists in the Modern Art sections are women, but 85% of the nudes are female." Emma's playfully innocent, slightly irreverent conversation with the statue in the museum will soon be complicated by a further question: does Emma want to get in? And will she then, like the Guerrilla Girls, have to mask herself in order to say what she sees?

Mame's eye for the disparity between outside and inside, between calm surface and explosive laughter, is evident as she describes the painting of *Reverend John Atwood and His Family*. His two oldest daughters, she writes, sustaining the possessive, "have no expression. They are just staring straight ahead, but one of them looks like she is going to burst out laughing." His wife, she concludes on a more somber note, "looks very worn and tired."

Standing on the edge of womanhood in a time and place of historical transformation, these girls see the lineaments of patriarchy and, at the same time, dwell in possibility. Emma imagines the statue leaving the museum; Mame envisions the daughter bursting out laughing in the grim portrait of Reverend John Atwood's family. And Malka, a gifted writer from a bicultural family, writes not one but two conversations between herself and the queen of Babylon.

The first is the official version. Speaking in the voice of a reporter, Malka addresses the queen in a manner befitting her station: "Hello Madam," she says to the woman in the painting, who is brushing her hair while receiving news of a revolt. "What is it like ruling so great a land?" "Glorious," the queen replies; "it is great fun, although," she adds with a yawn, "it does tax time and strength sometimes." In the second conversation, Malka speaks in her own voice to this bored, haughty queen, asking her simply: "Whatchya doing?" The queen, in a sudden reversal of priorities, replies: "Brushing my hair. I was interrupted this morning by a revolt." With this change in the voice of her question, Malka uncovers a funny, irreverent queen.

Like Emma, she is curious about the origins of these images that she is seeing. "Did these people, places, painted, sculpted, did they live? Did they live in the heart of the painter, sculptor?" Looking at the images and the statues of women, the girls are seeing into the hearts of men.

The depth of this perception is evident in Malka's description of her stories. In an interview earlier that spring, she tells me that she is writing a story about "someone during the Civil War" and making her story "a little bit sad" because when the father goes to war, the girl is "really upset." We have settled in a small room in her school; having observed her class during the year, I know Malka as an intelligent, tempestuous girl given to sudden outbursts of emotion. Sitting with me on a blue sofa, one leg folded under her, her dark bangs reaching to the top of her glasses, her olive face intent, she launches into a description of the girl, her father, and the relationship between them:

> He talks to her before he goes, about how he feels about leaving and that he is just as worried as she is, or more worried and more scared. . . . And, you know, she feels like he's never going to come back, which is possible, but, you know, it's not a fact yet. So she has a very, um, a very strange feeling sometimes.

I ask Malka about this strange feeling, and she explains:

> Before he left, she realized that he was not, um, totally powerful, but she didn't, um, feel angry at him for that, but she felt very, um, very sorry, sort of very sorry for him, and very shocked or surprised, mainly, and still upset that he was leaving. And, um, he was trying to comfort her when he told her about, um, about his own fears of going, but really she was just mainly surprised, and she hadn't realized that he could feel like this too.

When I ask why the girl in the story didn't know that her father "could feel like this too," she continues her carefully layered and nuanced description of the girl, her father, and the flow of feelings and thoughts between them, the "ums" and the "you knows" conveying her hesitation, and also the implicit question, do you know? Can she know what she knows about power, anger, sorrow, hurt, and fear, fathers and daughters and war?

> He had always been there for her, you know. She had been, um, she'd been hurt . . . and she had been humiliated because she was a girl. And he always understood her, and she was very close to him. Her siblings thought

it was really brave of him to [enlist] right away, but she knew that he was, he just, if he waited any longer he wouldn't be able to do it, he wouldn't have enough courage to do it.

(How did she know that?)

She knew because of the way he talked to her, that he was feeling really scared and upset, and he didn't want her to make it any harder or anything. After that, she didn't get so upset, or, she didn't show it.

By listening to "the way he talked to her," the girl picks up her father's fear and his upset feelings, and also his need to cover these feelings in order to enlist in the army. Knowing her father's vulnerability and also his wish that she not make it any harder for him, the girl also covers her feelings, and begins not to feel so upset or at least not to show how upset she is feeling.

The following year, when Malka is twelve and we resume our conversation, she tells me again about the stories she is writing—stories that are now winning prizes in local contests. But now the inner world of the Civil War story is only obliquely suggested, and she has become more reticent in speaking about her writing. Her prizewinning story captures this hesitation in an image: the story, she says, is about how "things would feel" if "they were able to see, like a pen with its cap off."

Malka is feeling the stirrings of new desires: to fall in love, to go on romantic adventures, to win prizes in writing contests and eventually, she hopes, a scholarship to college. In one of her stories, a girl "is trying to, well, she falls in love with this boy . . . and they have these adventures. It starts when they're at a dance, and then when she has to leave, his car gets stolen, and then they go to the gang. . . . This group has stolen it . . . and he has to fight one of the guys, and then they set off in the car, and there's a storm and the car stalls. It's a really good story," Malka says, "I can tell. It's a lot better than the ones I wrote a couple of years ago anyway." In another story, a queen who is "really a bad queen" is assassinated on the anniversary of her coronation. Three generations later, she is remembered as "a beautiful, wonderful queen." Sensing with me that something is missing, some understanding or even interest in the process of this transformation, Malka observes by way of explanation: "It's just the way memory covers up the bad things."

As the girl in the adventure story finds herself drawn into the world of the guys and the gang, the world of the good and bad guys, as this world is now linked with intimations of sexuality—the storm, the intimacy of the stalled car—so the stark description of the bad and good queen carries the threat that gives force to the process of initiation: as the bad queen in the story is assassinated on the anniversary of her coronation, so the bad girl is in danger of being cast out or abandoned. Malka at twelve is riveted by the split between good and bad women. By attributing the cover-up to an "it," to memory, she signals the onset of dissociation. What she is covering for the moment is her knowing of the human world—the knowing that sets the girl in the Civil War story apart from her siblings and also leads her to know what her father wants and doesn't want her to feel or to know or to show. Like Anne Frank, Malka sees this eclipse of a vibrant inner world as the good covering over the bad.

Since a girl's initiation into the world of good and bad women tends to take place at the time of adolescence, when her body becomes a woman's body and thus an object of men's desire and attention, and since a boy's initiation into the straits of manhood commonly takes place much earlier in childhood, girls who love boys find themselves entering a world to which boys have already adapted: an inner world rent by division and buttressed by the codes of honor and chastity. When the emotions and passions of adolescence bring a girl and a boy together in a new intensity of love and sensual excitement, a possibility opens between them at the same time that they are newly aware of the constraints placed on them by the ideals of manliness and womanhood that they strive to live up to. The opening into a confiding relationship is blocked by fears that if they reveal parts of themselves that are deemed unmanly or unwomanly, they will sacrifice the love and intimacy they desire so intensely. Thus a tragic story is enacted over and over again across the millennia as the heroism, the sheer courage, of love gives way to concerns about loss and fears of rejection and abandonment. The eye of the writer—Anne Frank and also Malka—spots this dilemma with astonishing clarity; it is the dilemma faced in one way or another by boys and by girls in the course of their initiation. To avert the tragic story of love, it is necessary—as Hester Prynne discerns—to take on the construction of manliness and womanhood, the underpinnings of a patriarchal society. Given the difference in the timing of their initiation, the vast emotional and intellectual chasm that separates four- or five-year-olds from adolescents, it is the adolescent girl who is likely to see this most clearly and to speak about what she is seeing. And yet the boy-become-man also knows the story.

In an extraordinary play, written in fifth-century B.C.E. Athens shortly after the *Oresteia,* Euripides fills in the voice missing from Aeschylus' trilogy: the voice of Iphigenia, the daughter whom Agamemnon sacrifices in order to gain the winds that will carry the Greek army to Troy. While the *Oresteia*—the story of Orestes—begins ten years after this sacrifice, when Agamemnon, returning victorious from Troy, is slain by his wife, Klytemnestra, Euripides sets his play at Aulis, the place where the sacrifice happens. As he insists that we listen to the voice of Iphigenia and the change in her voice that occurs when she aligns herself with her father, so also we see into the heart of Agamemnon, her father and the king. As the play opens, an absence of sound becomes startling. Agamemnon notices it: "there's no sound of either birds or sea. Silence, without wind, encloses this place." It is as if the natural world has receded to make space for an action that is profoundly unnatural: a father sacrificing his daughter. But the moment also presages what will be heard and not heard, heeded and silenced, as the tragedy unfolds. "I envy you, old man," Agamemnon says to the slave who accompanies him. "I envy any man who leads an unendangered life—unknown, unfamous. Those who live among honors I envy much less." The slave replies, "You give every sign of going mad. What are you struggling with? What's going on with you, my king? Bring out the story and share it with me. You'll be telling a good trustworthy man."

For a moment Agamemnon is clear. He tells the story, and as he tells it we begin to understand the psychology of the culture that is driving him, a psychology of shame and honor that is driving him mad, driving the relationships between women and men. So that in the end he cannot listen to his wife or his daughter without fearing that he will lose his manhood. The story starts with a rape. It is followed by marriage, adultery, a betrayal, and a loss that eventuates in the Trojan War. Leda, the woman raped by Zeus in the form of a swan, gave birth to three daughters, Phoebe, Klytemnestra, and Helen. It is Helen whom one of the richest young men in Greece came to seek in marriage.

It is a story about terrible threats, envy among men, competition for Helen, and finally the binding of the men together with an oath to punish whoever inflicted shame upon another by taking his woman, his wife. Helen, given her choice of suitors, chooses Menelaus, Agamemnon's brother. And then, "from the East, *he* came"—Paris, described in imagery that links racism with the assault on Menelaus' masculinity. Paris, "blooming in his fancy getup / sparking with gold—Oriental pansy," lusted after Helen and she after him. Quickly this imagery of mutual desire yields to the intimation of rape, as if it were inconceivable that Helen of her own free will would leave. Menelaus' shame becomes an assault on Greek honor, which Agamemnon, the king and Menelaus' brother, feels compelled to defend. "I had no intention of murdering my own daughter," he explains. It was Menelaus who "convinced me to do / this terrible thing." Agamemnon writes to his wife, Klytemnestra, telling her to bring Iphigenia to Aulis, lying to her, telling her that he has arranged a marriage. He changes his mind, takes back his word, writes again, but the letter is intercepted by Menelaus. A searingly honest conversation follows between Agamemnon and Menelaus as the brothers explore the psychology of leadership, its motivation, the linking of men's honor to their ability to control themselves and also their women, and the sickness of the situation. In the end Menelaus, out of love for his brother, tells him to send Iphigenia away from Aulis, so that the conflict then resides solely within Agamemnon, who feels trapped in a situation not of his making—like the father in Malka's story about the Civil War. Iphigenia, like the girl in the story, will sacrifice herself to protect her father, and it is Euripides' dramatization of the process of this dissociation—in Agamemnon and also in Iphigenia—that makes the play so psychologically astonishing.

Iphigenia arrives with her mother and the infant Orestes. Menelaus urges: "Send them away from Aulis! . . . I've changed / out of love for my brother." Agamemnon's ambivalence now becomes plain; the conflict he faces is an internal conflict: a conflict between love and honor, between being a father and being a king. Klytemnestra begs him to change his mind, asks him to envision what it will be like for her—the feelings she will have living in that house, Agamemnon gone to war, she seeing the chairs Iphigenia would sit in empty, "her bedroom empty, and I sit alone, in tears, always singing this lament. . . . Don't in the god's name! Don't make me become / wicked toward you! And don't you become wicked yourself." The chorus, women from the neighboring town of Chalkis, back up her words: "Be persuaded; it's a good thing to join together in saving a child, Agamemnon. No human being will contradict these words."

While the *Oresteia* begins with Klytemnestra murdering Agamemnon as he returns victorious from Troy and eclipses Iphigenia's voice completely—the chilling account of her sacrifice portrays her gagged—in *Iphigenia in Aulis,* Euripides insists on our hearing her voice. As she speaks to her father and then to her mother, first about love and then about honor, we also hear a change in her voice, a change that Aristotle, writing about tragedy, finds implausible and cites as an example of poor character development—a break in character for which he can find no motivation.

When Iphigenia discovers the ruse, that she has been brought not for marriage but to be a sacrifice, her first response is to speak to her father, telling him that he is mad. She is at a loss as to how to speak to him, how to move him with her words. She wishes she had the voice of Orpheus, which could move the stones to speak. She wants to break through to him, touch his emotions, his humanness, his memory. She re-creates in words their relationship, repeating to him words he has said to her, what she has said to him, giving voice to their love and relying on her tears to move him. Wrapping her body around his knees, she says, "It's sweet to look upon the light. Don't force me to look at the things beneath the earth." She reminds him that she was his first child:

I first called you "Father," you first called me "child,"
I was the first who sat upon your knees,
gave you sweet kisses, and got them in return.
This was what you said then: "Will I see you, daughter,

in the house of your fortunate husband,
living and thriving in a way that's worthy of me?"
This was my answer as I touched your beard
which I'm grasping now with my hand:
"What about me seeing you? Will I welcome you as an old man
with the sweet hospitality of my house, Daddy,
paying back the work of nurturing you gave while raising me?"
I still hold the memory of those conversations,
but you've forgotten them, and you want to kill me.
No! I beg you. . . .
What do I have to do with the marriage of Helen and Paris?
How does that result in my destruction, Daddy?
Look at me, give me a glance and a kiss . . .
this light is the sweetest thing for humans to see,
the things down below are nothing. Someone who prays to die
is mad. Living badly is better than dying well.

In this speech she joins her appeal to her relationship with her father with a challenge to the order of Greek culture that values men over women, Greeks over barbarians, death with honor over living with shame. Agamemnon faces a terrible dilemma: torn between his love for his child and his position, his duty as king and chief of the army, he resolves the conflict in favor of duty: "I love my children," he tells Klytemnestra. "Otherwise I'd be mad. / Taking this awful step fills me with horror, wife, but not to take it is horrifying too. *I have to do it.*" Turning to his daugher now, he concludes: "It's Greece for which I must sacrifice you, / whether I want to or not."

Iphigenia is overcome with shame. She has exposed her love, her pleasure; she has appealed to her relationship with her father, and he is seemingly unmoved. Urged by her mother to appeal to Achilles, the man she thought she was to marry and who now offers to help her, she withdraws, saying, "Women, open up the house for me, so I can hide myself . . . I'm ashamed to see Achilles. . . . This marriage that turned out wrong brings shame upon me." Klytemnestra turns to Achilles. "I'll hold him back," he tells her, urging her to "hold on to your daughter," to resist "a wicked choice to commit murder." But Iphigenia interrupts their conversation, urging her mother instead to listen to her:

Listen to my words, Mother!
I see you raging against your husband, but it's useless.
It's not easy for us to bear what can't be borne.
It's right to thank this stranger for his good intentions,
But even you must see this: he must not be attacked by the
        army.
We would gain nothing, while he'd meet with disaster.
Listen, Mother, what sorts of things have come to me as I've
        been thinking.
Death has been decreed—for me and by me.
I want to carry out this same act
in a glorious way, casting all lowborn behavior aside.
Look at it this way with me, Mother, see how well I reason:
All of Greece, great Greece, is looking at me now!
In me lies the setting forth of the ships, the ruin of the
        Trojans,
and women, in the future, even if barbarians try something,
never again to allow them to rob those happy women
        from Greece,
once they have paid for the theft of Helen, whom Paris stole.
I will fend off all these things by dying, and my glorious fame,
as the woman who made Greece free, will become blest.
Also, I should not love my life too much. . . .
This man must not go into battle with all the Greeks for
        a woman's sake or die.
It's more important for one single man
to look upon the light than a thousand women.
If Artemis wishes to take my body,
will I, a mortal, stand in the way of a goddess?

No! Impossible! I give my body to Greece.
Make the sacrifice. Eradicate Troy! For a long time to come
that will be my monument, my children, my marriage, my
*   fame!*
It's proper for Greeks to rule barbarians, Mother, not
*   barbarians Greeks,*
because they are slaves, but Greeks are free!

Feeling her powerlessness to affect her fate, Iphigenia begins a process of dissociation. She seeks an outlet for her anger, by placing the blame on Helen, the "bad woman," making her responsible for corrupting the social order. Iphigenia avoids knowing what she knows: as an outsider to that order herself, she is faced with hopelessness and isolation. In a desperate act of self-preservation, she throws herself upon the patriarchy and all that it asks of her. Thus she breaks her relationship with her mother, just as Orestes will also have to break his relationship with his mother as an initiation into patriarchy; this break will also be enacted by death, another family murder as he will kill his mother.

We have witnessed Iphigenia's heroic attempt to resist the exigencies of patriarchal society. When this resistance fails, she consoles herself as women for centuries will console themselves: with the "secondary gain" that in sacrificing herself she is allowed to participate in the society that makes the rules. Thus in her final role as willing sacrifice on behalf of Greece, Iphigenia is no longer in conversation with her father but has taken on his voice as her own.

The women of the chorus offer this commentary: "Your intention, young girl, is noble. / But what is happening here, and the goddess, are sick."

The change in voice is astounding, as Aristotle notices, but it is not unmotivated. Iphigenia has taken on her father's voice—seeking fame, aligning herself as he does with Greece, and beseeching her mother to "bring up Orestes here for me, to be a man." The chorus in the end will celebrate her glory as Iphigenia, bidding the day farewell, renounces life and the "sweet light of the sun." At the end of the play, a messenger arrives, describing how, at the moment when the knife struck, Iphigenia vanished and a deer lay on the altar. It is an Abraham-and-Isaac story. Agamemnon's willingness to sacrifice his child, his love, has been tested. That is all that is required. The Greek leaders and the messenger himself interpret this as a sign of divine favor toward Iphigenia, Agamemnon, and the Greek war effort, and the chorus rejoices at the news. Only Klytemnestra remains doubtful, suspecting that the whole story is a lie.

The word "myth" means story; it comes from the Greek *muthos*. Read positively, the ending of the play "seems to resolve all tensions . . . in favor of traditional values." Iphigenia becomes a savior: her sacrifice of herself restores the social order and reestablishes "proper contact with the gods through 'a politics of love.'" In this reading, Klytemnestra appears to be a woman for whom only domestic affairs matter, whose vision remains narrow, "who cannot see the issues from a civic or cosmic point of view. Her lack of understanding will result in unnecessary death for Agamemnon and herself, and unnecessary suffering for Orestes." But alternatively, as the classics scholar and translator Mary-Kay Gamel continues, "the conclusion of the play can be read negatively, with Iphigenia persuaded into willingly serving the traditional (though 'outworn') ideals of a masculine order that keep her and other women subordinated and manipulated in male struggles for power. Still another alternative is to see the ending not as resolving but maintaining these tensions, provoking the audience to thought and discussion."

It is a discussion that continues to this day. But more astonishing, given the sweeping changes of time and culture, place and history, is the similarity between the change in Iphigenia's voice as rendered by Euripides and the change we hear in the voices of contemporary girls. The ascendance of the split between good and bad women marks the moment of change and also fills in its motivation. With this split, pleasure—once associated with vitality, with love, with light, and with life—becomes the marker of the bad woman. The sexual woman, the curious woman, the funny, irreverent woman. The lusting Helen, the unfaithful wife, the woman who breaks with the values of patriarchy. "What I wanted from you, Mother, was this," Luce Irigaray, the French feminist, writes toward the end of the twentieth century, "That in giving me life, / You too remained alive."

OUR TENDENCY when we lose something is to hold on to an image of that thing, which often becomes the only thing, what we most wanted or value; or else to disparage what we have lost, seeing it as nothing, nothing of value. The pervasive images of women, idealized and degraded, reflect a pervasive loss of connection with women. Loving an image of woman rather than an actual person becomes a way of fending off the possibility of losing again, because an image can be held apart from relationship, and one woman can take another's place. "The voice of the Mother is the largest absence in literature," the writer Tillie Olsen observed in 1976; it is the voice that haunts the tragic love story.

THE OLD WIFE'S TALE about Psyche and Cupid looks unflinchingly at the difference between loving a woman and loving an image. But it also insists that we look head-on at the relationship between women within a culture where one woman can become a replica of another. Psyche and Venus, Cupid's lover and his mother, seemingly hopelessly enmeshed with each other in a bitter, angry quarrel, in fact stand in a position to take on and transform the situation. The envy and rivalry between them is essential, because their collaboration poses a threat to the patriarchy, given their intimate relationship with Cupid, the god of love. When Psyche is placed on the pedestal and crowned the New Venus, Venus turns to her son to avenge her. Having no effective way herself of exercising power in this situation, she tries to seduce Cupid into punishing Psyche for her. But the revenge is fundamentally displaced, because it is not Psyche who wanted to be New Venus—for Psyche, it was "as if I were already dead." The conflict is not really between the women but between the women and a practice of elevating one woman to a pedestal and worshiping her image—placing her in effect out of reach, out of relationship—and loving not her but the image of her, so that when she no longer fits the image, another woman can take her place.

As the myth highlights the triangle of the son, his mother, and his lover and zeros in on the encounter between Psyche and Venus that occupies most of the second part of the story, we see the roots of this myth in North African women's culture. Couched in the folk tradition, the women take on the seemingly impossible task of transforming a love story that is headed for tragedy and that plays up the rivalry between them into a story that ends with the birth of pleasure, with Venus dancing at Psyche and Cupid's wedding.

The transformation takes place through a series of seemingly impossible tasks that Venus sets for Psyche. Examined carefully, they are lessons in love, steps leading to psychological and cultural transformation. The old woman's dream interpretation is a deeply encrypted insight into the nature of love in patriarchy. She tells Charite—the perfect girl, heading into the seemingly perfect marriage—that when it comes to love, to dream of feasting and sexual pleasure is to court mental depression, physical weakness, and every other sort of loss. The road to pleasure leads through weeping, being beaten, and occasionally finding oneself unable to speak, because it requires finding one's way out of patriarchy.

In this reading, Psyche is neither hero nor victim, neither the good nor the bad woman. She lies to her sisters, she betrays them as they betray her, she tries to get other women to approach Venus rather than facing her herself; she becomes depressed when she is turned into an object, an image, and when she is forbidden to see and to speak; in the face of loss, she tries to kill herself and is stopped only by the intervention of nature, and the natural world steps in repeatedly to block the enactment of a tragic love story. The split between good and bad woman, the new and the old, the replacer and the replaced, is undone. As Psyche does both good and bad things, so Venus—angry, envious, vengeful, languorous, violent, and seemingly crazy—also is the one who in the end points the way out of an impossible situation.

The first task is sorting seeds. Seeds: small containers of great possibility, new life, different forms of life. It is hard to get more basic than this. Venus takes some wheat and barley and millet and poppy seed and chickpeas and lentils and beans—symbols of the great diversity of life—and jumbles them into a mound. Then, taking off for a party, she leaves Psyche with the task of sorting the seeds before she gets home. "To test your worth," she tells her.

There is no way that Psyche can do this. So the lesson must be of a different sort. What she learns is that the natural world will come to her aid, because she has aligned herself with love. Choosing love, choosing life, she is helped by country ants, simple creatures, who come up, wave after wave, and sort the seeds and disappear.

The second task is to bring Venus a hank of golden fleece from a flock of wild sheep. Golden fleece: the symbol of riches, money, patriarchal power. To obtain the fleece, Psyche must learn how to move safely in the face of danger. She is helped by a small green reed in the water of the river in which she intended to drown herself. "Poor Psyche," the reed says. "You are assailed by so many sorrows. Do not pollute my sacred waters with your pitiful suicide. And do not approach these fearsome wild sheep at this time of day." Wait, the reed tells her, until the afternoon breeze allays the heat and the flock settles down. Then, "if you shake the foliage in the adjacent woods, you will find some of the woolly gold clinging here and there to the bent branches."

The reed—something that bends, that is not rigid, that lives in water—shows her how she can get economic power from a flock of wild sheep. The lesson is simple but vital: do not go directly into the face of danger; pay attention to time, to the rhythms of the day and the cadences of emotional life.

The third task is going to the source. Venus tells Psyche to bring her water from the spring that feeds the river Styx—the river that carries the dead into the underworld. The spring is on a high mountain peak. Taking the pitcher that Venus gave her but intending to jump off the mountain, Psyche finds herself in a nightmare landscape of towering rocks, hideous streams, fierce snakes with long necks and unblinking eyes. The water screams at her: "Go away. What are you doing? Look out. What are you up to? Be careful. Run. You will die." Psyche stops in her tracks, frozen in terror. And then an eagle appears, Jupiter's bird; taking the pitcher from her hands, the eagle flies up and fills it with water from the spring.

Although the word "patriarchy" is descriptive of societies and cultures where fathers stand at the top of the hierarchy, serving as priests—the interpreters of truth, the dispensers of goodness, those with direct access to power, mediating relationships with power for those below—patriarchies are varied, and fathers are fathers and men and human as well. Here Jupiter acts through his bird to align himself with Psyche in her search for love.

The final task is to repair relationship. Psyche is to go into the underworld and bring Venus a day's worth of beauty in a jar from Persephone. But the task contains a deeper lesson: in repairing the break in her relationship with Venus that was caused by her beauty, Psyche also learns a vital lesson about relationship, a lesson that speaks directly to a change in the form of womanhood, because Psyche must resist sacrificing herself to help others, she must resist giving up her life in order to come to the aid of the dead. A tower, a symbol of culture and far-seeing, tells her what she needs to know.

In order to enter and leave the underworld safely, she must carry in each hand a barley cake soaked in mead for the three-headed dog that guards Persephone's chamber—one for the way in and the other for the way out. In her mouth she is to hold two coins to pay the boatman on the river Styx. Thus she must refuse the lame driver who asks her to lend him a hand and pick up some sticks that have fallen from his cart; she must not utter a single word but pass him in silence. She must refuse the entreaties of the dead old man floating in the Styx who begs her to pull him into the boat. And she must ignore the old women weaving at a loom who ask for her help in holding their wool. In Persephone's chamber, she must refuse the invitation to sit comfortably beside Persephone and eat a sumptuous meal; instead she must sit on the floor and eat common bread. Finally, she must not look in the jar. All of these are traps that Venus has set—traps that are the old forms of womanhood. Instead of sacrificing herself for relationship, she is to repair relationship and protect herself, to stay alive by doing what she needs to do in order to leave the world of the dead.

Psyche enters the underworld, obtains the jar, returns to the light, and then, despairing of finding Cupid, thinking perhaps that beauty will attract him, she opens the jar with the intention of taking some of the beauty for herself. But the jar contains nothing but a deadly sleep.

Cupid at this point reenters the story. Having recovered from his wound, he discovers that the separation he intended as punishment for Psyche is punishing for him as well. Immured in his mother's chamber, he cannot endure the long absence of Psyche. And so, in the most frequently misinterpreted part of the story, rather than going to rescue Psyche, Cupid goes to find her because he wants to be with her. When he sees her lying on the ground, overcome with the deadly sleep, he thinks, of course she would open the jar, Psyche with her curiosity. And wiping the deadly sleep from her face and putting it back in the jar, he is overcome with love for Psyche. The ambiguity surrounding Cupid's love—did he fall in love with Psyche, with New Venus, with the replica of his mother?—resolves. Coming to her in the full light of day and seeing her clearly as herself, Cupid loves her more and more. The love that began in darkness has now come fully into the light.

At the end of the myth, Jupiter, Cupid's father and the chief of the Olympian gods, enters the story to change the law. Approached by his son, the god of love, for help in arranging a marriage with Psyche, Jupiter acts to remove the ligaments of patriarchy, making their relationship "no longer uneven" and freeing their love from the threat that Cupid will leave Psyche if she does not obey him. "Drink this," he tells Psyche, having summoned her to heaven, and in the manner of Alice in Wonderland or, more accurately, Alice through the looking-glass, Psyche steps into a world where patriarchy is being dismantled. The celebration of a just and lawful and democratic marriage and a love not hedged by threats of leaving sets the stage for the birth of Pleasure.

III

The Birth of Pleasure

*In Arlit where I am sitting in my hotel room
writing this, I suddenly catch sight of a man
carrying an empty picture frame. . . . It frames
his whole person as he carries it, only his head
and feet outside it. It is strange to see the way
the frame separates him, brings him out, yes
even elevates him. When he stops for a moment
to move it from one shoulder to another, he seems
to step out of the frame. It looks as if that were
the simplest thing in the world.*

—SVEN LINDQVIST

*T*HE ROOM was white. White cushions on the sofa where
Psyche reclined, the pains coming now at shorter inter-
vals, Eros timing them. "Here," he says, cupping her shoulder, his wing brushing against the wall, gently bringing her
forward so he can replace the pillow that has slipped down,
plumping it up so that it cushions the small of her back. "Are
you curious?" he asks her and then smiles: of course. He too.
The physical labor a relief after the long psychic labor that has
brought them to this place where she can see and say what she
knows and he is no longer hiding his love. And now the final

mystery unraveling: the face and shape of the child. Her gaze is wild, distracted, turned inward, drawn outward fleetingly when he asks her, how are you feeling, do you want some water, water flooding and the child coming, the resistance of her body giving way now as with a final push she brings the child she has harbored within herself into the world. New life. Head coming first, torso following, shoulders turned, no wings attached, but beauty, yes, and dark like her mother and she like her mother, a girl, a daughter, and seeing her, delighting in her, they call her by the name Pleasure. The birth of pleasure seemed the most natural thing in the world.

I READ THE myth of Psyche and Cupid as I was listening to contemporary couples in crisis and tracing a road of development that had been surprisingly opaque. Like pleasure, girls and women are a perennial feature of the human landscape. An old wives' tale, rooted in North African women's culture, found its way into the heart of Western civilization; picked up by Shakespeare, repeated over the centuries, it begins at the time of a girl's adolescence. This is the edge I came to in my studies of development, the place where a mystery began to unravel. The familiar strains of the tragic love story haunted this journey like a siren's song. At the same time, Malka's question to the queen of Babylon, the age-old question "Whatchya doing?" became increasingly insistent as the research cast its illumination on losses that seemed necessary or inescapable and highlighted the possibility of resistance. "Isn't the honesty of things where they resist," Jorie Graham asks in her poem "The Age of Reason," "where only the wind can bend them back, the real weather. . . ." I had come upon evidence of pleasure that seemed ordinary, like wind and water, and I had witnessed the psyche's resistance to its loss.

It was this possibility that led me back to Psyche and Eros

(Cupid the boy becoming a man), to thinking about the soul and a love that springs from pleasure. Placing an ancient story about love alongside a contemporary psychological map, I saw an opening that like the tides has risen and receded over the course of history. I was writing on the swell of the liberation movements of the twentieth century, and I was reminded of a truism of psychotherapy: the volatility of the moment in the process of transformation when a person envisions the new, the moment of stepping out of an old frame. Suddenly there is no frame, no way to hold past and present together; it is the place where we find ourselves without a map, the most difficult place to be alone. My impetus to writing came from the realization that we have a map in the form of an old story and that this map converges with and is enlarged by what we have come to know about love.

Pleasure is a sensation. It is written into our bodies; it is our experience of delight, of joy. The English word "pleasure" is a sensual word, the z of the "s" and the sound of the "u" coming from deep within our bodies, tapping the wellsprings of desire and curiosity, a knowing that resides within ourselves. "Me," the loved two-year-old says with joy, sharing the delight in himself/herself—discovering with joy that I am me, my body, my feelings, my thoughts, my desires and my curiosity, exulting in the exuberance of language, the pleasure of naming myself, my family, my friends, my love, my anger, my joy, my sadness, my world, the power of saying "no" and asking "why." "Mine," the two-year-old proclaims, embracing life and the world in all of its weathers. "I'm sad," two-year-old Nora says, "I'm crying out of my eyes"; and then, following the rhythm of her emotions, "I'm all done crying now." This knowing becomes a taproot, anchoring the psyche in the body, in relationship, in language and culture. Pleasure will become a marker, a compass pointing to emotional true north.

But why a daughter?

What allowed me to open a door and see into love was my experience of finding in girls an honesty that I remembered and had learned to dismiss. "When we were nine, we were stupid," thirteen-year-old Tracy says; I am meeting with her and her classmates at the end of a five-year study in which they took part. "You know," I say, "it would never have occurred to me to use the word 'stupid,' because what struck me about you when you were nine was how much you knew." "I mean," Tracy says, "when we were nine, we were honest." As I began to explore the roots of this honesty and to consider its implications, I was taken back to the infant research and the studies that show that our maps start in a place of relationship. As babies, we know the rhythm of relationship—turning to, turning away, turning back again; know without knowing we know it the pleasure of moving in synchrony with another person. This delicate knowing of relationship is our first experience of love. The very openness and vulnerability of relationship—standing out in the rain of love—exposes us to disappointment, betrayal, loss, and trauma.

As I watched girls weather the strains of relationship and followed their increasingly intricate strategies for repairing the inevitable breaks in their connections with others, playing games of inclusion and exclusion, testing their mettle, honing their skills, I saw the development of the ability that was caught by the films of infants and mothers: the ability to know when love is real and when it is not. This deep knowing depends on staying connected with our bodies. Judy, at eleven, locates her mind in her stomach; she will describe the split between what she knows in her gut and what she calls "the brain knowledge." Seeta, also eleven, readily locates her emotions in her body; asked where anger lies, she replies, "In the pit of my stomach and in my throat"; sadness, she says, "is in my heart." Describing a tense Sunday dinner at the home of her father and stepmother, Lily explains that the fight that broke out when her younger brother refused to eat the carrots "was not about the carrots." Just as five-year-old Nick knows that his father's remorse carries his fear that in hitting Nick, he was repeating a cycle that he had vowed to break: "You are afraid that if you hit me, when I grow up I will hit my children."

The Abolitionist Feminists of the nineteenth century sought to free love from the constraints of racism and patriarchy. This political agenda contains a deep psychological wisdom: patriarchy drains pleasure because hierarchy leads us to cover vulnerability. The symptoms of dissociation (loss of voice, difficulty in seeing or saying what one knows, dizziness, a sense of dislocation or the "as if" feeling of alienation—not really living one's life) are so often revealed through the body because the body is our strongest barometer of our consonance with or dissonance from the world around us. Through the experience of sensual pleasure, we come into associative relationship with ourselves, unless the body becomes divided within itself, as when we separate our minds from our hearts.

I have highlighted a map showing a divergence between two paths that we can trace in the development of men and women, one branching off earlier than the other, breaking off in the last years of early childhood, while the other branches off at adolescence; and I have identified these splits as times of initiation. These are the times when boys enter the play of the good guys versus the bad guys; when girls are beset with the division between good and bad women, taking on a legacy that is not of their making. When a man and a woman join later in life, we often see this history played out in games of love. But we also see the power of love to unglue hierarchy, as association opens the way to undoing dissociation.

While each person brings a unique history of love with them into adulthood, and while significant differences exist within cultures that fall under the overarching rubric of patriarchy, it is also true that men's histories frequently chronicle a sacrifice of relationship made earlier in childhood, often in the name of love and for the sake of manhood. We know this story; it is the quest story, the hero with a thousand faces. It is the quintessential story of patriarchy, the story of men's initiation into the battle between the good and the bad guys. Whereas the initiation of girls typically occurs later, their participation in patriarchy becoming essential only at the time when they become young women, the time when the continuation of patriarchy depends on women being with men. The opening I found in my research with girls lay in the question that they asked in a variety of forms: what does it mean to be with someone? What they knew in their bones, in their gut, by heart, is that it means being present. They were resisting the invitation to absent themselves from relationship in the name of love, as Psyche resisted becoming New Venus, knowing that by fitting herself into an image, she was barring the way to love. I'd rather die, she said, in a voice that travels across the centuries, than live this death-in-life existence.

When I began to explore the roots of girls' honesty and to consider the implications of their resistance, I saw what at first seemed a terrible dilemma. It was a dilemma I remembered from my own adolescence: the sense of having to choose between being in relationship and having relationships, between living in synchrony with another person and fitting oneself into a form. It was an exquisitely paradoxical choice: the invitation to give up relationship in order to have relationships. At the time, I did not see this as an initiation, but only as confusing and ultimately painful, a paralyzing sense that there was no way to move forward without falling into an abyss of loss.

It was when I discovered that being with girls as they approach the cusp of adolescence took me back to a time before a dissociation I was coming to remember, and also discovered that my experience was shared by many women from a variety of backgrounds and cultures, that I saw that an answer is in our midst. Because girls are older, more experienced and articulate, at the time of their initiation, their voices can lead us out of what otherwise becomes a tragic dilemma by reminding us that a way out is always there. Once we can see a path, following it becomes an option.

Thus we come to the question of choosing pleasure. Choosing, so to speak, to give birth to pleasure. It would seem, on the face of it, an irresistible choice. Suddenly duty looms, work, obligation, law and order, all the things that appear to stand in the way of pleasure along with the internal obstacles, such as guilt and shame and fear. Dostoevsky, in the scene of "The Grand Inquisitor" in *The Brothers Karamazov*, explores the question of why we willingly give up freedom, giving ourselves over to the power of the Inquisition, whatever form that might take. Freud, in his essay "Beyond the Pleasure Principle," asks why we repeat a traumatic experience, or whatever version we tell ourselves of the tragic story. He sees this as an attempt at mastering loss—the fantasy that it will come out right this time. I see our predilection for living on the far side of loss, east of Eden, as a way of protecting ourselves from the seemingly overwhelming vulnerability of finding ourselves standing again in the place before the loss happens. Knowing the end of the story, knowing the tragedy, we have vowed never to repeat it. And yet of course we repeat it over and over again, until we know it by heart.

I remember from the time of my own adolescence losses so shocking to me that I literally could not speak of them at the time (my grandfather leaving, my mother sending him away). My shock came in part from the realization that others around me, mainly my parents, were not registering the loss I was experiencing, so that I suddenly felt out of touch with them. I remember submerging myself, as if I were a whale or a dolphin, a mammal that could live under water. Later, in the In Our Own Voices workshops, when I drew the river of my life and placed stepping-stones in it, I saw that the stepping-stones in my life were places where I had surfaced: when I fell in love, in an openness of love that was breathtaking to me, joining the play of relationship that I knew from my childhood with a woman's experience of joy; when I fell into my work with a passion and a pleasure that was all-encompassing; when I experienced with new intensity the pleasures of nature, the sounds of words and music, the excitement of knowing, the bite of discovery, the sensuousness of my own body. I found that when I made a real commitment to my own experience, staying with my sense of what was happening within and around me, I came into powerful connection with other people and also came into conflict. Finding relationship, losing relationships. It was a dilemma I remembered, but being played out backward. As I walked out of my own dissociation, I walked back into my relationship with my mother.

I had often felt that she did not want me to see what I was seeing or to say what I wanted to say; she wanted to tell me how I should see things, and also what I should say. You could say that she had the best of intentions; she was trying to teach me how to live in the world, and she knew that I was heading for trouble in challenging the rules of the game. And this was true. In claiming freedom, I often came up against the voice of restriction—in school, at camp, and at universities, where I was a leader of various movements for social justice. But what I felt at the time and also later was something I understood fully only when I was working with girls and other women and saw that in the presence of girls who will speak freely and say what they are seeing and hearing, thinking and feeling, women begin to know what they know. I don't know how to talk about this kind of knowing, since it so readily seems suspect. It is the way animals know. Through vibrations. Something that passes between people. We pore over novels and poems because this is what writers put into words. Truths that have until recently escaped the nets put out by science. Speaking truth truly, in Emerson's phrase; knowing what rings true.

I remember standing with my mother at a bus stop on First Avenue, she reciting a poem and I knowing I was in the presence of love, feeling the affinity between us. Which I did not feel when she became Mother. But since I knew this deep sense of connection with her, I was shocked when she would suddenly change into what seemed to me another person. Or a shark. And come at me, telling me what I wanted, what I should say or do. How were we going to be in relationship with each other now that I was walking into what had seemed her territory: sex, love, money, marriage, making one's way in the world. How were we going to love each other? How would we know each other, and what could we allow the other to know?

I have watched the silent pact that women often make with girls—in families, in classrooms, in therapy rooms. It goes something like this: if you don't say what you see me doing, I won't say what I see you doing. It is an eye-rolling, turn-a-deaf-ear collusion that also exists among women: like, girl, you gotta do your stuff. It is a tacit agreement about living and participating in patriarchy. In Edith Wharton's novel *The Age of Innocence,* when Newland Archer says to Ellen Olenska that he wants to go away with her into a world where "we shall simply be two human beings who love each other," where words like "wife" and "mistress"—"categories like that"—won't exist, she sighs and then laughs, saying, "Oh, my dear—where is that country? Have you ever been there?" In the Metropolitan Museum of Art, they stand amid the relics of Troy. The objects are so old that it is impossible to tell what they were ever used for; and yet the Trojan War and the story of Helen, the consummate bad woman—the woman who leaves her marriage and runs off with a barbarian—have not lost their grip.

In the United States, the divorce rate now hovers around 50 percent; a recent survey finds that the woman most often initiates separation. My impression, from the study of marriages in crisis, is that she is often seeking pleasure, moving out of dissociation, knowing what she knows: the difference between presence and absence, between love and not love.

But men know this too. My grandfather came to live with us just after I was born, when his wife died. He was my father's father, and my mother welcomed him into her house. But he did not really live in her house. He lived on the edge, where I would join him. He was a man who retired as soon as he could, an immigrant who had worked in the sweatshops, had a small store, then another, saved his money, bought some property, along the way married a woman he loved as he loved my father, their son. He was a man given to parrots—to teaching birds how to talk. He did not want my father to go away to college, because he did not want him to leave home. My father had to win a Regents scholarship to go upstate to Cornell. And his brilliance, his tenderness, because he too was a gentle and sensitive man, lifted him from the world of his childhood, where he lived above the store, to the high offices of Wall Street and the inner sanctums of capitalism. He was a lawyer, and his sense of people—together with his razor-sharp analytic mind and also perhaps his sense of timing and love of theater—led him to do most of the trial work for his firm. He rose to the top of his profession, or at least very near the top. His mother had encouraged her brilliant son; my mother encouraged him as well and also helped, bringing her charm, her warmth, her generous hospitality, opening her home to their friends and acquaintances, many of whom became my father's clients.

Growing up, I saw one man rising through the patriarchy and another who had turned his back on that world. Each sacrificed something, as one does with any choice. What I knew without knowing it, growing up, is that my father, who had a huge appetite for life, who relished the winter and water and breakfast, had also covered himself in ways that my grandfather had not. I was my father's companion; he would take me swimming with him, or walking in the winter; I went to his office and played with all the different colors of paper. I adored my father; I felt adored by him. When I asked him late in life about his father, he—old and depressed at this time— didn't have much to say. Or perhaps didn't want to talk about it. I asked him about Popsy's relationship with me, and my father said, "He couldn't take his eyes off you."

What I remember is running through the apartment, playing hide-and-seek, shrieks of delight as I would open the door of the hall closet and find him, or he would find me. I remember sugar sprinkled on toast in the morning, a little coffee stealthily poured into my milk; sitting on the edge of the high sink watching him shave, he giving me a razor with no blade so I could shave too; and playing school, I the teacher, he the pupil; and the animals—the bird that flew out of the window one day, the turtle, the fish, and the dog. When I found the letters he wrote me at camp—letters I carried with me without looking at them for years and years, through many moves—that whole world came back with the sound of his voice. "My dear sweet big girl"—I was twelve that summer. My parents were away; he was alone in the hot apartment with the animals. In his letters, they all spoke, like the parrots he used to train. They said how they felt about my being away. My grandfather was a man of relationship, and my father was also a man of relationship who climbed the hierarchy of the patriarchy.

I PROMISED to return to the question of whether the tragic love story is the watermark of patriarchy, the way it goes into our souls, becoming the default option—the story we are set to repeat unless we change the settings. Perhaps because of my relationship with my grandfather, I know a love that is filled with play, and my father's phrase "He could not take his eyes off you" comes back to me as I think about times I have loved with my eyes wide open, when there was no bar to seeing and being seen.

The psychological separation between children and mothers has been seen as a mainstay of development. It has been associated with the establishment of the child's sense of self, the awareness of being a separate person. And yet the new infant research calls this formulation into question. The evidence of relationship shows that from the beginning the baby has the rudiments of a self: a voice, the ability to initiate action and to register experience, what Antonio Damasio in his study of "body and emotion in the making of consciousness" calls "a core sense of self." Damasio, one of the leaders in the new field of cognitive neuroscience, adapts a line from Seamus Heaney's poem "Song" in titling his book *The Feeling of What Happens.* Heaney's line is "the music of what happens," and music underlies Damasio's discussion of consciousness, despite his preference for visual imagery.

"Stepping into the light," Damasio writes in introducing his book, is

> a powerful metaphor for consciousness, for the birth of the knowing mind, for the simple and yet momentous coming of the sense of self into the world of the mental. How we step into the light of consciousness is precisely the topic of this book. I write about the sense of self and about the transition from innocence and ignorance to knowingness and selfness. My specific goal is to consider the biological circumstances that permit this critical transition.

Consciousness, Damasio observes, "often seems the last mystery in the elucidation of the mind."

But coming into consciousness is not simply the replacement of innocence and ignorance with knowingness and selfness. It is also the coming out of dissociation—our ability to remain unconscious or unaware of what otherwise we know. Dissociation differs from denial in that denial signifies a kind of blindness or obtuseness in the face of the obvious—consequences of actions that we are fully aware of but would rather not face. The alcoholic denies that he or she is drinking; the overeater may deny the consequences of obesity; the adolescent may deny the fact of mortality. In dissociation, we literally don't know what we know; and the process of recovery, now illuminated by the biological and psychological studies of trauma, centers on the recovery of voice and, with it, the ability to tell one's story.

Works by two novelists writing in the last years of the twentieth century explore the phenomenon of recovered memory—not in the controversial arena of trauma studies, but in telling a tragic love story. Both writers span Eastern and Western cultures, and their insight and acute sense of language reflect the eye and ear of the traveler who retains the sense of foreignness, of strangeness, and also the voice of the post-colonial writer, tracking the emergence from colonization. The question that haunts both novels has to do with the costs of love. It seems strange that love would lead to tragedy, and yet this story is so familiar that it is only by setting it against the forces of nature—the monsoons of southern India and the Libyan desert—that we begin to make the crucial separation between losses that are a part of nature and losses imposed by civilization. The narrative device that caught my attention was the decision to tell the tragic love story backward, to set it not in the present but in the past; to start with the dissociation and to unravel the skein of associations through which we, the readers, along with the characters in the novel, come to an understanding of what happened. Thus the tragedy becomes in the end surprising. Why, we ask, does this have to happen? Or, more radically, does this have to happen? In Michael Ondaatje's *The English Patient* and Arundhati Roy's *The God of Small Things*, we see the tragic love story through the eyes of the next generation, who inadvertently have witnessed the tragedy.

The final chapter of *The God of Small Things* is called "The Cost of Living." Ammu—the name means "mother"—is a divorced woman in her late twenties, the mother of seven-year-old "two-egg" twins, a boy and a girl. Rising from her chair one night, she "walked out of her world like a witch. To a better, happier place." She "moved quickly through the darkness, like an insect following a chemical trail." This instinctive reaction is catalyzed by a knowing that has passed silently between her and Velutha, a young man, black, one of the untouchables, a carpenter, a man of exceptional competence who carries with him from his childhood only his smile.

A glimpse of pleasure has released the chemistry of love. A vibrancy awakens one afternoon when Ammu sees her daughter, Rahel, and Velutha playing:

> She was surprised at the extent of her daughter's physical ease with him. Surprised that her child seemed to have a sub-world that excluded *her* entirely. A tactile world of smiles and laughter that she, her mother, had no part in. Ammu recognized vaguely that her thoughts were shot with a delicate, purple tinge of envy. She didn't allow herself to consider who it was that she envied. The man or her own child. Or just their world of hooked fingers and sudden smiles.

Velutha glances up and catches her gaze. And in that moment history "was caught off guard." The god of small things takes over; laughter, pleasure, the color of envy, the god "of goosebumps and sudden smiles." The god of small things is also the god of loss—often said to be a small thing. The novel is a refutation of that thought.

Loss is huge. It casts its shadow over generations. My mother's loss of her twin at the age of thirteen hung over our relationship; it was the mystery behind a pattern of painful separations, as if she were signaling something to me in code. All the women in Roy's novel have suffered losses: loss of sight, loss of love, loss of a leg to stand on. The untouchables in the past had to erase even the trace of their presence, walking backward and brushing away their footsteps so that no touchable would have to step in them, covering their mouths when they spoke so as not to infect the touchables with their breath. When the untouchable Velutha touches Ammu, when she, a luminous woman in a clouded world, opens herself to him, a luminous man, their love sets off the psychological equivalent of a nuclear chain reaction, leading through a series of small things—the misplaced loyalty of a drunken father, the spitefulness of an embittered old aunt, the petty ambitions of a local police chief, and the pretensions of the police—until it explodes in terror. The horrifyingly brutal beating of Velutha by the policemen, Ammu locked in her room by her mother and aunt, and the twins, Rahel and Estha, lured into a trap, lied to by the aunt, who tells them that the only way they can save their mother is by betraying Velutha. Either way, they are forced to betray love.

It is only after we see the magnitude of the loss, a world reconstructed and then blown apart, that we are allowed to see the love. The usual order has been reversed: first we see the tragedy, and then we see the pleasure that caused it. The question hangs at the end of the novel: how could love—an innocent love at that, except that it crossed the uncrossable line of caste—how could love lead to such loss? It is a child's question, though a question that the child cannot answer until she becomes an adult. Rahel is the central character in the novel; it is her return to Ayemenem, the scene of her childhood, to be with her brother, who has become mute, that leads her to reenter what had become an emptiness inside her. Quietness and emptiness: this was the fate of the twins, the price paid for the loss of their childhood. But the brilliance of dissociation as an adaptation to trauma is that it keeps alive what had seemingly been lost. What is known and then not known remains out of reach, buried in the depths of the psyche; an innocence and ignorance that become frozen in time, suspended by what Robert Jay Lifton has called "psychic numbing": sustaining a false consciousness and also a false rendering of history. It is necessary for Rahel to go back and remember the pleasure of her childhood in order to understand what was lost and how and why.

"The Love Laws"—Arundhati's phrase. The laws that "lay down who should be loved. And how. And how much." The tragic story of love is the watermark of patriarchy because it enacts the enforcement of its love laws. We begin to understand why the freeing of love is so inflammatory. Why pleasure is the seed, the spark that must be stamped out. Or brought under control, its vibrations deadened, bottled and sold like the mangoes in the Paradise Pickle and Preserves factory that Rahel's grandmother started and her uncle took over.

On the day when Velutha glances up and catches Ammu's gaze, "coins of sunshine dancing on his body, holding her daughter in his arms," history vanished, leaving "an aura, a palpable shimmering that was as plain to see as the water in a river or the sun in the sky. As plain to feel as the heat of a hot day, or the tug of a fish on a taut line. So obvious that no one noticed."

In that brief moment, Velutha

saw things that he hadn't seen before. Things that had been out of bounds so far, obscured by history's blinkers. For instance, he saw that Rahel's mother was a woman.

He saw too that he was not necessarily the only giver of gifts. That she had gifts to give him, too.

This knowing slid into him cleanly, like the sharp edge of a knife. Cold and hot at once. It took only a moment.

Ammu saw that he saw. She looked away. He did too. History's fiends returned to claim them. To rewrap them in its old scarred pelt and drag them back to where they really lived. Where the Love Laws laid down who should be loved. And how. And how much.

Ammu walked up to the verandah back into the Play. Shaking.

Velutha looked down at [Rahel] in his arms. He put her down. Shaking too.

OVER THE centuries, physicists have been mystified by phenomena exhibiting action at a disance. Newton was puzzled by gravitational forces; Einstein could not understand how a measurement of one particle could affect measurements of a correlated particle thousands of miles away. Scientists were observing connections that they could describe but could not satisfactorily explain without fundamentally changing their picture of the universe. Gravitational action at a distance remained a complete mystery until Einstein introduced the concept of curved space/time, thus showing what mediates the relationship. We know from chaos physics that a butterfly flapping its wings in Rio de Janeiro can cause a shift in the weather leading to storms on a distant continent. And so it is with love. As its vibrations elude our usual forms of explanation, so it threatens our sense of boundaries. Like the twinship of Rahel and Estha, like the affinity between Ammu and Velutha, the "I" becomes part of a "we" that, rather than erasing the sense of self, calls it fully into existence. Like voice is called forth by resonance.

Ammu and Velutha are vibrant souls in a dying world. The Play Ammu walks out of is unbearably racist; the return of the almost blond, almost white Sophie Moll (the child of Ammu's brother and his English former wife, Margaret) displacing the twins in everyone's attention and affection. Sophie Moll (the word means "daughter") also walks out of the Play to join her cousins, the life-filled twins; she drowns because, unlike the twins, she was never taught how to swim by her father. Although the accidental death of Sophie becomes the central event of the Play, the deaths of Velutha and Ammu are the tragedy, ending the play of the children as well as of the lovers. When the sour and jealous aunt falsely accuses Velutha of raping Ammu and abducting the children, and the ambitious police chief seizes the moment to show his power and secure his position against his rival, the twins and also Ammu are sacrificed in order to cover the truth of what actually happened.

It was like the butterfly flapping its wings. "A luminous woman opened herself to a luminous man. She was as wide and deep as a river in spate. He sailed on her waters." The hierarchy vanished: brown, black, touchable, untouchable, woman, man—each had gifts to give the other.

[His] carpenter's hands lifted her hips and an untouchable tongue touched the innermost part of her. Drank long and deep from the bowl of her. She danced for him. . . . She lived. . . . Seven years of oblivion lifted off her and flew into the shadows on weighty, quaking wings. Like a dull, steel peahen. And on Ammu's Road (to Age and Death) a small, sunny meadow appeared. Copper grass spangled with blue butterflies. Beyond it, an abyss.

Choose life, choose love. The novelist plays with the words "viable" and "die-able," placing them next to each other. "The cost of living had climbed to unaffordable heights." The aunt, Baby Kochamma, would say that "it was a Small Price to Pay." Was it? the narrator asks. It is Rahel, reconstructing her mother's life, entering finally what could be called the holy of holies: the place where her mother experienced pleasure—not the pleasure she knew as a mother, which was considerable, but a woman's pleasure. In her body, in her soul, she felt joy.

The price was two lives (hers and Velutha's), two childhoods (Rahel's and Estha's), and "a history lesson for future offenders."

What was the lesson? It is the question posed by the book. The epigraph is a quotation from John Berger: "Never again will a single story be told as though it's the only one." It is an epitaph to hierarchy. Returning twenty-four years later to the scene of the terror, Rahel sees herself and her brother as "a pair of actors trapped in a recondite play"—racist, imperial, patriarchal. The therapy they are offered only compounds the problem by further confusing their knowledge of what actually happened ("You're not the Sinners. You're the Sinned Against. You were only children. You had no control. You are the *victims*, not the perpetrators").

Well-intentioned, perhaps, but missing the point. These divisions were the very terms of the world they walked out of—a world filled with hate and betrayal, sorrow and grief. The children knew what had happened to Velutha, even though they did not know the whole story. They knew that his love had been betrayed, and that they (for good reason) were among the betrayers, although not the only ones. As children will, they blamed themselves for what happened to their mother; it was only later that they understood the full story.

As a child, Ammu learned very quickly that the story told about love was not the real story; it covered the truths of what went on in her family, her father beating and humiliating his wife and children, who were then "made to suffer the envy of friends and relations for having such a wonderful husband and father." As a divorced woman, a single mother in a caste-ridden, patriarchal society, she had no leg to stand on. Forced back into her family, moored by the need to support her twins, she contained an "unmixable mix" inside her: "the infinite tenderness of motherhood and the reckless rage of a suicide bomber." This is the understanding that Rahel comes to: it was this explosive mix that led her mother "to love by night the man her children loved by day."

IDEALIZATION and denigration are the hallmarks of loss. When we lose pleasure, we idolize Pleasure, or else we disparage it, making it tawdry. And the same is true with love. But when we have lost love, the hurt we have suffered and the vulnerability of loving come to feel so overwhelming that we often turn to loving images as a bulwark against loss, because an image can be replaced, unlike a person.

Asked whether he has experienced a love that has the feeling of chemistry, Cal, a friend, speaks about his relationship with Angie. He is an actor in his early forties, handsome, with the finely chiseled features of a leading man. Divorced and raising his teenage son, he has fallen in love with Angie, a member of the same theater company. It is the middle of summer, and the conversation about love and chemistry takes place on a long afternoon. Cal and Angie are lovers, and Cal speaks of their love as an ineluctable joining. And then, breaking off in midstream, he says, "But she is not my ideal woman." Angie has large breasts, he explains, whereas the ideal woman has small ones. Being in therapy, he makes the connection to his small-breasted mother.

We all carry images of love from childhood, images of the people we loved as children, and also familiar rhythms of love that move us like an old song. But the abruptness of Cal's shift catches me off balance and becomes dizzying, like a sudden fall. I know this sensation in relationships with men, the dizzying turn from lover into mother and the sudden feeling of losing relationship and becoming eclipsed by an image. I have taken refuge in this image—finding the role of mother easy to assume, a safe haven of sorts. But the presence of a close woman friend whose dislocation I also register leads me to stay with my dizziness and, in the spirit of the conversation about love, to ask Cal "What just happened?"—a question echoed by my friend. Cal was interested although puzzled by the question, and as we came back from swimming and settled inside, the three of us pursued it. How to understand the shift from closeup to distance, from his description of the chemistry between him and Angie to saying that she was not his ideal woman. It was like suddenly stepping out of relationship. I said it was like a shade coming down. He thought for a moment and said it was like a film, and a shade had come down over one of the frames. It happened so quickly, he couldn't catch it.

It is a woman's nightmare to discover that although she feels loved she doesn't fit the image: her breasts are too large, too small, some part of her is not right. And most women have a ready script for blaming themselves for why they are left. They should have called, shouldn't have called, should have slept with him, shouldn't have slept with him, should have said, shouldn't have said or done this or that. Whatever it is, they seem to have made a fatal error.

What I have noticed in hearing one or another version of this story over and over again from women is that the woman is left feeling confused. She had picked up the chemistry, felt the connection, experienced the joy of love, and then it was as if it had never happened, as if she was deluded or crazy. And yet she resists letting go of the relationship. The honesty I found in girls, the honesty I remembered and learned to dismiss, as girls would dismiss it, calling it stupid, led me to suspect that the woman was not crazy or out of touch with reality; what she experienced happened, but reality had shifted. She was holding on, in Damasio's or Heaney's words, to the feeling or the music of what happens, so that while she may have seemed crazy or pathetic, like Psyche holding on to Cupid, in danger of losing herself, she was holding on to a core sense of self, her ability to register her experience. Rather than her being left because she or the relationship had some intrinsic flaw or failing, I suspected that it was the very intensity of the connection that was responsible for his leaving. The shift in reality covered his tracks. So that while she might be sad about losing what had felt so magical, I did not think she had lost her sense of reality.

Women disappear from relationships as well as men; the vulnerability of loving is universally shared. The birth of pleasure in itself is simple, but staying with pleasure means staying open, and this is where history tends to kick in. Volumes of psychology have been written about the ways we defend ourselves against love and loss, often giving up what we have most wanted. The experiments with infants where mothers are asked to put on what the researchers call a "still face" show the baby turning to her, trying to elicit a response, running through the repertoire of relationship—the moves that have worked in the past—and then, in the absence of any response, becoming puzzled, then distressed, then turning away. When repair follows, relationship resumes, and these cycles of break and repair build a growing vocabulary of love and trust. But when something impedes the process of repair, the core sense of self recedes from relationship and begins to build a wall of protection.

I have seen this wall going up in young boys when their faces no longer register their emotions or let only a few emotions show through, when they steady their voice and adjust its pitch to a few notes that carry the image of themselves they want to project (strong, tough, invulnerable). I have watched girls at adolescence masking their faces, putting on a face that a year or two earlier they had identified as a false face, hiding anger with smiles, boredom with a look of interest, a feeling of being ordinary with a look of specialness. And take on a voice that they had gleefully mimicked as a woman's false voice in hilarious skits where they demonstrate the acuity of their listening. What I found extraordinary among girls was their ability to name this process of masking. In an exercise on masks developed by Normi Noel, who brought her expertise in theater into the project with girls, ten- and eleven-year-old girls in an urban public school, from a variety of ethnic and social-class backgrounds, showed remarkable facility in masking their faces and naming the feelings in the mask as well as the feelings that the mask was hiding. In skits where one girl stood behind another and played "her thoughts," the girls revealed how closely they listen to the conversation behind the conversation.

The difference in the timing of initiation that leads boys to take on the mantle of manhood earlier than girls put on the masks of womanhood suggests that this process will be more readily articulated by girls and also remain closer to the level of their consciousness. Thus girls in general are more apt to speak about an experience that for boys is rawer and more inchoate, although no less deeply felt: an experience of loss or inner division, which leaves a sense of distance and alienation. But also a deep knowing of love that is sparked, like a chemical reaction, by the sensation of pleasure. When a man and a woman fall in love, this history is caught off guard, love disassembling the internal structures of patriarchy in a way that can be profoundly unsettling.

Among the married couples in crisis who took part in my study or who came for consultation with Terrence Real and me, it was the women who commonly spoke of an experience of love that had come to seem incredible, naming a reality that otherwise remained hidden under the flak of argument and accusation. Eileen spoke of the fire and chemistry between Rick and herself, Jude of "the two Dans," and Sonya named Phil's "stonewalling" as the impediment that came between them. By providing resonance for these women who in one way or another had experienced an impending sense of craziness (feeling crazy, walking through a fog, double-thinking themselves), I found an opening into stories about love that men had buried within themselves: Dan's pleasure in his relationship with his mother, his saying that they had been buddies or pals; and the ultimate nightmare that lay behind Phil's seemingly implacable hurt and rage at the thought of Sonya in the arms of another man: "I guess the ultimate nightmare really for me was to never have the opportunity to show her how I really feel . . . to open my heart and to love her."

Give me a map and I'll build you a city. Give me a pencil and I will draw you a room in South Cairo, desert charts on the wall. Always the desert was among us. I could wake and raise my eyes to the map of old settlements . . . and surrounding those the shades of yellowness that we invaded, tried to lose ourselves in. . . . You do not find adultery in the minutes of the [Royal] Geographical Society. Our room never appears in the detailed reports which chartered every knoll and every incident of history.

IT IS the oldest of stories, this story of hidden, forbidden love. Almasy, the desert explorer, tells it midway through *The English Patient.* His love affair with Katharine follows the path of romantic tragedy: an illicit love that leads to death. But as we listen to this story, told retrospectively by a man who has literally been burned beyond recognition, we enter an interior missing from the myth of Psyche and Cupid: the inner world of a man burned by love.

A detail from the myth—oil falling from Psyche's lamp, burning Cupid on his shoulder. He wakes to discover that she has seen him; he leaves without saying a word. He had told her she must not try to see him. Seeing him, she falls in love.

When Almasy falls in love with Katharine, she tells him she will not lie about their love.

"What do you hate most?" he asks her.

"A lie. And you?"

"Ownership," he says. "When you leave me, forget me."

She had picked up a cushion and placed it on her lap "as a shield against him." She "moves the cushion against her heart, as if she would suffocate that part of herself which has broken free." When he speaks of her leaving him and forgetting him, she hits him. Then "she dresses and leaves."

He begins to look at himself in a way that he has not for years. He becomes curious about the shape of his face, the color of his hair. "He who has never felt alone in the miles of longitude between desert towns . . . wants [only] the minute and secret reflection between them, the depths of field minimal, their foreignness intimate like two pages of a closed book."

"How does this happen?" he asks himself. "To fall in love and be disassembled." A first-person voice answers:

I was in her arms. I had pushed the sleeve of her shirt up to the shoulder so I could see her vaccination scar. I love this, I said. This pale aureole on her arm. I see the instrument scratch and then punch the serum within her and then release itself, free of her skin, years ago when she was nine years old, in a school gymnasium.

It is the "I" coming out of dissociation: "I was in her arms . . . I had pushed . . . I could see . . . I love this, I said . . . I see."

In his study of consciousness, Damasio describes core consciousness or a core sense of self as the film that runs continually inside us, registering our experience from moment to moment and also our awareness of watching the film, the "extended consciousness" that carries the sense of self into time and history, memory and identity. He contrasts this "core self" with what he calls "the autobiographical self," the self that is wedded to a story about itself. It is a useful way to think about dissociation: our ability to register experience, know it even and yet not know it, the experience not becoming part of our story.

In the story Almasy tells himself, Katharine has left him, insisted on their parting, saying that her husband would go mad. And while he does go mad, some months after the love affair has ended, attempting to kill all three of them and succeeding only in killing himself, the tragedy lies not in the events that follow. Like the death of Sophie Moll in Arundhati Roy's novel, Katharine's death and Almasy's burns turn out to be the result of an accident. The seeming tragedy is not the tragedy. The tragedy lies in the silences that Almasy registers and records in his journal without seeing at the time that in his silences he had left Katharine.

> In the street of imported parrots in Cairo one is hectored by almost articulate birds. . . . We stood among them. I was showing her a city that was new to her.
>
> Her hand touched me at the wrist.
>
> "If I gave you my life, you would drop it. Wouldn't you?"
>
> I didn't say anything.
>
> "I think you have become inhuman," she said to me.
> "I'm not the only betrayer."

"I don't think you care—that this has happened among us. You slide past everything with your fear and hatred of ownership, of owning, of being owned, of being named. You think this is a virtue. I think you are inhuman. If I leave you, who will you go to? Would you find another lover?"

I said nothing.

"Deny it, damn you."

"She had always wanted words," Almasy explains. "She loved them, grew up in them. Words gave her clarity, brought reason, shape. Whereas I thought words bent emotions like sticks in water. She returned to her husband."

Paintings of swimmers on the walls of a cave in the desert reveal that the desert had once been a lake. "A love story," Almasy writes in his journal as he is falling in love with Katharine, "is not about those who lose their heart but about those who find that sullen inhabitant who, when it is stumbled upon, means the body can fool no one, can fool nothing—not the wisdom of sleep or the habit of social graces. It is a consuming of oneself and the past." The coming alive of love carries with it the sensation of finding oneself in a place where no one has walked before. And while it is true that love is always a once-upon-a-time story, that relationships like snowflakes and people are unique, it is also true that lovers enter a place that has a history. When Almasy discovers the lost oasis of Zerzura, its acacia trees in full bloom, he is

walking not in a place where no one had walked before but in a place where there were sudden, brief populations over the centuries—a fourteenth-century army, a Tebu caravan, the Senussi raiders of 1915. And in between these times—nothing was there. When no rain fell the acacias withered, the wadis dried out—until water suddenly reappeared fifty or a hundred years later.

Sporadic appearances and disappearances, like legends and rumours through history.

A love story is not about losing but finding a part of oneself. Pleasure blooms like the acacia trees when water suddenly appears. We speak of falling in love. But perhaps it would be more accurate to speak of finding rather than losing our balance. Coming into our bodies, our senses electric, our hearts incapable of lies. The central insight in Ondaatje's novel comes with the realization, late in the story, that when Almasy holds Katharine's life in his hands, he does not drop it, nor does he replace her when she leaves him. The tragedy loses its cast of inevitability. Instead, we are left with an old question: why didn't he want her to see him?

Ondaatje has set his novel in an abandoned villa in Italy during the closing months of the Second World War. Poised at a moment of political liberation (the victory of the Allies over the Germans), it explores the psychic impediments to freedom. The characters in the present time of the novel are all in varying states of shock. Hana, a young Canadian nurse who has followed her father into the war, has drawn "her own few rules to herself." Coming out of what has happened to her during the war—an avalanche of loss culminating in the news of her father's death—she "would not be ordered again or carry out duties for the greater good. She would care only for the burned patient." She is joined by Caravaggio, the "uncle" of her childhood, a thief who worked as a spy for British intelligence until he was caught by the Germans and maimed; and also by Kip, a young Sikh sapper trained by the English, an expert in defusing bombs.

Each of these men has acute sensitivity. The desert explorer, the spy, and the sapper pick up the subtlest shifts in the landscape; they read the nuances of emotion and character and intuit the mind of another as Kip intuits the tricks of the bomb-maker. These skills, honed in the service of civilization, are the skills of a lover: sensing changes in the emotional weather, tuning in to the rhythms of another's psyche, following the turns of another's mind. And yet these men, who span three nationalities and two generations, who differ in class and color, all place a barrier between themselves and love. Manhood, a hatred and a fear of ownership, an autobiographical story, a desire for self-sufficiency. We are in the world of Odysseus and Aeneas, Abraham and Agamemnon—men who were called upon to sacrifice their love.

"Women want everything of a lover," Almasy says to Caravaggio in what begins as a familiar man-to-man conversation but then takes a surprising turn. "And too often I would sink below the surface. So armies disappear under sand. And there was her old fear of her husband, her belief in her honour, my old desire for self-sufficiency, my disappearances, her suspicions of me, my disbelief that she loved me. The paranoia and claustrophobia of hidden love."

"Her old fear . . . my old desire"—my disappearances, her suspicions, my disbelief that she loved me. Only when we begin to tell a new story can we see rather than be enveloped in the old. In the world of *The English Patient,* the fathers are dead; the older men are burned or maimed. Hana the nurse and Kip the sapper are members of a new generation, disillusioned with war and empire.

When Kip falls in love with Hana, he thinks of his ayah—the one he loved most, the source of all comfort and peace in childhood. He also had comforted her, rubbing her back when she grieved over her mother's death, as he will comfort Hana in a love that moves freely across the boundaries of race and nationality, mixing tenderness and wild play, celibacy and passion. Hana and Kip will discover that "in lovemaking there can be a whole civilisation, a whole country ahead of them. The love of the idea of him, or her. I don't want to be fucked, I don't want to fuck you." But Hana will realize later that "he never allowed himself to be beholden to her, or her to him"; she "will stare at the word in a novel, lift it off the book and carry it to a dictionary. *Beholden. To be under obligation.*" She lies next to him in his tent at night, unable to sleep, "irritated at his self-sufficiency, his ability to turn so easily away from the world. . . . 'Kiss me,'" she says. "Kip? Do you hear me? I'm so happy with you. To be with you like this." She wishes for rain, for a river they could swim in. She wants to take him to meet Clara, her stepmother, who lives out on a lake in Canada, "that demon for pleasure who became so wise," who was "not fooled like us . . . My father forsook her for a war."

Hana would break the old codes of honor that have bound men to war and women to chastity. She would free herself and also Kip from the grip of a tragic story, wash its imprint from their psyches. She will repeat a line the burned man read to her: "Love is so small it can tear itself through the eye of a needle."

But when Kip hears on his shortwave radio that the Allies have dropped atom bombs on Asia, he leaves her abruptly, "say[ing] nothing, looking through her." He had loved the English, been loved by the English; unlike his father and brother, he believed it was possible to transcend empire. Betrayed in his love, his manhood under siege, he picks up his rifle and revs up his motorcycle. "His name is Kirpal Singh and he does not know what he is doing here."

"Kip, it's *me*," Hana says. "What did we have to do with it?" He is "a stone of silence" in front of her. She leans the side of her head against his chest: "A beating heart." He leans away from her, his face "a few inches from a rain puddle." Ondaatje comments: "A boy and a girl."

What are we to make of this pattern that repeats across generations? Or, to put it differently, once we understand the history behind this pattern, what stake do we have in repeating it? In a novel where love crosses nationality and color, class and culture, where it vaults the walls of marriage and a woman's honor, manhood becomes the final obstacle. Or, more precisely, a particular story about manhood, because there is no inherent contradiction between manhood and love, or love and civilization. But manhood—the manhood that pits honor against love—is the mainstay of patriarchy.

"In the Cave of Swimmers we talked," Almasy says. Katharine's husband was dead, having crashed his plane; Katharine was wounded but not fatally. Almasy will set out for a jeep to bring her to safety.

Things fall apart just as they are coming together. It is an old question as to whether a love that feels earthshaking depends for its intensity on the presence of an obstacle, so that once the barrier is removed, a kind of domesticity sets in or the relationship goes up in flames. But maybe this is not the right way to frame it. It may be that an obstacle is necessary because love *is* earthshaking, disassembling an order that links manhood with self-sufficiency, taking apart the world of Odysseus and Aeneas, reversing the choices of Agamemnon and Abraham. Perhaps the relationship must fall apart precisely for this reason. Since pleasure, like a lost oasis, is always waiting in the desert, part of our bodies, part of our nature, an obstacle to love becomes necessary to ensure the continuation of an old tragic story.

In a small desert town, in sight of a jeep, Almasy gives his name to the British MPs, saying that Katharine is his wife and telling them that she is injured. "No one listened," he says; "I didn't give them a right name." War was breaking out in the desert, and everyone with a foreign name was suspect. "The only name I should have yelled, dropped like a calling card into their hands, was Clifton's"—Katharine's husband. Almasy is mistaken for a spy and imprisoned. Katharine dies because of this mistake, and Almasy is burned when he returns for Katharine, the plane carrying them out of the desert "years too late" bursting into flames.

There is no betrayal more wounding than the betrayal of

love. The pattern of men turning away from love, leaving without saying a word, suggests that they have already been burned. It is a history that bears the hallmarks of trauma: a heightened vigilance, a loss of voice, the inability to tell one's story. Given this legacy of betrayal, what becomes surprising is the staying power of love.

Hana will carry the sound of Kip's beating heart, as her mind will repeat "the line of movement [his] body followed out of her life." Knowing him in the way she was privy to, but that becomes like a secret room. Not shown on the map, not part of the story about himself to which he is wedded. Holding a love for which there is seemingly no evidence, she will search for a way to live in the world.

Ondaatje's novel catches a moment of transition in the history of empire and between men and women. It opens with Hana standing in the garden of the villa, sensing a shift in the weather; it ends with Kirpal back in India. The final section is filled with questions. "Now where does he sit as he thinks of her . . . the girl he has fallen in love with?" Kirpal sits in his garden and watches her, "her hair longer, in her own country." He thinks of going down to the telephone depot and phoning her, but he doesn't. He is a doctor working in a clinic, he is "permanently busy"; he has "two children and a laughing wife"; at his table "all of their hands are brown." The lines between manhood and womanhood, white and colored, have for the moment been redrawn.

And Hana? Like Clara, her stepmother ("the darkest bean"); like Kip's ayah, the woman from South India who lived with his family and knew all the children better than their "real parents"; like so many young women of varying colors and castes and sexualities, Hana does not fit into this picture. At nine she walked out of a hospital, refusing to have her tonsils removed; at sixteen she stood on a table in a café in Toronto singing "The Marseillaise"; coming out of the war, she chose to live by her own few rules: she would not abandon those who were burned. On the day after the Allies drop atom bombs on Japan, she wrote to Clara, "If we can rationalize this, we can rationalize anything." She was sick of Europe; she wanted to come home. She, "even at this age, thirty-four, has not found her own company, the ones she wanted. She is a woman of honour and smartness whose wild love leaves out luck, always taking risks."

But then, like the wind that blows across the Sahara, picking up red sand and depositing it as far north as the coasts of Cornwall, like the butterfly flapping its wings and causing a disturbance on a far continent, or the particles that retain their affinity across time and space so that a measurement taken on one will reveal the position of the other, which may be thousands of miles away, love moves through the universe of the novel. In Canada, Hana's "face turns and in a regret she lowers her hair. Her shoulder touches the edge of a cupboard and a glass dislodges. Kirpal's left hand swoops down and catches the dropped fork an inch from the floor and gently passes it into the fingers of his daughter, a wrinkle at the edge of his eyes behind his spectacles."

"Edges, Borders, Boundaries, Brinks and Limits"—the capitalized words of Arundhati Roy's novel define the world that love disassembles. The laws that hold love captive hold this world in place. In telling a tragic love story as a story of the past and seeing it through the eyes of Hana and Rahel, Ondaatje and Roy invite us to imagine a world more hospitable to a daughter named Pleasure. Re-creating the love story we have fallen in love with but associating it with a history of colonization, they register the costs of loss and trauma and encourage us, the readers, along with the characters in their novels, to embrace the love and step out of the tragedy. Like the wind that carries pleasure (along with a fork) into the hands of a daughter at the end of *The English Patient*, the final word of *The God of Small Things* is the lovers' promise: "tomorrow."

. . .

WHAT I first notice about Zoe is that she seems to have vacated her face. A philosophy graduate student in her late thirties, the mother of three children, ages two, four, and five, she has come to talk about her marriage as part of my study of marriages in crisis. A slight woman with short dark hair and steady brown eyes, she has a grace about her, a spiritual quality of tuning in to a world other than the one she is living in. She is a dancer, deeply into the practice of meditation, and as I begin to see signs of animation, I suspect that what I had taken for absence was also the calm of detachment. She seems to be hesitating as to whether she really wants to be in this world. But the choice she has come to talk about concerns her marriage, whether or not she wants to be in that. "I am confused," she says. With her children, she finds "a great potential for joy"; with Peter, her husband, although they have "only been married six years, there's very little of that in our relationship. Very little intense joy." This becomes less surprising when Zoe explains that she knew before she married him that "I didn't really love this man," and then she adds, "which probably makes me different from some people you might talk to."

I ask her how she knew. "I knew from the minute, from the first day that I met him." In her early twenties, Zoe had married a "man whom I really loved and who had a lot of difficulties, which I managed to convince myself were all his problems and of course they weren't."

I see Zoe's shrewdness: she's onto herself. Her intelligence and her honesty draw me in. I am curious about the other man. Sam, she says, the man she "adored and had everything in common with, married for the right reasons, I suppose, which is that I loved him." They were friends before they married; she worked in the legislative office in which he was a lawyer, and then she went back to school, having previously dropped out several times. When one of her cousins was severely injured in a motorcycle accident, she dropped out again to take care of him, finally placing him in a long-term care facility. "That summer I got engaged to Sam, and we married in the fall the following year."

The puzzle, the confusion at the center of Zoe's seemingly endless struggle over whether to stay in or leave her marriage to Peter, swirls around her realization that she had left the man with whom she was in love ("and he with me"), a man with whom she got along "incredibly well," and married a man with whom she doesn't get along "on almost any level, but I'm sure that's part of the reason I picked him." On some level of consciousness, she knew what she was doing.

Speaking of Sam, Zoe says, "We have the same sense of humor, we had the same sort of humor, I don't know if I should use present or past tense. We, uh, had very similar likes and dislikes, similar hobbies that we liked. . . . And we liked each other, we liked spending time together. Our families were very, very different." Different in religion, her family Catholic, his Jewish; his family intellectual, her family—"in many ways we had sort of the normal family, normal family weirdness being together, but fun. It was in many ways a typical family." For the moment, the "weirdness" remains unaddressed or, rather, is addressed in the context of Zoe's current relationships, her confusion about her situation.

Sam, like Oedipus, had a problem with his feet. He was born with a deformity that was subsequently corrected, but in the process he spent months in a cast, his legs held apart, his lower body immobilized. This left him with a nearly overwhelming sense of vulnerability when it came to sex. After struggling with this for some time with Zoe, he finally decided that he wanted to be celibate. Coming from a Catholic family where sex "was certainly not discussed and not a joyous activity," Zoe held back from taking the lead and also was moved by Sam's story, protective of his vulnerability.

The problem was that "I was definitely interested in having sex. I certainly wasn't going to be the one to initiate it or talk about it or to laugh about it or anything like that. And he had a really hard time sort of figuring out what he wanted and coping with his own desires and, in my guess, was fairly judgmental about his fantasies or about his thinking about sex, his feelings about sex. We used to have enormous fights about sex, which was the only thing we would have fights about, really the only thing."

When Zoe moved to Palo Alto to begin her graduate studies at Stanford, she just decided that "if I didn't have sex, I was going to go crazy. It gave me an insight into what it must be like for a teenage boy. I felt there was just this biological imperative. . . . I thought I was going to explode, and I'd never felt that way. It was very funny. . . . I clearly didn't feel that strongly when I was with Sam, because he probably would have welcomed this rapacious female."

Although at the time I don't pick up this comment, listening now to the "I" in this sentence—the way Zoe enters the first person—I hear implicitly the question that was forming in my mind as I listened to her:

> *I thought*
> *I was*
> *I'd never felt*
> *I clearly didn't feel*
>
> *[I was] this rapacious female.*

Behind her impassive surface, Zoe is a passionately sensual and sexual as well as a highly intelligent and scrupulously honest woman. The "I poem" answers the question of why she had not acted on her feelings: if she felt the intensity of her own desire, she would become "this rapacious female."

Initially, when Zoe moved to Palo Alto, she and Sam were

planning to stay together, although they weren't sure. Sam was concentrating on building up his legal practice in preparation for moving, should Zoe decide to continue her studies. He more than she was leaning toward continuing the marriage. But by Christmastime, Zoe had decided that she "was going to, uh, have an affair with somebody." There was nobody in the picture at that time; she wanted to tell Sam before she acted and not betray or lie to him about what she was doing. She went back over Christmas to tell him, and then they officially separated.

Zoe returned to Palo Alto, and the next day she called Peter. "Thinking about you," she said, and he "pulled up to Palo Alto and we started having an affair, which was not very satisfying sexually or emotionally, and here I am."

"So, Zoe," I say, "what's your question?"

She begins to talk about her research, which is on the subject of knowing. It leads her back to her marriage with Sam: "He was such a good friend and yet, enormous joy together and clearly I didn't see it.

"You asked me how I knew," she continues, "how I knew that I was in love with Sam and he was in love with me? In the way that you're absolutely certain of things. I knew."

"And with Peter?"

"I had such a strong gut sense of unease, dis-ease, which is sort of interesting, because I'm sick a lot more now than I was. . . . Most of the time that we have conversations I have a very basic-level sense of sort of unease, needing to sort of defend myself. . . . It's almost a visceral sense of unease."

Zoe's mask of detachment serves to keep her from knowing what otherwise becomes unbearably obvious. She remembers that when Peter proposed, "my first thought was 'Oh no.'" Her second thought was "I can't say no and hurt this man."

The reluctance to hurt has traditionally been seen as the mark of the good woman. It is the essence of moral sensibility, an awareness of human vulnerability. But Zoe is living within cultures, both religious and secular, that have led women to experience their own desires as rapacious—wounding to others, like an act of violence. Consequently, she buried her desires. With Sam, she tried to bury her sexuality, keeping it hidden within herself.

In an early short story, "An Unwritten Novel," Virginia Woolf addresses this buried self. "When the self speaks to the self, who is speaking?" the narrator asks, and then answers: "The entombed soul, the spirit driven in, in, in to the central catacomb; the self that took the veil, and left the world—a coward perhaps, yet somehow beautiful as it flits with its lantern restlessly up and down the dark corridors."

In "The Fullness of Life," an early story, Edith Wharton draws an extended simile:

> I have sometimes thought that a woman's nature is like a great house full of rooms: there is the hall, through which everyone passes in going in and out; the drawing room where one receives formal visits; the sitting room where the members of the family come and go as they list; but beyond that, far beyond, are other rooms the handles of whose doors are never turned; no one knows the way to them, no one knows whither they lead; and in the innermost room, the holy of holies, the soul sits alone and waits for a footstep that never comes.

Within the great house of civilization, the woman's soul seeks sanctuary within her own nature. As she sits alone listening "for a footstep that never comes," she discovers that no one has noticed her absence, no one has followed her.

Wharton finds the voice of this early story troubling. Writing to her editor, she explains her wish not to include it in her first published collection: "As to the old stories of which you speak so kindly, I regard them as the excesses of youth. They were all written 'at the top of my voice.' . . . I may not write any better, but at least I hope that I can write in a lower key, and I fear that the voice of those early tales will drown all the others. It is for that reason that I prefer not to publish them." "'The Fullness of Life,'" she says, "is one long shriek."

This adaptation on the part of women—taking the veil, leaving the world, retreating to an innermost room—allows the world they could not live in to continue. A move impelled by a desire for change becomes in this sense an act of futility, like a tragic love story. Wharton returns repeatedly to this theme in her novels, creating women characters who resist "the deadening process of forming a 'lady,'" and exploring the potential for transformation. In *Summer*, her rewriting of the Psyche and Cupid myth, the lovers—Charity (a dark girl from "the Mountain") and Lucius (the golden ass)—follow the path of resistance laid down in the ancient tale, up to a point. "How I hate everything," Charity begins, echoing the voice of Psyche in naming the "prison-house" of her existence. Her love affair with Lucius, told as a story of nature, breaks societal conventions, awakening her desire, which blossoms into a fully sensual, sexual womanhood, and freeing his manhood to find expression in an openhearted and tender love. When Lucius returns to the city and Charity, pregnant (with Pleasure, we assume), discovers that he is engaged to the blond and blue-eyed Annabel Balch, the promise of transformation is held in abeyance, remaining a dream, a possibility perhaps for the next generation as Charity decides on her own to have the child and to marry her adoptive father, the lawyer Royall.

I have set my book in the time of the present, in the years following the civil rights movement, the anti-war movement, and the women's and gay liberation movements that swept through America in the twentieth century, precipitating a series of radical changes, so that by the end of the century a war resister was elected president and most families no longer fit the model of the nuclear family, the family that Zoe calls "typical." Collectively, we are stepping out of an old frame, and the volatility of this moment in history arises from the sense of vulnerability: suddenly finding ourselves without a frame. Nothing to separate us, make us stand out, even elevate us. The old story beckons as new ones are written. It is not possible to talk about pleasure without talking about trauma, the shock that drains the capacity for joy; just as it is not possible to talk about trauma without talking about pleasure, the way life returns even in the face of the most terrible adversity, like a plant pushing its way through the sidewalk. And herein lies the center of Zoe's confusion: the "weirdness" she brushed off as "normal" in her family.

Zoe is the articulate knower who brought the question of trauma into my study of pleasure—not in its extreme manifestations but as part of a seemingly ordinary story. When she couldn't say no to Peter's proposal, she relied on her parents to stop her from entering into a marriage that was in all senses an act of abandonment—most deeply, Zoe's abandonment of herself. In one sense, Peter seemed the ideal husband. Like Zoe, he was Catholic; his father too was a rancher; their families lived in the same part of the West. Zoe's fantasy reflects the child's wish to be known and loved by her parents; she hoped her parents "would know me well enough and they would say no, this is not going to work out. . . . In my fantasies, they would save me from marrying him." Save her from abandoning herself.

Zoe suspects that she chose Peter because she felt guilty; "picking somebody so awful for me was my way of atoning." For wanting pleasure, for freeing herself. "There wasn't very much denial of what I knew; maybe I was denying how much I knew, but I had a deep-down feeling, a very gut-level sense, that Peter was wrong for me from the first morning after he drove up and we spent the night together, and that next morning, I can remember where we were sitting, and I just had the sense that I really didn't like this guy, and that's never changed. I've seen aspects of him that I appreciate a lot more than I did then; he can be very kind, and there are other aspects that I've grown to appreciate, but not anything close to the sort of spiritual kinship that I know I had with Sam and that I know is possible and that I think is important in life."

She wonders to what extent the problems she and Peter are having are her own "baggage," things "that I need to work on so that I will be better off, that I will be a better mother for having worked out, and that might give Peter and me a chance. So how much is that, and how much are things that have to do more with the relationship and that I can leave."

Can she leave? She knows that a divorce would be acrimonious; "Peter feels he's really been taken advantage of," and he would be "losing a lot of contact with the children." They both have "really strong feelings" about the children, who are young and vulnerable.

On the other hand, she says, "it might be better." I ask why she thinks this, and she explains, "It's better because it gives us all a capacity to really live life, to be joyful." "You know," she explains, "that's probably my most important job as a parent, certainly one of my most important jobs, to not lock my children into a life where that doesn't happen."

Choose life, for the children. The old terms are breaking down: pleasure versus duty, freedom versus the family. To free the children "to really live life" means freeing herself and Peter "to be joyful."

The clarity of this thought sends her back into confusion. The "I poem" from a long, convoluted passage captures the essence of Zoe's struggle:

> *I'm stuck*
> *I had been digging*
> *I'm not certain*
> *I don't know.*

I'm not certain
I don't think
I can
I know.

I'm not certain
I'm not certain
I don't know.

In counseling, she and Peter have decided for the moment to put the decision on hold so that they can learn to get along better or at least learn how to talk with each other in the ways they will need to if they are to divorce, to minimize the hurt to their children.

But Zoe is skeptical of this endeavor. Like Anna in *Private Confessions,* she has a history of throwing away pleasure, overriding her own sense of truth with what others call the truth. While Peter is "very committed to staying married," Zoe has no sense that he knows about joy, or at least not what she means by joy. "When I've tried to talk about it, I get a real, a real fog. There's a fog between us that feels like we have separate vocabularies."

Joy for Zoe is something that comes and goes through a fog—the weather of dissociation. She speaks of her mother as a woman with "an enormous capacity for joy," but then says, "I feel very conflicted about that. More of my memories of my mother are bad ones rather than good ones." Her memories of her mother as joyful are completely dissociated from their relationship; or, rather, the connection between them, their shared capacity for joy, is held by an image of pleasure that they both know but experience separately.

Possessing the Secret of Joy is the title of Alice Walker's novel about female genital mutilation. In *Working with Available Light,* written by Jamie Kalven after his wife, Patricia Evans, was violently assaulted and raped, the loss of pleasure is at the center of "a family's world after violence." The title comes from photography, Evans' work, and her eye is evident throughout the book. In a conversation she initiates with her husband in the second year after she was attacked, she speaks of what she knows and what she is still trying to sort out. "I'm in terrible shape. . . . I feel like there are a thousand broken pieces inside me. I feel so isolated. I can't talk to others. I don't *want* to talk to others. It's gone on for too long, I hate myself for feeling this way. So weak." She had been depressed before; she had had problems with sex; but this was different. "What I *do* know, what *is* different, is the loss of pleasure—never being able to experience anything with genuine relaxation or pleasure." Her voice—the voice of a white woman—resonates with the voices recorded by Charlotte Pierce-Baker in *Surviving the Silence: Black Women's Stories of Rape*; the loss of pleasure is everywhere in its pages. As Kalven joins his voice with those of his wife and other women who have become experts on the subject of rape; as Pierce-Baker joins her experience of rape with the experiences of other black women and with the voices of black men, including her husband, an old conversation that pits men against women, women against men, blacks against whites, gives way to a joining that addresses the source of the problem.

Kalven tells a story that he heard from a friend, the eminent professor A. K. Ramanujan—a poet, translator, and scholar at the University of Chicago, known to his friends as Raman. He was working on Indian folk tales at the time, collecting stories that change form, and had become particularly interested in "exploring the counterrealm of what he calls 'women-centered tales.'" Tales where men are the protagonists often end with a marriage, whereas women-centered tales "frequently start with a marriage. That's when the woman's troubles begin. For example, she must domesticate an animal husband or contend with the cruelties of her husband's family. The resolution of such tales, he says, often turns on the woman telling her story and being heard." Like Psyche and Cupid.

IT IS THE STORY of a daughter that catches Kalven's attention and my own; it is a story about transformation and also about pleasure and creativity; it is about "the question of when a woman is safe." In the story, a poor woman has two daughters; at puberty, the younger daughter tells her older sister that she will turn herself into a flowering tree. The sister can pick the flowers, and they will sell them to make money for their mother. Her sister is to go the well and bring two pitchers of water. "You pour the water from the first pitcher all over my body. I'll turn into a flowering tree. Pluck as many flowers as you want, but take care not to break a sprout or tear a leaf. When you're finished, pour the water from the other pitcher over me and I'll become a person again."

The king's son learns of the young woman's remarkable ability; he marries her and bullies her into turning herself into a tree for him. He learns how to pour the water, and they sleep on a bed of flowers. When his younger sister wants to see how this happens, she assembles her friends and forces her sister-in-law to show them. But they are careless, pouring the water haphazardly and breaking the sprouts and leaves of the tree. The flowering daughter turns into a wounded carcass, losing her hands and her feet. She is found in the gutter by a cart driver, who deposits "the thing with a beautiful face" on the outskirts of the town where the prince's older sister and her husband live. The women servants take her into the palace and persuade the queen to let them bathe her in oils, dress her, and care for her wounds. The prince, despairing over the loss of his wife, sinks into deep grief and becomes an ascetic. Wandering through the world, looking like a madman, he ends up outside his sister's palace. She has him brought in, recognizes his face, and instructs her servants to bathe him, clothe him in finery, and feed him good food. They bring him beautiful maids, but he refuses them. Finally, they bring "the thing" to him; he realizes that it is his wife.

"What shall we do now?" he asks. She tells him to get two pitchers of water, and now, "with great care and gentleness," he pours the water, turning her into a tree, sets the broken branches right, and mends the torn leaves. Then he pours the second pitcher over the tree. "And his wife stood before him, shaking the water from her hair."

To Kalven, this story was a great gift, "a fresh idiom, cast in images, for thinking about violence and healing, about creativity in general and sexuality in particular. One is most vulnerable, the story suggests, at the moment of greatest creativity, the moment of opening to the world, the moment of flowering. To offer one's special gift is to be exposed to danger and to be dependent on the care of others." Raman, his friend, observed that "girls in folktales are often described as being twelve years old. This is a way of saying the girl has reached puberty. He added that in Tamil and Sanskrit the word for 'menstruation' and the word for 'flowering' are the same." It is a feature of such women-centered tales that "a woman's agency—her capacity to act—is bound up with her recovery of her voice, with her telling her story and having it heard. The story of the healing of a woman is thus often also the story of the education, by way of loss and grief, of a husband." Evans, Kalven's wife, observes that part of the logic of the story is that "you could avoid harm by shutting down." It is also part of the logic of the story, Raman explains, "that the violated woman—the ravaged half-human thing—can only be healed by becoming a tree again, by becoming vulnerable and flowering again, by trusting another to mend her broken branches." He thought it was a mistake to focus too narrowly on the violence of men against women. "The violence that occurs in families takes various forms. We should focus on the violence adults do to children, the violence the strong do to the weak."

Zoe witnessed violence in her family; she speaks first about the humiliation she suffered at the hands of her siblings, who would tease her for finding pleasure in reading, so that she learned to cover her pleasure. She associates this with her fears of "combining sex with being really intimate." I ask her how old she was at the time, and she remembers that it was at the farmhouse, "this house on the road that we lived in from when I was nine. I don't remember a lot of stuff before then," she says, and then she remembers, walking the edge of dissociation:

> What I remember before then is physical abuse by my parents, all of my siblings and me, but I think my oldest brother Zach . . . My parents called it spanking, but it was really all with a belt, repeatedly, it was very vicious beating. It wasn't spanking, it was beating. It's funny to have those images be much more dominating in my mind than joyous images, but I'm also very clear that my mother had this capacity for joy.

In her mind, she holds the image of her mother in the bathtub: "I'm pretty sure I never saw her in the bathtub, but we've talked about this, so I guess that's why." The pleasure in water is a pleasure they share, but not when they are together.

> We both lay on our bellies in the bathtub and play with little boats. She loved it. She floats around and blows bubbles and we both did that and now my daughter . . . And I can picture my mother in the bathtub on her stomach, just sort of laying and having fun and then turning upside down and even submerging herself, and

then you come up and you can sort of float, and it feels like, not really like you're swimming, but enough like you're swimming that you can play with that whole experience of being in the water, buoyant. I loved that.

A simple joy. Like Zoe's joy in being in the ocean, "the whole sensory experience of being underwater and having fish come up to you with colors . . . My mother, she had that, she's very simple because joys are very simple." It is something they share, "the joy of being alive and aware, aware of the colors in the sky."

How to reconcile this image of her mother as a joyful woman with her memories of her mother taking part in the beatings or watching them? Zoe remembers being "terrorized" when her parents beat her younger brother Paul:

It was worse than being actually hit myself, because I could hear him crying and it was awful. I remember hiding out. I remember that as much more the dominant atmosphere in our house than joyousness. My mother had joy, but it was, maybe it was a separate thing like it was for me. . . . So maybe I witnessed [joy] and learned this was something you do separate from this other thing, they could coexist.

As Zoe circles around her mother and her memories of a joy she heard about but did not witness, she describes her father "as a thinker who is completely uneducated and did not ever show much capacity for joy. . . . I think his main joy is being with—his biggest joy, I was going to say pleasure, is being with my mother, because she's such a vibrant light."

Zoe explains that the photographs of her mother, "up to when we were mid to late teens, were of this beautiful, very young, blond athletic horsewoman." Images of her mother as joyful and a vibrant light, and a visceral sense of being terrorized. A picture of "the normal family, normal family weirdness being together, but fun . . . a typical family," and memories of very vicious beatings. How to associate these images of her mother and family life with her memories of what actually happened?

The dissociation between image and memory, between the look of things and the feeling of what happens, holds two worlds in place simultaneously: what you know and what you really know, what you feel and what you really feel, the story you tell about yourself and the experience of what happened. I have been following the voice of pleasure, and it has led me into a discussion of trauma. Babies in the infant studies are not taken in by false images of relationship. I heard young boys tracking the human weather, differentiating happiness and anxiety, fear and anger. But it was with girls that I saw most deeply into how the ability to trust one's experience can be systematically undermined and, at the extremes, broken as an inner compass gives way to an outer reading that is at once adaptive and misleading.

The undermining of trust that I observed among girls was subtle. The very strategies they had used so effectively in naming and repairing breaks in relationship (with parents and teachers, friends and siblings) began to undermine their relationships. To say what was happening often made things worse. "I called my mother up and said 'Why can't I talk to you?' and she hung up on me." "I went up to my friends and said, 'Why are you angry at me?' and it only made them madder." Thus girls learn not to talk about the breaks in their relationships and to cover their anger and hurt or puzzlement. Sita, who picks up her friends' anger at her, feigns ignorance and says to them innocently, "So hi, what's up?" At adolescence, girls learn a new language of pleasure, a new vocabulary of the body. They often carry with them into adolescence a knowingness about love that serves as a compass, an invaluable guide at a time when relationships are rapidly changing.

When Proust found that the taste of a madeleine brought back a lost world of childhood, he discovered that it is through sensory experience that we recapture the past, opening "the vast storehouse of recollection." Because we have the capacity to examine the relationship between our experience and the images or stories we carry with us, the psyche is able to free itself from captivity, or at least to reopen a gap that has closed. For Zoe, pleasure becomes the marker of loss, the dye that floats on the surface of grief.

As Zoe pieces together the images of her family with memories whose trace was a feeling of weirdness and a dissociated sense of joy, she thinks about grief. "I guess I want to try to think, I've been thinking that with Sam it's filled with grief, because I'm keenly aware of an enormous loss." To know her sense of loss is "to know what I know." Like many people, she had put loss "in a box." Now her question for herself is "What happens if you feel the enormous loss, what can't I know about it?"

"I think you do know about it," I say.

Zoe continues, "I have not let myself be really upset over losing Sam." I think of the phrase "careless with joy." She says, "I thought that I wouldn't really lose it, that I would be able to find other ways to do it." And in many ways, she had: with her children, in her work, with meditation and with friends— up to a point. "So grieving is related to knowing, then," she says, knowing pleasure without dissociation.

We are back to the story of Adam and Eve. A story held up as a cautionary tale about sin and punishment and curses. But it is also a story that reveals the tension between knowing pleasure and living in patriarchy. When Eve eats the fruit of the tree of knowledge, good and evil, she knows the good as well as evil. *Eitz ha'daat, tov v'ra*—tree of knowledge, good and evil. The Hebrew word *daat* means embodied knowledge, the knowledge that comes through experience, what you know in your bones, in your gut, by heart. When Eve eats from the tree of knowledge, she knows what she knows: her life in the garden with Adam. In the beginning, Eve knows pleasure and love. And the first thing she does is to give the fruit to Adam, so that he will know too.

It is when Adam has eaten that the story of shame and hiding begins. Adam and Eve know that they are naked; they see their vulnerability and feel afraid. God comes into the garden calling for Adam: "Where are you?" Adam says that he is hiding, ashamed of his nakedness, afraid of God. Adam blames Eve, and Eve blames the serpent. God punishes Adam and Eve by making them labor in sorrow, but God also punishes Eve by binding her desire to Adam's, so that from this time forth she will want only what he wants and know only what he knows ("Toward your husband will be your lust, yet he will rule over you"). But in the beginning, Eve and Adam know love, and for a brief moment, they know that they know it.

Read historically, the Garden of Eden story records the move into patriarchy; we see its hierarchy being established: God over Adam, Adam over Eve, the serpent at the bottom. It is a hierarchy secured by the prohibition against knowing what you know through experience, a prohibition that creates the need for a priesthood. In the beginning, in the opening of Genesis, God is *ruach*—a breath, a wind, a voice, a spirit that pervades the universe. God has no image, no body, no sex, no place in the human world of male and female. Once God becomes "He," *melech*—king of the universe, or Father—we know that we are in patriarchy.

In a recent feminist reading, the story of Adam and Eve becomes a story about the breaking of relationship. The original sin is not disobedience but Adam and Eve's covering themselves, hiding their desire and knowledge from God. I am intrigued by this reading, and it leads to the suggestion that the banishment from Eden occurs when it becomes impossible to repair the relationship. Once Adam and Eve have covered their desire and their knowledge, once they blame others for the actions they have taken, the way to repairing relationship is barred. Shame and blame become the two flaming swords that keep them from reentering the garden.

THE TIME is ending. I ask Zoe, "Have you let yourself grieve for losing joy?"

It's a sweet question and also a sad question, she says. "No. I think I said to myself that I wouldn't really lose that." And in fact, she hasn't lost it, but she has boxed it within herself, keeping it separate, and boxed herself in in the process.

IN MOMENTS of epiphany—moments of sudden, radical illumination—we see through the categories that have blinded our vision. These are the moments when we step out of a frame. The tale of Psyche and Cupid ends with the birth of a daughter named Pleasure. Her birth becomes a moment of epiphany when we read the myth as showing a way out of patriarchy, because a daughter holds the promise of transformation, and pleasure lies at its center. The essence of love is love, and love by its very nature is free. Freeing love means releasing it to find its own form. Like wind and water, love crosses borders and boundaries: when we fall in love, we fall into relationship and out of categories, because love is always particular. This person.

In telling the story of Psyche and Cupid, I am telling *a* story, not *the* story, and more specifically a story that shows a way out of the Oedipus tragedy, the quintessential story of patriarchy. It is in this sense a transitional tale, and I am writing at a moment in history when the tension between democracy and patriarchy has become explosive, the driving force of fundamentalism signaling the power of the threat. Freeing love means freeing the voice so it can carry the full range of emotion and the subtleties and nuances of thought; it imposes psychic equality in the sense of everyone's having a voice and feeling free to speak. To say this is to see the affinity between love and democracy; to see that love is the psychic grounding for a democratic society—not an idealized love, but the actual gritty pleasure of living in relationship.

I am zeroing in on the role of the daughter. Like trick pictures that at first glance appear to be a mass of lines and swirls, until you let your eyes go out of focus and then suddenly an image is revealed, patriarchy creates an optical illusion, focusing one's eyes in a way that makes it difficult to see its presence. To see patriarchy means to look at the world in a different way from the way we are taught to see it. Since culture is what we do not completely see, because it is the lens through which we are seeing, an outsider's eye is needed. To some extent, girls have this eye until adolescence, and, loving girls, we begin to see it.

But this insight, which is grounded in contemporary research, has a long history, dating back to Apuleius and the old wife's tale, going back further to Iphigenia and Eve, and brought forward into the heart of the present not only by feminists but also by Shakespeare. Once we unfocus our eyes and let go an accustomed way of seeing, we recognize that a path has been laid out in our midst. *A* path, not *the* path. If we mark the places where pleasure is buried and the seeds of tragedy are planted, then when we arrive at these places, we can take an alternate route.

APULEIUS' *Metamorphoses* was a prime source for Shakespeare, and most specifically the tale of Psyche and Cupid: the young woman who breaks taboos on seeing and speaking, who insists on having a voice and not becoming an object, and the daughter named Pleasure who holds a promise of transformation. These are familiar characters on the Shakespearean stage. The universality of Shakespeare's plays, their translation into a myriad of languages, their appreciation across a vast range of cultures, as well as their growing popularity at the present time, suggest that they are tapping into what we have come to call the human condition and also showing the possibility of transformation, heightened in Shakespeare's time and also at the present moment.

Twelfth Night is Shakespeare's play about epiphany. Written for the night of epiphany in the Christian tradition—the night when the magi bring the news that the child born twelve days previously is the messiah—it is a celebration of light in darkness: the light of revelation and also the light that returns with the turn of the seasons. The messiah, so to speak, is Viola, a girl on the edge of womanhood, a twin rescued from a shipwreck in which she fears her brother has drowned. Her name is the name of a musical instrument, and her voice becomes the instrument of love.

"If music be the food of love, play on," the lovesick duke begins in the opening scene of the play, and as the music continues, he speaks of love's appetite filling and waning, love's spirit fresh and then stale, love's passion rising and falling, and finally of his love for Olivia, who will not admit him to her presence. Following the deaths of her father and brother, she has become the head of her household; cloistering herself in a seven-year mourning, she abjures the company and the sight of men. Her removal and perhaps her position of power only fuel the duke's desire. He is the ultimate romantic, consumed with "love-thoughts," in love with an image of his beloved, a man sick with love, though his love, we notice, is preoccupied with loss.

In the second scene, Viola enters. Arriving on the coast of Illyria, she asks the sailors who are with her, "What country, friends, is this?" and then "What should I do in Illyria?" A girl arriving at womanhood, she has landed in the country of romantic legend, the land of the "noble duke" and the "virtuous maid." Viola would prefer to serve the lady and be not "delivered to the world" until she knows her estate. But since Olivia will receive no petitions, Viola sets out instead to serve the duke—which she can do only by disguising herself as a boy. Dressing as Cesario and presenting herself as a eunuch, a man with a woman's voice, she qualifies for the duke's service because she "can sing/ And speak to him in many sorts of music." Thus Viola/Cesario becomes Orsino's messenger, and more specifically, the voice of his love, its composer and also its instrument. Ironically, Viola falls in love with Orsino while Olivia falls in love with Cesario. In the midst of this tangle of age and gender—the coordinates of a patriarchal order—Viola/Cesario teaches Orsino and Olivia truths about love.

She is the daughter named Pleasure; we have seen her everywhere—in Euripides' Athens, in Harriet Jacobs' fugitive-slave narrative, in an attic in Amsterdam, in Antigua, Jamaica, in endless films and novels, her face arresting in its steady gaze, her honest voice unmistakable, Iphigenia speaking to Agamemnon, Psyche speaking to her parents, Anne Frank writing her diary, Claudia in *The Bluest Eye*—girls speaking about love and pleasure, taking the pulse of relationships in stories and poems, families and schools. On the face of it, it seems incredible: what do girls know about love? It is common knowledge, and then not.

For Shakespeare, for anyone living in patriarchy, the way in which love is gendered is deeply problematic. The natural difference of sex supports the imposition of a seemingly natural imagery of love: male and female, hunter and prey, king and subject, lover and beloved. Until we realize that there is nothing natural to this human order: it is patriarchy masquerading as nature—it is the enemy of love. This is the epiphany of *Twelfth Night,* the radical light in this dark comedy: if patriarchy is antithetical to love, then love holds the potential to uproot patriarchy. The key has to do with loss.

Romantic love feeds on loss; it relies on absence to create the space for fantasy—an image of the beloved replacing the reality, thus setting the stage for tragedy. Shakespeare's comedies unmask this tragedy by revealing its origins in not knowing, self-deception, and folly. But the deeper insight lies in the revelation that if it is a woman who has been lost, then only a woman can change the story. Since her actual presence would revivify the loss, arousing feelings that threaten to become overwhelming, she must appear not as a woman but as a girl dressed as a boy. Thus Viola presents herself as Cesario, the little Cesar, claiming authority and the protection of power where otherwise she has no estate. But she is also in the poetic license of the play an identical twin, indistinguishable from her brother Sebastian: "One face, one voice, one habit and two persons, / a natural perspective, that is and is not!"

This sums up the riddle of love: it has one face, one voice, one habit and two persons. It is the riddle of relationship—a natural perspective that is and is not. Love dispels a naturally occurring optical illusion, overriding the visual separation of persons, revealing a connection that both is and is not. One face, one voice, one habit, and two persons. In contrast, the world of tragedy is a one-person world: Hamlet, Macbeth, Othello, Lear. The women who love and are loved by these tragic heroes go mad (Ophelia), unsex themselves (Lady Macbeth), are strangled (Desdemona), say nothing (Cordelia). In *Romeo and Juliet* and *Antony and Cleopatra* we see the forces arrayed against love in the ongoing battle of Montague versus Capulet, Rome versus Egypt.

Perched on the edge of tragedy, *Twelfth Night*, the last night of celebration, is a lesson in love, composed by Shakespeare and orchestrated by Viola. Arriving on the coast of Illyria at the time of her own adolescence—before the customs of that country have become her own—she speaks from the heart, says what she sees, keeps silent where she must, puts out riddles that are notoriously overlooked, and becomes the voice of emotional truth. As such, she is irresistible. To her, Orsino and Olivia open their hearts. "Thou know'st no less but all," the duke tells her; "I have unclasped / To thee the book even of my secret soul." Olivia takes the veil away from her face, including the veil of her beauty, to show a less perfect, more human countenance—her love, her fears, her desire, her vulnerability. "What might you think?" she asks Viola/Cesario, wanting to hear her "unmuzzled thoughts." "Let me hear you speak . . . prithee tell me what thou think'st of me." And Viola tells the truth.

This is the essence of her lesson in love: loving means knowing, it means opening your gates. Unrequited love makes no sense, because there is no connection with the other person. How can love be love and leave the other unmoved? Viola/Cesario tells Olivia, "If I did love you in my master's flame . . . In your denial I would find no sense, / I would not understand it." When Olivia asks her, "Why, what would you?" Viola tells her:

> Make me a willow cabin at your gate
> And call upon my soul within the house,
> Write loyal cantons of contemned love
> And sing them loud even in the dead of night,
> Hallow your name to the reverberate hills
> And make the babbling gossip of the air
> Cry out "Olivia!"

As the string of verbs makes clear (call . . . write . . . sing . . . hallow . . . cry out), voice is the instrument of her love, carrying her soul through Olivia's gates until it resides within her house, shouting Olivia's name to the reverberate hills until the world resounds her presence.

With Orsino, Viola/Cesario breaks through the walls of his self-enclosure by revealing to him what he does not know. He is comparing women's love with that of men, who are more constant, who more skittish, whose love is stronger, more capacious, less likely to suffer "surfeit, cloyment and revolt." Swerving in and out of contradiction, Orsino ends with an insult that reveals his ignorance. "Make no compare," he says to Cesario, "Between that love a woman can bear me / And that I owe Olivia."

"But I know," she says. She knows "too well what love women to men may owe," and then, covering her tracks, Cesario explains, "My father had a daughter lov'd a man / As it might be / perhaps, were I a woman, / I should your Lordship." Now the duke is curious. "And what's her history?"

> *A blank, my lord; she never told her love,*
> *But let concealment, like a worm i' the bud*
> *Feed on her damask cheek; she pin'd in thought,*
> *And with green and yellow melancholy*
> *She sat like Patience on a monument,*
> *Smiling at grief.*

"I am all the daughters of my father's house," she tells him, "and all the brothers too—" But when the duke does not pick up on what she is saying, she recedes into silence ("and yet I know not"), offering "Sir, shall I to this lady?" And he answers, "Ay, that's the theme."

In the long final scene of the play, when Olivia, having married Sebastian, whom she mistakes for Cesario, finally comes face-to-face with the duke and discovers that Cesario, whom she mistakes for her husband, is in love with Orsino, the confusion of sex and identity reaches full pitch and threatens to explode into tragedy. Publicly shamed by Olivia's rejection, Orsino goes into a rage. He threatens to kill her, or even better, to sacrifice Cesario, "whom I know you love." But

Cesario is the light of his life as well, "the lamb that I do love." Inching toward the imagery of Othello ("Put out the light, and then put out the light"), Orsino speaks about sacrificing Cesario "to spite a raven's heart within a dove," and Viola anticipates Desdemona in suddenly proclaiming her willingness to die for love. But *Twelfth Night* veers back into comedy with the epiphany of the twins.

With nature providing the solution to the otherwise insoluble riddle—how to untie the patriarchal knot—-the liberated Olivia marries the man/girl she loves, while the lovesick duke will marry his boy/woman. On close inspection, we see the grounds of patriarchy eroding: Olivia has married a younger man, who will not seek to mold her to himself, whose affection is "more likely to hold the bent," while Orisino will wed his saucy page, his little Cesar who loves him, who "hast said to me a thousand times / Thou never should'st love woman like to me." We notice the duke delaying to the last possible moment risking his love for a fantasy love by changing Cesario's name to Viola: "Cesario, come— / For so you shall be while you are a man; / But when in other habits you are seen, / Orsino's mistress, and his fancy's queen." Mothers, strikingly absent from this play about families, are still not mentioned, but Olivia now says to Viola, "A sister! You are she."

Twelfth Night has been called a dark comedy; like lights in winter, it offers a respite. Love is an epiphany, a moment of sudden, radical illumination. Yet Malvolio—ill will—runs off at the end; humiliated, seeking vengeance, he is loose in the world. Feste, the fool, ends the play by singing a song about manhood. The song traces the life of a man from when he was but "a little tiny boy . . . and a foolish thing was but a toy," to the time when he "came to man's estate . . . [and] 'gainst knaves and thieves men shut their gate," to when he "came, alas, to wive" and found that "by swaggering could I never thrive." The song's refrain—"With a hey ho, the wind and the rain / For the rain it raineth every day"—holds the possibility, held out in the play, that love can weather the storms of change.

WITH THE epiphany of *Twelfth Night,* Shakespeare plunges into the world of tragedy. Manhood becomes the central theme. *Hamlet* is written around the same time; *Othello, Macbeth,* and *King Lear* follow in rapid succession In all of these tragedies, the heroes are men who resist patriarchy; their heroism lies in their resistance, the tragedy is they are chewed up in the process. Hamlet resists avenging his father's murder, Othello resists placing honor over honesty, Macbeth resists the promptings of "vaulting ambition," and Lear moves to give away his kingdom. This resistance meets such force of opposition, putting their manhood on the line, that Hamlet, a sensitive poet, becomes a killer; Othello, a man of music and stories, sacrifices Desdemona for the sake of honor; Macbeth, a man of loyalty and conscience, separates his eye from his hand and becomes one of the most terrifying murderers of the Shakespearean canon; and Lear, seeking love, banishes the daughter who loves him. In the classical form of tragedy, what is noblest in their character catches on the hook of fate; all these men go mad, and in their madness, they see into the structure in which they were caught.

How is it possible to see and not go mad; can a man be a man and not avenge his father's murder, and yet in becoming an avenger, he loses his humanity; can a man be a man and not seize power, and yet in seizing power at the expense of an older man, he loses his humanity; can a man live with a woman who is rumored to be with another man and still be a man, and yet when Othello gives up love for honor, he throws away "a pearl richer than all his tribe"; can a man be a man and give away his power to his daughters—the lesson in *Lear* is that to invite love, it is necessary also to know love, and both fathers in *King Lear* are blinded.

The women who love these tragic heroes illuminate the tragedy. Before she goes mad, Ophelia says, "O, woe is me / T' have seen what I have seen, see what I see." In her madness, in songs and riddles, she will tell the truth about the goings-on at court. In the scene before Othello suffocates her, Desdemona sings the willow song; it was sung by her mother's maid Barbary, and it tells the story of a woman who loved a man who went mad and killed her. Desdemona sings but she does not listen, as she will shut the door on Emilia, her maid, who offers to tell her what she needs to know about men and marriage in order to protect herself. Lady Macbeth, in her madness, illuminates the impossibility of erasing one's actions; she cannot wash the blood off her hands. And Cordelia in *Lear*, in saying nothing, in refusing to make false promises of love or vie with her sisters for her father's kingdom, reveals the true nature of love. All these women die, and when Gertrude, Hamlet's mother, offers a detailed description of Ophelia's drowning, we are left with the impression that she has watched her drown, without lifting a hand to save her.

The depths of human suffering and the brilliance of Shakespeare's insights into what has become the human condition drive his poetry to a pitch of passion and beauty that sustains us so that we can stay in the presence of emotions and thoughts that are otherwise unbearable. Shakespeare shows us the tragedy and makes it possible for us to take in the dimensions of the trauma both men and women suffer when manhood stands in the way of humanity. The power of the tragedies, their greatness, lies in allowing us to see the tragedy and also to see beyond it.

The ending of *King Lear* is a requiem for patriarchy. Spoken by Edgar, Gloucester's loyal son, or in the quarto version by Albany, Lear's son-in-law who steps out of the battle for succession, it is a younger man's tribute to the fathers whose insight has been gained through so much suffering:

The weight of this sad time we must obey,
Speak what we feel, not what we ought to say:
The oldest hath borne most; we that are young
Shall never see so much nor live so long.

There is no talk of restoration, no mention of honor; instead, we hear about sadness; speaking what we feel takes precedence over saying what we ought to say, and the suffering of fathers, the insights they have come to, become part of a history that is ending. In the fourth act, a gentleman reminded Lear, "Thou hast one daughter / Who redeems nature from the general curse / which twain have brought her to," and this potential for redemption becomes the subject of Shakespeare's romance plays.

Set on disant islands or in fairy-tale kingdoms, they are filled with daughters: Miranda in *The Tempest,* Marina in *Pericles,* Imogen in *Cymbeline,* and Perdita in *The Winter's Tale.* The plays dramatize the possibility of repairing relationships that seem irrevocably severed. Perdita's name means "loss," and in *The Winter's Tale,* Paulina tells the mad king Leontes, who had set his daughter on a hillside to die, that what has been lost must be found.

At the present moment in history, the possibility of repairing long-standing ruptures in relationships between people and between nations is in our midst. The birth of pleasure vies with the repetition of tragedy. And it is the very volatility of this moment that leads me to retrace a history of finding and then losing and then finding again an old map of love now joined by contemporary psychological wisdom. More specifically, I have read the Psyche and Cupid myth as showing a way out of the Oedipus tragedy, and the tension between these two myths, the way in which one eclipses the other, offers us a way of locating our position in the historic struggle to end the contradiction between democracy and patriarchy.

AT THE END of the nineteenth century, Psyche comes for psychoanalysis. In a relatively short time, the human psyche opens to a remarkable investigation. Insights into the human condition carried by folk tales and writers across the centuries begin to gain a footing in science, so that we see not only what happens or how it happens, but also why it happens over and over again. Freud is at the center of this story, and it is his relationships with women that provide the opening.

Psyche, the young woman who became an object, who was barred from seeing or speaking about love, stands at the center of *Studies on Hysteria*. In a rush of discovery, Josef Breuer and Freud, its co-authors, uncover the profound connection between our minds and our bodies by tracing the conversion of psychic pain into physical pain; they describe the process of dissociation, the splitting of the mind so that parts of our experience become absent from our consciousness; and in their treatment of hysterical young women, they discover the power of relationship, the way in which association heals dissociation, the power of the talking or listening cure. They have discovered the power of a confiding relationship.

We see how quickly these discoveries become fraught. Freud referred to his early women patients as his teachers, and what they taught him gave him an insight not only into the workings of the psyche but also into the connection between inner and outer worlds, the psyche and the culture in which it is living. The implicit relational knowing of the human infant becomes the knowing that is carried by hysterical symptoms, and in the course of these early forays into psychoanalysis, it becomes the explicit relational knowing of young women and also of their physicians. We begin to see the drama of the

Grand Inquisitor played out in this psychological arena, the tension that arises with the possibility of freedom.

It was the separation of women from their own stories that initially caught Breuer and Freud's eye; "her love had already become separated from her knowledge," Freud writes in the case history of the woman he calls Fräulein Elisabeth von R. Since women's love is connected to men's, the seeming conflict between love and knowledge that becomes the center of this psychological case history also raises a series of larger questions: Is it possible to know and also to love? Is it possible to love and also not know? It is the tension between tragedy and comedy, loss and pleasure.

In connecting women with their own knowledge, Freud became a virtual Eve or, more accurately, the serpent in the garden. He was breaking a cultural taboo, undoing a process of initiation by forging a method of inquiry that placed him in direct opposition to the fundamental rule of patriarchy: the claim on the part of fathers to authority.

I am reading from the case of Ilona Weiss (Elisabeth von R.), from the passage near the beginning where Freud describes the difficulty of the journey he was undertaking. Elisabeth, a young woman of twenty-four, had been referred to him for treatment of the pains in her legs, which made it difficult for her to walk. The referring physician suspected that her symptoms were hysterical in origin, and Freud's impression confirmed this suspicion, along with the failure of neurological treatment. When he proposed psychic treatment to Elisabeth, he was met with "quick understanding and little resistance." He writes:

> The task on which I now embarked turned out, however, to be one of the hardest that I had ever undertaken. . . . For a long time, too, I was unable to grasp the connection between the events in her illness and her

actual symptom. . . . When one starts upon a cathartic treatment of this kind, the first question one asks oneself is whether the patient herself is aware of the origin and the precipitating cause of her illness. If so, no special technique is required to enable her to reproduce the story of her illness.

From the beginning, Freud has the impression that Elisabeth's "mask reveals a hidden sense." At first he considers her knowledge a secret that she was withholding from him rather than a "foreign body" within herself, but this formulation yields to revision as he comes upon the signs of dissociation: gaps in memory, points at which "some train of thought remained obscure or some link in the causal chain seemed to be missing." He realizes that Elisabeth herself has become separated from her knowledge. It is at this point that Freud turns his attention to method. Some special procedure was required in order to repair this dissociation, which was held at an unconscious level rather than in conscious awareness.

Pierre Janet had relied on hypnosis to unlock the dissociation of trauma; Breuer's way was made easy by Anna O's ability to sink into periods of "absence," thus essentially hypnotizing herself. Freud, never good at hypnosis and facing a patient whose *"belle indifférence"* reflected a wait-and-see attitude, decided on a more straightforward approach. His "special technique" was to press his hand on his patient's forehead at those moments when she fell into silence or claimed not to know her thoughts and feelings, and to suggest that in fact she knew. Thus Freud discovered that Elisabeth's love had become separated from her knowledge, and in reconnecting them, he also came to know what she knew.

Freeing women to see and to speak about love, he was using his picklock, his psychoanalytic method, to unlock one of the deep secrets of patriarchy: what daughters know about their fathers, including the secret of father-daughter incest.

Trauma, seen by Janet and others to be the bedrock of hysteria, became in Freud's understanding a sexual trauma, a traumatizing of love that leads the psyche to disassociate itself from the body, which then becomes the repository of experiences that cannot be known or spoken.

As Freud discovered the power of association to undo dissociation—the associative stream of consciousness and also the touch of relationship—the psyche opened to his investigation. In short order, he learned the indirect discourse of symptoms, and this language led him to understand the mechanism of conversion, how psychic pain becomes physical pain; he discovered the symbolic nature of human consciousness, the power of resistance, and also the power of voice to bring dissociated parts of the self back into relationship.

THE DIFFICULTY Freud faced in his early work lay in relinquishing the voice of the father; as a physician he had a claim to authority, and yet his method depended on giving up this claim. His authority lay in knowing a way—a method that could unlock his patient's dissociation. Knowing the way but not the endpoint of the journey. In a stunning moment with Elisabeth, when she breaks off her stream of consciousness, declaring that nothing has occurred to her, Freud decides to proceed as though he is convinced that his method never fails. When she says she does not know, he assumes that she knows; when she says that nothing has occurred to her, he—observing her "tense and preoccupied expression"—assures her that something has occurred to her. Perhaps she has not been sufficiently attentive; perhaps she thought that "her idea was not the right one," or was concerned as to whether it was "appropriate or not"; perhaps she was concealing what had in fact occurred to her because she was reluctant to share her thoughts with him or to bring herself face-to-face with thoughts and emotions that felt unbearable. Thus he was systematically undoing a process of initiation by replacing a father's authority with her own. In staying with his method, he ceded to Elisabeth the position of knower and, in doing so, freed her own desire and curiosity. And then with Elisabeth he discovered what she knew.

> I derived from this analysis a literally unqualified reliance on my technique (of applying pressure to the patient's head to encourage her to continue her train of association). It often happened that it was not until I had pressed her head three times that she produced a piece of information; but she herself would remark afterwards: "I could have said it to you the first time."—"And why didn't you?"—"I thought it wasn't what was wanted," or "I thought I could avoid it, but it came back each time." In the course of this difficult work I began to attach a deeper significance to the resistance offered by the patient . . . and to make a careful collection of the occasions on which it was particularly marked.

"I could have said it . . . I thought it wasn't what was wanted . . . I thought I could avoid it, but it came back each time." The knowledge from which she had dissociated herself, which she thought she could avoid or keep out of relationship, bore the telltale sign of dissociation: it was at once familiar and surprising.

DESCRIBING Elisabeth, Freud cites her giftedness, her ambition, her moral sensibility, her excessive demand for love "which, to begin with, found satisfaction in her family and the independence of her nature which went beyond the feminine ideal and found expression in a considerable amount of obstinacy, pugnacity and reserve." He is describing the character of a resister, "the features which one meets with so frequently in hysterical people," the qualities Breuer noted in Anna O:

> She was markedly intelligent, with an astonishingly quick grasp of things and penetrating intuition. She possessed a powerful intellect. . . . She had great poetic and imaginative gifts, which were under the control of a sharp and critical common sense. Owing to this latter quality she was *completely unsuggestible;* she was only influenced by arguments, never by mere assertions. Her willpower was energetic, tenacious and persistent; sometimes it reached a pitch of obstinacy which only gave way out of kindness and regard for other people. One of her essential traits was sympathetic kindness.

Breuer also observes the hallmark of sexual trauma: "The element of sexuality was astonishingly undeveloped in her."

Psyche had come for psychoanalysis, and these stubborn, intelligent, gifted, and sympathetic young women were irresistible. They also were suffering from hysterical blindness, losing the range of their sight and hearing, experiencing nervous tics and paralyses, choked by nervous coughing, and suffering most commonly from "a loss of voice." Judith Herman in *Trauma and Recovery* and Bessel van der Kolk and his colleagues in their neurological and psychological studies of *Traumatic Stress* identify loss of voice as the psychic core of traumatic experience: the loss of the ability to tell one's story. It is the wisdom of the women-centered folk tales that Professor Ramanujan found so striking. But as the folk tales show and as we have repeatedly discovered, people do not lose their voices; they lose the desire or the courage or the will or the ability to use their voices to tell their stories.

They have swallowed their voices, or as Sandor Ferenczi observes in his paper "The Confusion of Tongues between Adult and Child," they have taken on the voice of another as their own. The "loss of voice," which Freud cites as the most common symptom of hysteria and which Ferenczi explicitly links with trauma, was the sign I followed in suggesting that as young boys take on the voices of fathers, the heroes and superheroes of their play, and as adolescent girls take on the voices of good and bad women, the angelic mother or the slut or whore, we can speak of a process of initiation that is akin to trauma in that a voice is seemingly lost or confused with another voice that finds more cultural resonance and thus carries more authority.

In inviting Normi Noel to join the research with girls, I sought the guidance of her ear, trained in the voice work of Kristin Linklater and thus tuned to the vibrations of the voice, and also her acute understanding of resonance—Noel's ability as a voice teacher and theater director to pick up the subtlest manifestations of the impulse to speak. Listening to girls' voices as they approached and crossed the border into adolescence, she followed their impulse to speak the truth of their thoughts and emotions and thus to stay in association with themselves and with others. She identified a series of steps leading from full speaking voice to half-voice to breathiness and into silence. In the silence, she picked up the almost imperceptible vibration of the impulse to speak, which remained alive, vibrating in what she called "an inner cello world or resonating chamber." In the journal she kept in the course of this work, she records her observations:

> Just as the acoustics for the strengthening of sound require certain physical properties, so too do the voices of the girls depend on a sympathetic "sounding board" or environment. . . . [A patriarchal culture] is filled with a dissonance that separates intellect from feeling. When there is no longer a "place" or "room" to strengthen their truth or practice speaking directly what they know, the girls then leave the vibrations of their speaking voice and

move from breathiness to silence. In this silence, an inner cello world or resonating chamber keeps alive the energy of the initial thought/feelings, preserving an integrity that risks everything if taken back onto the speaking voice in a culture still unable to provide a resonance for such clarity, subtlety and power.

As Freud initially offered himself as a sympathetic sounding board to his women patients, so he heard a voice that had receded into silence. It is the voice Euripides heard in imagining Iphigenia; it is the voice I heard in girls and women across a range of personal and cultural backgrounds, crossing ethnicity and class, sexuality and nationality. It is so common that the surprise is that it remains surprising. It is the voice of Psyche, the voice of the A version of Anne Frank's diary, the voice of the daughter named Pleasure. It is the voice I picked up in Eileen and in Sonya.

We know how this voice gets lost. But with Freud, what we can see so clearly is how this loss becomes yoked to the ascendance of the Oedipus story—the quintessential story of the wounded son. Like Shakespeare's tragic heroes, Freud was a man resisting patriarchy, taking arms against a sea of troubles and seeking by opposing to end them. And then he found himself in the sea. His early case histories, which "read like short stories" and seemingly "lack the serious stamp of science," in fact reflect a boldness of method whose claim to science lies precisely in their narrative style. In the heady days of discovery, Freud had set out from a position of not knowing, and the evidence he came upon through a process of relationship required that he report the process of relationship— hence the case histories that read like short stories. Robert Alter, in *The Art of Biblical Narrative,* observes that the ancient Hebrew writers had to invent a narrative art in order to convey a view of human life as lived reflectively, "in the changing medium of time, inexorably and perplexingly in relationship." To capture the relational and responsive nature of the human psyche, Freud developed a narrative art for his scientific writing.

The drama of his early case histories is a drama of relationship. We watch with the same fascination evoked by the films of mothers and babies as Freud and Elisabeth move in and out of touch with one another, finding and losing and finding, the process of discovery resembling the rhythms of love. "Psychoanalysis is a cure through love," Freud will subsequently write to Jung, and here we see love unfolding. Freud writes of the "deep human sympathy" he feels with Fräulein Elisabeth, although he notes that this in itself does not illuminate the cause of her symptoms. As she comes to connect her love with her knowledge, she remembers her hidden love of her sister's husband, their affinity with each other (so obvious that nobody noticed), and most shockingly, the thought that came unbidden into her consciousness as she stood at her dead sister's bedside ("Now he is free again, now I can be his wife"). The relationship with Freud, his ability to stay in the presence of such thoughts and feelings, releases Elisabeth from what Jean Baker Miller will subsequently call "condemned isolation": the feeling of being too bad to be human. As Elisabeth discovers that she can be with herself and also with Freud, as she responds to his interest in what she knows, we see a process of initiation reversing itself: knowing replacing not knowing, the touch of relationship speaking directly to the fear that in knowing what she knows, she will find herself condemned and isolated. As "her frozen nature" began to melt, the pains in her legs subsided, and Elisabeth regained the capacity to move forward.

Freud goes to her mother, Frau von R., encouraging her to become Elisabeth's confidante. He is encouraging a confiding relationship between them, and also pressing Frau von R. to arrange a marriage between Elisabeth and her brother-in-law now that he is free to marry her. Frau von R. rejects this proposal, citing the family's concerns about her son-in-law's health and also the state of his fortune. As for Elisabeth, she is angry at Freud for having broken her confidence. But Freud trusts the relationship, trusting more specifically that Elisabeth knows his intentions, the deep sympathy that led to his actions, and his continuing affection for her becomes evident several years later when he wangles a ticket for a ball she is attending: "I could not resist seeing my former patient whirl by in a lively dance."

BUT FREUD is a man and also a father, and as he aligns himself with women, he finds himself in the position of women, isolated and embattled in his claim to knowledge. It is a position I have seen parents and teachers and therapists come to when they align themselves with a child or adolescent's perceptions and join their resistance to a dissociation that is part of a process of initiation. In aligning themselves with such resistance and opting for relationship, they are coming into conflict with voices of authority and risk being called bad parents or jeopardizing their positions as teachers and therapists. Just as when I aligned myself with Eileen's fears of losing her grounding in relationship or took on Jude's question about the two Dans or pursued Dan's description of the affinity he felt with his mother or asked Phil what his real question was and why his worst nightmare was Sonya in the arms of another man, I was encouraging them to explore what they knew and also the obstacles to that knowing.

In 1896, the year following the publication of *Studies on Hysteria,* Freud's father dies. On the night after the funeral, Freud dreams that he is in a barbershop and a notice on the wall reads, "You are requested to close the eyes." It is a service commonly performed for the dead. But it is also a message whose meaning Freud registers as he begins to identify with Oedipus—the son who closes his eyes, blinding himself.

Now we can watch how the ascent of the Oedipus story begins to eclipse the tale of Psyche and Cupid. The familiar characters rearrange themselves like stars forming different constellations. The wounded son who became Psyche's lover will now become Oedipus, the lone solver of riddles, the man who universalizes his situation rather than looking at his feet and asking where he has come from and where he is going. And along with Oedipus, we see Antigone and Jocasta—Psyche, the seeing and speaking young woman, and Venus, the outraged mother, becoming the daughter summoned by her father to accompany him in his blindness and the complicit wife/mother of the Oedipus tragedy. If the Psyche and Cupid myth is the polestar of democracy, the story that shows a way leading to freedom and to equality between men and women, the conditions for the birth of pleasure, the Oedipus tragedy is the lodestar of patriarchy.

IN THE YEAR following his father's death, Freud begins his self-analysis. His discoveries become the basis for *The Interpretation of Dreams*. This is the work where Freud introduces the Oedipus story, finding in his own dreams the same themes that he finds in the great tragedies of Sophocles and Shakespeare—seeing them now as universal. Interpreting the dreams of his women patients, he aligns himself with Oedipus the king, the solver of riddles, or as Jonathan Lear reminds us, Oedipus Tyrannus, the tyrant who usurps authority. With this break in relationship, Freud's scientific method comes into question. Because now, instead of proceeding from a position of not knowing, he has seized the position of knower, the interpreter of dreams, the conquistador of the unconscious. He begins to override the voices of others; we see him becoming embattled with those who disagree with him. We are witnessing the birth of tragedy, repeating a history that began in fifth-century Athens or before that in the book of Genesis: the alignment of knowledge with fathers.

In the short span of time between the publication of *Studies on Hysteria* in 1895 and *The Interpretation of Dreams* in 1900, Psyche disappears from psychoanalysis. For much of twentieth-century psychology, she remains screened or hidden behind images of Madonna mothers and silent infants, the iconography in Western culture of female devotion and compliance. The figures of Antigone and Jocasta come to the fore. In the story commonly retold, Freud writes to his confidante Wilhelm Fleiss that he no longer believes in his "neurotica"—the theory linking hysteria with sexual trauma. He takes the position that there are "no indications of reality in the unconscious, so that one cannot distinguish between truth and fiction that has been cathected with affect." The role of traumatic experience in psychic illness once named by Freud as *"caput Nili,"* the head of the Nile, although still recognized, will no longer occupy the place of prominence in his theory. But the continuing argument about the relative roles of reality and fantasy in the inner workings of the psyche misses a point that becomes obvious when we retrace Freud's steps in this critical period.

When Freud disavows what has come to be known as "the seduction theory" and questions the pervasiveness of incest, he places an incest story—the Oedipus story—as the cornerstone of psychoanalysis. In doing so, however, he introduces a central displacement. In place of the young woman speaking about her experience of an incestuous relationship with her father, Freud puts the young boy, fantasizing about an incestuous relationship with his mother. The shift in emphasis from reality to fantasy follows this displacement, and with it we see Freud shift his alignment from the young women hysterics to the young Oedipus, the son who will grow up to be Oedipus Tyrannus, the father in the Oedipal drama.

Freud's teachers will become *Freud's Women,* the title of John Forrester and Lisa Appignanesi's book, in which they note that when Freud abandons his seduction theory, he "felt it as a sudden loss." For a variety of reasons, including arguments having to do with the relationship between wish and reality, fantasy and experience, and the seeming improbability of his finding that "in all cases, the *father,* not excluding my own, had to be accused of being perverse." Freud receded from the psychically intimate, pleasurable, and fruitful relationships that he had established with his women patients. The rush of discovery Freud experienced in these relationships and the deep human sympathy he felt with the women had become associated with danger and vulnerability, including the risk of appearing gullible or intellectually naïve in the eyes of fathers. With the death of his father, he became the father, identification replacing a lost relationship, and with this replacement, Freud became the hero of his own tragic story.

What is known and then not known, dissociated or repressed, however, tends to return. In 1900, the voice Freud repressed returns in the person of Ida Bauer—the eighteen-year-old he calls Dora. She was sent by her father to Freud for analysis, suffering from a range of hysterical symptoms, including nervous coughing that interfered with her speech. Freud's internal battle over his relationship to women's voices will become the battle of her analysis. This disturbing and fragmentary case history is the most widely read and discussed of Freud's cases, perhaps because the battle is so shockingly familiar. We watch with a mixture of horror and fascination as Freud repeatedly overrides Dora's voice with his own, claiming to know her inner world better than she does. In stark contrast to his method with Fräulein Elisabeth, Freud will connect Dora's love with his knowledge rather than hers until, in protest, she leaves him. When Dora breaks off her treatment and leaves the analysis, the door that was opened by *Studies on Hysteria* closes for almost a century. Psyche—not the "eternal feminine," but the seeing and speaking young woman—disappears from psychoanalysis, and pleasure becomes a principle.

KNOWING WHAT we know. The Psyche and Cupid myth has been in our midst for almost a millennium. Psyche, the young woman who resists becoming an object, who insists on seeing and speaking about love—when we lose her voice, we lose a story about love that is deeply instructive. And Cupid, also known as Amor or Eros, the young man whose name means "desire" or "love"—when we cannot see or speak about his humanness, his vulnerability, we lose a crucial part of the story. Which is also a story about his mother and women's relationships with one another in a world where one woman is seen to take the place of another. When we cannot see the sources of women's envy or anger, when all that we see is an angry or envious woman, Venus—the outraged mother of the Psyche and Cupid tale—becomes the silent and complicitous Jocasta.

Metamorphosis—changing the shape, overcoming the form—is the essence of creativity. It is by its very nature improvisational, taking off from the familiar and heading into the unknown. Like art, like science, like love. The road leading to the birth of pleasure skirts the tragic love story, veering off at critical moments, illuminating a path of resistance: a young woman refuses to become an object, a stand-in for a fantasy, a replacement for an older woman; a young man refuses to become Oedipus, his mother's lover or the instrument of her revenge; a mother refuses to risk sacrificing her child, instead arming herself against monsters; and love—at its heart a seemingly impossible task—leads to the birth of pleasure. Thus a relationship fired by erotic passion leads in the end to a relationship between a man and a woman that uproots its history in patriarchy, becoming no longer uneven. Falling in love is associated in this story with bleeding and burning, curiosity breaking through a surface that seemed impermeable but which turns out, like skin, to be porous.

I will never lie to you, I will never leave you, I will never try to possess you. These became the vows of relationship that Terrence Real and I came to in the course of our work with couples in crisis. They hold a promise not necessarily to stay married but to stay in relationship by creating the grounds for trust—making it possible to open oneself freely to another and to find the other again after the inevitable breaks in connection. It is the condition for living with change.

I am curious about the connection between love and democracy, the intimate joining of private and public life. Both love and democracy depend on voice—having a voice and also the resonance that makes it possible to speak and be heard. Without voice, there is no relationship; without resonance, voice recedes into silence. As the resonances of our common world are changing, as more voices come into the human conversation, we are rewriting our collective story, our history, coming to hear and to see ourselves and one another differently. Thus we step out of a frame. I write at a time when frameworks are shifting. The framework of love, the framework of marriage, what it means to be human—a man, a woman, a person, a couple, a family, a member of the human community. Collectively, we have moved to an edge of possibility; it has become possible to envision a democracy that is not patriarchal; it is more difficult to imagine a love that is passionate without becoming tragic.

The pursuit of happiness stands innocently alongside life and liberty in the Declaration of Independence, the ordinariness of the word "happiness" perhaps masking the revolutionary nature of the claim to psychic freedom. When pleasure threatens an order of living that has come to feel both essential and stifling, the dangers of pleasure are conjured up and magnified, so that pleasure comes to connote chaos and riot. But there is nothing intrinsically chaotic in pleasure. It has its own rhythms and cadences; finding and losing and finding again. It is the music of love. We have learned, although it is still hotly contested in many places, that love and family take many forms. From Hannah Arendt we know that the enemy of freedom is not structure but totalitarianism, which sets out systematically to destroy freedom, co-opting voice and confusing language in a public enactment of terror. It is the politics of Inquisition, the opposite of the policy adopted in the sixteenth century by Elizabeth I, whose approach to freeing her people and her country from the extremes of both Rome and the Reformation was to say, "We do not seek windows into men's souls."

Leaving patriarchy for love or democracy sounds easy, even inviting, but it is psychically as well as politically risky; at least at first, it seems to mean giving up power and control. Hope is the most dangerous emotion: it invites us to imagine an escape from tragedy, it tempts what we have come to think of as fate. The hope of the new, the nakedness of standing without a frame heightens our awareness of vulnerability and, with it, the temptation to return at whatever cost to the known. The birth of Pleasure, like any new life, is an invitation to creativity. In *Talking Jazz: An Oral History*, Ben Sidran, a journalist and jazz musician, writes: "At the heart of jazz . . . is a terrific contradiction: nothing is what it appears to be, but everything is exactly what it is. There are no secrets, and that, of course, is the secret. It is the art, then, of circumlocution, of learning to approach the truth from many sides."

I DREAM THAT my father has come back. He has been dead for several years. In the dream, he is standing in a small hallway, wearing his brown tweed overcoat, a little unsteady on his feet—the way he was when he was old. He smiles uncertainly, holding a bouquet of balloons or flowers, brightly colored, like fireworks. He has come for my birthday. I am so happy to see him. "Daddy," I say, "I am so happy you have come." His smile brightens; he looks a little sheepish. "It wasn't easy," he says. I look at the bouquet and see that it is made of long-stemmed tulips—that he has made them for me out of thin wooden sticks and paper cups painted yellow and orange. Playful, silly. "Daddy," I say, filled with joy, "I am so happy to see you."

A door opens in the hallway where we are standing, and we turn to the right. My father is younger now, and we are in the dormitory I lived in during my senior year in college. I had found joy in my work that year, found my own rhythm of working. We enter my room; my mother is there. I had climbed out of the window of that room late one night to meet my boyfriend, releasing the bans on pleasure, saying to myself as we lay on the small bed in the apartment he had rented that I was not going to live the way my mother had lived. Or maybe, thinking back now to that moment, I was going to live in the way I knew that she wanted, for which she had prepared the ground.

The three of us are in my room together—it is like the best of when we were together, my mother, my father, and I. The nights when we would sing in the car, or sit at the kitchen table together, the formality of life ebbing away. The room leading off mine is empty; my suitemate is away for the weekend. "There is room," I say to the two of them. "Plenty of room for you to stay."

My parents have entered the world of my pleasure. They have come to celebrate my birthday. My father, his father's son, has come back to play. "It wasn't easy," he says, taking off the trappings of the life that enclosed him. And my mother, sitting in the room in which I stayed up all night writing papers on poetry and perception, the window open, the ground with its leaf-smell only a small jump away. She sits in the dream in the way she sat when we sewed in my childhood, her face absorbed in her concentration, pleasure easing the lines of distraction, as if we are swimming in an ocean of time.

THE SEEMINGLY impossible tasks assemble. Sort, practically on an unconscious level; find economic sustenance, learn how to move safely in the face of danger, pay attention to the cadences of emotional life; take water, go to the source, repair relationships, know what you know; listen to the stirrings of nature, remember the culture, face mortality and choose life—this is an old wife's wisdom.

Maybe love is like rain. Sometimes gentle, sometimes torrential, flooding, eroding, joyful, steady, filling the earth, collecting in underground springs. When it rains, when we love, life grows. To say that there are two roads, one leading to life and one to death and therefore choose life, is to say in effect: choose love. We have a map. We know the way.

A Note on Sources

WHILE ALL THE QUOTATIONS from interviews and therapy sessions are taken verbatim from recorded transcripts, I have changed people's names and some details of their lives to protect their identity, with the exception of the eleven-year-old girls who, as young women, wanted their names in this book.

The line about the psyche on page 8 was suggested by Stephanie Levine and is quoted directly on page 131; the quotations from Freud on pages 219–20 are from his 1908 essay, "Civilized Sexual Morality and Modern Nervous Illness"; the lines by Jorie Graham on page 6 are from her poem, "The Age of Reason"; the evidence I refer to on page 15 is presented in my 1996 paper, "The Centrality of Relationship in Human Development: A Puzzle, Some Evidence, and a Theory," as well as in *Meeting at the Crossroads* (Brown and Gilligan, 1992) and *Between Voice and Silence* (Taylor, Gilligan and Sullivan, 1995); in telling the Psyche and Cupid myth, I have drawn on J. Arthur Hanson's translation in the 1989 Loeb Classics edition and most of the quotations come from this edition; I have also drawn from the previous Loeb Classics edition as well as on my own reading of the Latin; the excerpts from Proust are from D. J. Enright's revision of the Kilmartin and Montcrieff translation; the passages from Anne Frank's diary

A Note on Sources

are from the English version of the Critical Edition, translated by J. Pomerans and B. Mooyart-Doubleday; the excerpts from the five missing pages of the diary are quoted from the *New York Times* (10 September 1998). Lawrence Langer's observation on page 81 was made at a Facing History and Ourselves seminar in Brookline, Massachusetts, in 1999. A description of the Listening Guide method mentioned on page 130 and referred to on page 8, can be found in "On the Listening Guide" (Gilligan, Spencer, Weinberg, and Bertsch, in press); Iphigenia's speeches and other excerpts from Euripides, *Iphigenia in Aulis,* are from Mary-Kay Gamel's translation; for the line from Sophocles' *Oedipus* on page 33, I am indebted to Robert Fitzgerald's translation; the quotation from the *Oresteia* on page 34 is from David Slavitt's translation. The quotations of Freud and of Breuer are from the Standard Edition, edited by J. Strachey.

Earlier versions of some of the material in this book appeared in the *Michigan Quarterly Review, The Inner World in the Outer World* (edited by E. Shapiro), and the *Lincoln Center Theater Review* (summer 1998).

Bibliography

Aeschylus. *The Oresteia,* edited and translated by David R. Slavitt. Philadelphia: University of Pennsylvania Press, 1998.

Amichai, Yehuda. *A Life of Poetry, 1948–1994,* translated from the Hebrew by Benjamin and Barbara Harshav. New York: Harper-Collins (Wild Peace), 1994.

Appignanesi, Lisa, and John Forrester. *Freud's Women.* London: Weidenfeld and Nicolson, 1992.

Apuleius. *Metamorphoses,* edited and translated by J. Arthur Hanson (originally edited and translated by W. Adlington, 1566, and revised by S. Gaselee, 1915). Cambridge: Harvard University Press Loeb Classical Library, 1989.

Arendt, Hannah. *The Origins of Totalitarianism.* New York: Harcourt Brace Jovanovich, 1973.

Berger, John. *Ways of Seeing.* London: British Broadcasting Corporation and Penguin Books, 1972.

Bergman, Ingmar. *Private Confessions,* SVT Kanal 1 Drama, First Run Features and Castle Hill Productions, Inc., 1996.

Blondell, Ruby, Mary-Kay Gamel, Nancy Sorkin Rabinowitz, and Bella Zweig (eds. and translation). *Women on the Edge: Four Plays by Euripides.* New York: Routledge, 1999.

Boland, Eavan. "What We Lost" from *Outside History.* New York: W. W. Norton, 1990.

Breuer, Josef, and Sigmund Freud. *Studies on Hysteria, 1893–1895,* translated from the German and edited by James and Alix Strachey. London: Penguin Books, 1974.

Brown, Lyn Mikel, and Carol Gilligan, *Meeting at the Crossroads: Women's Psychology and Girls' Development.* Cambridge: Harvard University Press, 1992 (paperback, New York: Ballantine, 1993).

Chu, Judy Yi-Chung. "Learning What Boys Know," Ed.D. dissertation, Harvard University, 2000.

Cliff, Michelle. *The Land of Look Behind: Prose & Poetry.* New York: Fireside Books, 1989.

Damasio, Antonio. *The Feeling of What Happens: Body and Emotion in the Making of Consciousness.* San Diego: Harcourt, 1999.

De Costa, Denise. *Anne Frank and Etty Hillesum: Inscribing Spirituality and Sexuality,* translated by Mischa F. C. Hoyinck and Robert E. Chesal. New Brunswick, N.J.: Rutgers University Press, 1998 (Dutch edition, 1996).

Debold, Elizabeth. "Toward an Understanding of Gender Differences in Psychological Distress: A Foucauldian Integration of Freud, Gilligan, and Cognitive Development Theory," Ed.D. dissertation, Harvard University, January 1994.

Dickinson, Emily. *Complete Poems of Emily Dickinson,* edited by Thomas H. Johnson. New York: Little, Brown, 1955.

DuBois, W. E. B. *The Souls of Black Folk,* edited by Henry Louis Gates Jr. and Terri Hume Oliver. New York: W. W. Norton, 1999.

Edwards, Lee R. *Psyche as Hero: Female Heroism and Fictional Form.* Dartmouth, N.H.: University Press of New England, 1984.

Ferenczi, Sandor. "The Confusion of Tongues between Adult and Child," pp. 156–67, in Michael Balint, ed., *Final Contributions to the Problems and Methods in Psychoanalysis.* London: Hogarth Press, 1955.

Frank, Anne. *The Diary of a Young Girl,* translated by B. M. Mooyaart. New York: Doubleday, 1952.

———. *The Diary of Anne Frank: The Critical Edition* (prepared by the Netherlands State Institute for War Documentation, edited by David Barnouw and Gerrold Van Der Stroom), translated by Arnold J. Pomerans and B. M. Mooyaart-Doubleday. New York: Doubleday, 1989.

————. *The Diary of a Young Girl: The Definitive Edition,* edited by Otto H. Frank and Mirjam Pressler, translated by Susan Massotty. New York: Doubleday, 1995.

French, Marilyn. Introduction to *Summer* by Edith Wharton (1917). New York: Scribner's, 1998.

Freud, Sigmund. *The Standard Edition of the Complete Psychological Works of Sigmund Freud,* edited and translated by James Strachey. London: The Hogarth Press, 1961.

————. *The Complete Letters of Sigmund Freud to Wilhelm Fliess, 1887–1904,* edited by Jeffrey Moussaieff Masson. Cambridge: Harvard University Press, 1986.

Five Books of Moses: Genesis, Exodus, Leviticus, Numbers, Deuteronomy, vol. 1, translation by Everett Fox. New York: Schocken Books, 1997.

Gamel, Mary-Kay. Introduction to *Iphigenia in Aulis* by Euripedes, in R. Blondell et al., eds. and trans., *Women on the Edge: Four Plays by Euripides.* New York: Routledge, 1999.

Garcia-Coll, Cynthia, Janet L. Surrey, and Kathy Weingarten, eds. *Mothering Against the Odds—Diverse Voices of Contemporary Mothers.* New York: Guilford Press, 1998.

Gilligan, Carol. "The Centrality of Relationship in Human Development: A Puzzle, Some Evidence, and a Theory." In G. Noam and K. Fischer, eds., *Development and Vulnerability in Close Relationships.* New York: Erlbaum, 1996.

Gilligan, Carol, Annie G. Rogers, and Deborah Tolman. *Women, Girls and Psychotherapy: Reframing Resistance.* New York: Haworth Press, 1991.

Gilligan, Carol, Renee Spencer, Katherine M. Weinberg, and Tatiana Bertsch. "On the Listening Guide: A Voice-Centered Relational Method" in P. M. Camic, J. E. Rhodes, and L. Yardley, eds., *Qualitative Research in Psychology: Expanding Perspectives in Methodology and Design.* Washington, D.C.: American Psychological Association Press, forthcoming, fall 2002.

Graham, Jorie. *The Dream of the Unified Field: Selected Poems, 1974–1994.* Hopewell, N.J.: The Ecco Press, 1995.

Hart, Ellen Louise, and Martha Nell, eds. *Open Me Carefully: Emily*

Bibliography

Dickinson's Intimate Letters to Susan Huntington Dickinson, Ashfield, Mass.: Smith Paris Press, 1998.

Hartman-Halbertal, Tova. *Appropriately Subversive: Modern Mothers in Traditional Religions.* Cambridge: Harvard University Press, in press.

Hawthorne, Nathaniel. *The Scarlet Letter* (1850). New York: Random House, 1950.

Herman, Judith. *Trauma and Recovery.* New York: Basic Books, 1993.

Irigaray, Luce. *Et l'une ne bouge pas sans l'autre.* Paris: Les Editions de Minuit, 1979.

Jacobs, Harriet. *Incidents in the Life of a Slave Girl, Written by Herself* (1861). Cambridge: Harvard University Press, 1987.

Kalven, Jamie. *Working with Available Light: A Family's World After Violence.* New York: W. W. Norton, 1999.

Kincaid, Jamaica. *Annie John.* New York: Farrar, Straus & Giroux, 1983.

Langer, Lawrence L. *Versions of Survival: The Holocaust and the Human Spirit.* Albany, N.Y.: State University of New York Press, 1982.

Lear, Jonathan. *Love and Its Place in Nature: A Philosophical Interpretation of Freudian Psychoanalysis.* New York: Farrar, Straus & Giroux, 1990.

————. *Open Minded: Working Out the Logic of the Soul.* Cambridge: Harvard University Press, 1998.

LeVine, Robert. *Culture, Behavior and Personality.* Seven Oaks, Kent: Pondview Books, 1973.

Levine, Stephanie. "Mystics, Mavericks, and Merrymakers: The Inner Worlds and Daily Lives of Hasidic Adolescent Girls," Ph.D. dissertation, Harvard University, 2000.

Lifton, Robert Jay. *The Broken Connection: On Death and the Continuity of Life.* Seven Oaks, Kent: Pondview Books, 1979.

Lindqvist, Sven. *Exterminate All the Brutes,* translated by Joan Tate. New York: The New Press, 1996.

Linklater, Kristin. *Freeing the Natural Voice.* New York: Drama Book Publishers, 1976.

———. "Undertones, Overtones and Fundamental Pitch of the Female Voice" in F. Armstrong and J. Pearson, eds., *Well-Tuned Women: Growing Strong Through Voicework*. London: The Women's Press, 2000.

Lipper, Joanna. *Inside Out: Portraits of Children*. New York: Ruby Slipper Productions, 1999.

Merrill, James. *Collected Poems*. New York: Alfred A. Knopf, 2001.

Morrison, Toni. *The Bluest Eye* (1970). New York: Alfred A. Knopf, 1993.

Miller, Jean Baker. "Connections, Disconnections and Violations," *Work in Progress No. 33*. Wellesley, Mass.: Stone Center Working Paper Series, 1988.

Muller, Melissa. *Anne Frank: The Biography,* translated by Robert Kimber and Rita Kimber. New York: Henry Holt, 1998.

Murray, L., and C. Trevarthen. "Emotional Regulation of Interactions Between Two-month-olds and Their Mothers," in T. M. Fields and N. A. Fox, eds., *Social Perception in Infants*. Norwood, N.J.: Ablex Publishing, 1985.

———. "The Infant's Role in Mother-Infant Communication." *Journal of Child Language* 13 (1986): 15–29.

Noel, Normi. Unpublished journals, 1990–1992.

Neumann, Erich. *Amor and Psyche: The Psychic Development of the Feminine: A Commentary on the Tale by Apuleius*. Seven Oaks, Kent: Pondview Books, 1956.

Olsen, Tillie. *Mother Daughter Daughter Mother: Mothers on Mothering*. New York: Fireside Books, 1984.

Ondaatje, Michael. *The English Patient*. New York: Vintage, 1993.

Pierce-Baker, Charlotte. *Surviving the Silence: Black Women's Stories of Rape*. New York: W. W. Norton, 1998.

Proust, Marcel. *In Search of Lost Time,* vol. 1, *Swann's Way,* translated by C. K. Scott Moncrieff and Terence Kilmartin, revised by D. J. Enright. London: Chatto & Windus, 1992.

Real, Terrence. *I Don't Want to Talk About It: Overcoming the Secret Legacy of Male Depression*. New York: Fireside, 1997.

Richards, David A. J. *Women, Gays, and the Constitution: The*

Bibliography

Grounds for Feminism and Gay Rights in Culture and Law. Chicago: Universitiy of Chicago Press, 1998.

Rodgers, Richard, and Oscar Hammerstein. "If I Loved You," 1945.

Rogers, Annie G. "Voice, Play, and a Practice of Ordinary Courage in Girls' and Women's Lives." *Harvard Educational Review* 63 (1993): 265–95.

Roy, Arundhati. *The God of Small Things.* New York: Random House, 1997.

Saliers, Emily. "Galileo," Epic Records, 1995.

Shakespeare, William. *The Riverside Shakespeare,* edited by G. Blakemore Evans and Herschel Baker. Boston: Houghton Mifflin, 1974.

Sidran, Ben. *Talking Jazz: An Oral History,* expanded edition. New York: Da Capo Press, 1995.

Sophocles. *The Oedipus Cycle,* translated by Dudley Fitts and Robert Fitzgerald. New York: Harcourt, Brace and Co., 1949.

Stern, Daniel N. *The Interpersonal World of the Infant.* New York: Basic Books, 1998.

Surrey, Janet. "Relational and Cultural Reconstructions of Motherhood: Clinical Implications." Paper presented at the Harvard Medical School Learning from Women Conference, April 1996.

Suttie, Ian. *The Origins of Love and Hate* (1935). New York: The Julian Press, 1952.

Taylor, Jill McLean, Carol Gilligan, and Amy Sullivan. *Between Voice and Silence: Women and Girls, Race and Relationship.* Cambridge: Harvard University Press, 1995.

Tobin, J. J. M. *Shakespeare's Favorite Novel: A Study of* The Golden Ass *as a Prime Source.* Lanham, Md.: University Press of America, 1984.

Tolman, Deborah. *Dilemmas of Desire.* Cambridge: Harvard University Press, in press.

Tronick, E. Z. "Emotions and Emotional Communication in Infants." *American Psychologist* 44 (2) (1989), 112–19.

Tronick, E. Z., and A. Gianino. "Interactive Mismatch and Repair Challenges in the Coping Infant: Zero to Three." *Bulletin of the Center for Clinical Infant Programs* 6 (3) (1986), 1–6.

Tronick, E. Z., and M. K. Weinberg. "Depressed Mothers and Infants: Failure to Form Dyadic States of Consciousness," in L. Murray and P. J. Cooper, eds., *Postpartum Depression and Child Development.* New York: Guilford Press, 1997.

Van der Kolk, Bessel, Alexander C. McFarlane, and Lars Weisaeth, eds. *Traumatic Stress.* New York: Guilford Publications, 1996.

Walker, Alice. *Possessing the Secret of Joy.* New York: Harcourt Brace Jovanovich, 1992.

Way, Niobe. *Everyday Courage.* New York: New York University Press, 1998.

Wharton, Edith. "The Fullness of Life" (1891–1896), in *Complete Short Stories* by Edith Wharton, edited by R. W. B. Lewis. New York: Scribner's, 1968.

———. *Summer* (1917). New York: Scribner's, 1998.

———. *The Age of Innocence* (1948). New York: Scribner's, 1968.

Woolf, Virginia. "An Unwritten Novel," in *A Haunted House and Other Stories* (1921). London: Grafton Press, 1981.

———. *Mrs. Dalloway* (1925). San Diego: Harcourt Brace, 1981.

———. *Three Guineas* (1938). San Diego: Harcourt Brace, 1966.

Wolff, Cynthia Griffin. *A Feast of Words: The Triumph of Edith Wharton.* Radcliffe Biography Series. Reading, Mass.: Addison-Wesley, 1995.

Zimlicki, Birute. "Speaking of Love: From a Study of Relationships in Crisis," Ed.D. dissertation, Harvard University, 1991.

Index

Index

Index

Index

A NOTE ON THE TYPE

THIS BOOK was set in Adobe Garamond. Designed for the Adobe Corporation by Robert Slimbach, the fonts are based on types first cut by Claude Garamond (c. 1480–1561). Garamond was a pupil of Geoffroy Tory and is believed to have followed the Venetian models, although he introduced a number of important differences, and it is to him that we owe the letter we now know as "old style." He gave to his letters a certain elegance and feeling of movement that won their creator an immediate reputation and the patronage of Francis I of France.

Composed by Stratford Publishing Services,
Brattleboro, Vermont
Printed and bound by R. R. Donnelley & Sons,
Harrisonburg, Virginia
Designed by Virginia Tan